The
Strange Case
of Dr. Etienne Deschamps

The Strange Case

of Dr. Etienne Deschamps

Murder in the New Orleans French Quarter

Christopher G. Peña

PELICAN PUBLISHING COMPANY
Gretna 2017

The word "Pelican" and the depiction of a pelican are
trademarks of Pelican Publishing Company, Inc., and are
registered in the U.S. Patent and Trademark Office.

Library of Congress Cataloging-in-Publication Data

Names: Peña, Christopher G., author.
Title: The strange case of Dr. Etienne Deschamps : murder in the New Orleans
   French quarter / Christopher G. Peña.
Description: Gretna : Pelican Publishing Company, 2016. | Includes
   bibliographical references and index.
Identifiers: LCCN 2016007459| ISBN 9781455621958 (hardcover : alk. paper) |
   ISBN 9781455621965 (e-book)
Subjects: LCSH: Deschamps, Etienne, 1834-1892. | Murderers--Louisiana--New
   Orleans--History--19th century. | Murder--Louisiana--New
   Orleans--History--19th century.
Classification: LCC HV6248.D47 P46 2016 | DDC 364.152/3092--dc23 LC record available
at https://lccn.loc.gov/2016007459

Printed in the United States of America

Published by Pelican Publishing Company, Inc.
1000 Burmaster Street, Gretna, Louisiana 70053

For
DeeDee

Contents

Acknowledgments

I won't say that I have a macabre fascination with homicide, but for some odd reason I've always wanted to chronicle a famous murder case. One day I stumbled upon the Web site Murderpedia: The Encyclopedia of Murderers. As I scrolled through its alphabetized listings, I came across Etienne Deschamps. What particularly interested me about this case was that the murder occurred in New Orleans. Though I currently live in the Volunteer State, I was born in Louisiana. For many years I lived and worked in Thibodaux, a small college town approximately sixty miles southwest of New Orleans. Over time, I also became very familiar with the Crescent City. With my love of history, and the fact that the murder occurred more than 125 years ago, I was hooked. This was a story I was destined to write, for better or worse.

The first person I contacted about my book project was DeeDee Denise DiBenedetto, a dear friend and a private investigator who lives in St. Amant, Louisiana. I deeply appreciated her unique abilities to access research materials online and her willingness to go the "extra mile," which included visits to Louisiana State University's Hill-Memorial Library, and they are the reason why I dedicated this book to her. She never said no and always sought to do more. I could never have accomplished what I did without her assistance. Thank you so much, DeeDee.

I would be remiss if I did not mention the following people whose assistance is greatly appreciated. Thanks to family members Gerard and Patricia "Trisha" Peña, of Slidell, Louisiana; Michael Peña, of Irvine, California; and my daughter, Pamela P. Smith, of Knoxville, Tennessee. Many thanks to Gloria Borum, of Knoxville, Tennessee, for proofreading my first draft and your words of encouragement. Special thanks to Beth Davis, Vital Records Section, Louisiana State Archives, Baton Rouge; Judy Bolton, former Head of Public Services for L.S.U. Special Collections, Jennifer Mitchell, Head of Manuscripts Processing, Hans Rasmussen, Coordinator of Special

Collections Technical Services, Tara Zachary Laver, Curator of Manuscripts, and Jason Ford, former Cataloging Associate in Special Collections, all at Hill-Memorial Library, Baton Rouge; Danny Gamble, librarian at the *New Orleans Times-Picayune;* Anna Gospodinovich, Assistant Registrar, Louisiana State Museum, New Orleans; my cousin and Louisiana Supreme Court Justice John Weimer, Thibodaux; Sandra Vujnovich, Judicial Administrator, Betsy Gundorf, Secretary, Judicial Administrator's Office, Georgia Chadwick, former Director, and Sara V. Pic, Reference Librarian, all of the Law Library of Louisiana, Louisiana Supreme Court, New Orleans; Irene Wainwright, former Head, Louisiana Division/City Archives, New Orleans Public Library; Mary Lou Eichhorn, Senior Reference Associate, Williams Research Center, The Historic New Orleans Collection; John DeSantis, senior staff writer, *Houma (LA) Times;* Andrew Hunter, New Orleans; Dorenda Dupont, staff, Office of Archives and Records, Archdiocese of New Orleans; and many thanks to owner Dustin Palmisano and employees Carissa Rael and Dawn Johnson of The Old Coffee Pot Restaurant, New Orleans, for allowing me unfettered access to the building's second-floor rooms and exterior walkway. Finally, I would like to specially thank my wife, Linda, for putting up with me during this project.

Author's Notes

Going over various accounts of the murder and its aftermath, I often found that people's version of the truth became modified or remembered differently from one year to the next, or even one day to the next. This, in and of itself, is not unusual. Days, months, and years after the fact, people often see and remember things differently. Even two people who shared an experience may recall different versions of what they saw or heard. As a result, their recollections, as true as they believe them to be, often contradict other eyewitness accounts. With that said, I attempted to take everything into consideration as I chronicled the history of this murder, especially the dates when comments or testimonies were recorded. I hope that I have presented the storyline with a clear focus so as not to confuse the reader, while pointing out discrepancies whenever appropriate.

The victim's last name was often spelled *Dietsch* or *Deitsch* in various newspaper articles and *Deitsh* in the defendant's first legal brief filed with the Louisiana Supreme Court in late 1889. I prefer to use *Dietsh,* which was the spelling that appeared in some personal letters; the victim's burial record; the January 31, 1889, Orleans Parish coroner's report; the first trial in late March 1889 (the summation of which was printed in the *New Orleans Daily Picayune*); the defendant's second legal brief filed with the Louisiana Supreme Court during the second quarter of 1890; and *Soards'* New Orleans city directories from 1891 through 1898 (except for 1897, when it was spelled *Deitsh*).

I have one final note. In 1893-94, the New Orleans street-numbering system underwent a major overhaul. There was no standardization to the numbering process prior to that. Thus, for all pre-1893-94 street addresses, I have included the current block number or address to orient the reader to its approximate or exact present-day location.

Prologue

In New Orleans during the latter years of the nineteenth century, a hideous crime was perpetrated upon an innocent twelve-year-old girl. It sparked outrage in the city and attracted an unprecedented amount of local, state, and national press coverage. For many people across the country, but especially for the folks living in the Crescent City, the guilty verdict and the sentence of death that followed were not only justifiable; they were righteous judgments. The perpetrator had not only murdered a child. He had stolen her innocence while betraying her trust and the trust of her father.

But not everyone during that time desired the death penalty as adjudicated by the court. Was the murder a premeditated act as the State successfully argued, or was it a horrible experiment gone awry, given the strange set of circumstances under which the young girl met her death? Also, was the condemned man sane or insane at the time of this appalling deed? These were perplexing questions that were raised during that time.

Complicating the matter for the defendant was the physical evidence and the words he uttered outside the courtroom that portrayed him as a sexual predator, though that did not directly contribute to the young girl's death. The man was never charged with rape, a capital offense. Nevertheless, that fact alone did not aid in his defense, nor did it create a swell of sympathetic supporters once he was convicted of his crime.

In essence, the condemned man was clearly guilty of something, but did his crime—premeditated murder by chloroform poisoning—rise to the level of a capital offense? At that time, the answer was a resounding yes, though it was far from a universal sentiment. Even now, the question of guilty as charged, or guilty of manslaughter, or innocent by reason of insanity begs a renewed look, a new perspective, and a reexamination of the facts. Only then can the mysteries surrounding this bizarre murder be brought to light and the persistent misconceptions about this case be properly addressed.

The
Strange Case
of Dr. Etienne Deschamps

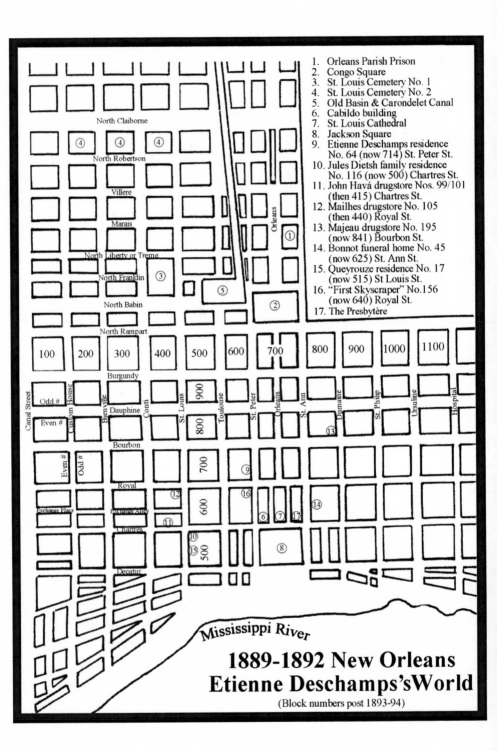

1. Orleans Parish Prison
2. Congo Square
3. St. Louis Cemetery No. 1
4. St. Louis Cemetery No. 2
5. Old Basin & Carondelet Canal
6. Cabildo building
7. St. Louis Cathedral
8. Jackson Square
9. Etienne Deschamps residence
   No. 64 (now 714) St. Peter St.
10. Jules Dietsh family residence
    No. 116 (now 500) Chartres St.
11. John Havá drugstore Nos. 99/101
    (then 415) Chartres St.
12. Mailhes drugstore No. 105
    (then 440) Royal St.
13. Majeau drugstore No. 195
    (now 841) Bourbon St.
14. Bonnot funeral home No. 45
    (now 625) St. Ann St.
15. Queyrouze residence No. 17
    (now 515) St Louis St.
16. "First Skyscraper" No.156
    (now 640) Royal St.
17. The Presbytère

1889-1892 New Orleans Etienne Deschamps's World
(Block numbers post 1893-94)

Chapter One

Execution Day

The head jerked to the right, the feet swung forward, and then the figure straightened and swayed a bit from the strain of the rope.
New Orleans Daily Picayune, May 14, 1892

When dawn broke on Friday morning, May 13, 1892, a heavy fog hung over the Crescent City. This was not an unusual spring occurrence in New Orleans, which was often plagued with high humidity and progressive heat, though the city would be spared record warmth that day. It wasn't until twenty or thirty minutes later that the first burst of sunlight pierced the eastern horizon, slowly dissipating the mist. By all accounts it would be a gorgeous, cloudless day, with the temperature rising no higher than eighty-three degrees. As the sun rose higher in the sky, commercial carts rumbled on the brick-lined streets of New Orleans, and foot traffic slowly began to clog the downtown area as people went about their business. There seemed to be "an easy and sweet contentment" that morning, according to the *New Orleans Daily City Item*, as delightful floral fragrances inundated the air.

But not every quarter in the city shared in that pleasant moment. Fronting Orleans Street and bordering Marais, North Liberty (or Treme), and St. Ann streets, a block behind Congo Square in what is now Louis Armstrong Park, stood a massive and foreboding three-story, gray, stucco building—Orleans Parish Prison. The main prison complex, which housed male inmates, ran along North Liberty Street. It was accessible only through an iron gate. The portion of the prison along Marais Street was used as the New Orleans Police Department Fourth Precinct. The women's prison was located to its rear. In essence, the massive structure, built in 1834 of brick and iron, was divided in half by an enclosed walkway, with male prisoners on one side and females on the other. White and African-American inmates of both genders were segregated.

Orleans Parish Prison (1834-95). (Courtesy NOLA.com/The *Times-Picayune*)

Inside the main entrance of the men's prison on the right was a visitor's room—visiting hours were from 9:00 A.M. to 3:30 P.M., Monday, Wednesday, and Friday. Next was the clerk's office, followed by a private apartment for the criminal sheriff. Situated on the left were the sleeping quarters for the captain, deputy sheriffs, prison keepers, and watchmen.

A second iron gate led to a long corridor, which served as a dining room for prison officials. The kitchen was located at one end of the passageway. To the right of the kitchen, a third iron gate led directly to the interior prison yard and to cells occupied by African-American inmates. To the left of the kitchen were the cells and yard for white prisoners. A stairway at the end of the corridor led to the second-floor infirmary and "rooms for prisoners able to pay board and enjoy all the comforts of life, except liberty," according to a *Daily Picayune* story about the prison.

Beyond that, in the middle of the hallway through another iron gate, ran a gallery that skirted a double tier of cells allocated for condemned criminals only. Any inmate who received a sentence of death, regardless of whether that sentence was under appeal, was immediately transferred to this isolated section of the prison. There were eight cells, grouped in pairs. Condemned Box No. 1 and 2 ran along the third-floor gallery and No. 3 and 4 along the second floor. All of the cells, isolated from one another, overlooked the prison yard below. During the day, occupied cells were left open, giving the prisoner access to

Orleans Parish Prison interior. (Courtesy NOLA.com/The *Times-Picayune*)

his individual gallery in front. He could exercise there, if desired, or converse with the general population in the yard below. No visitors were allowed in the condemned person's cell, except in the presence of a prison official.

Once the governor had signed and transmitted the death sentence, the condemned prisoner was placed under constant watch and frequently searched for any contraband that might be used for self-destruction. Prisoners were locked in their cells at sundown and placed under constant surveillance by a jail keeper or watchman. This ritual constituted the "death watch." Prisoners slept on a mattress placed on the floor and were provided with a pillow, bed linen, and mosquito netting. No other furniture was allowed, though there was some means for toileting. When the prisoners ate, only a spoon was furnished, no knife or fork. All meat was cut into small pieces by an attendant prior to serving.

On this particular Friday in May 1892, Etienne Deschamps was the only condemned prisoner at the facility. He was scheduled to be executed that day for his crime. His cell, identical to the adjoining one in Condemned Box No. 1, was a gloomy ten-by-twelve-foot space. It rarely saw direct sunlight, and graffiti from past occupants covered its walls. Deschamps referred to his cell as no more than a stall.

Originally housed on the second-floor condemned area, Deschamps had been transferred to the third floor sometime after mid-March 1891. There he remained isolated, except for an eleven-month period starting in mid-May 1891 when a fellow condemned prisoner, Philip Baker, occupied the adjacent cell. He went to the gallows on April 22, 1892.

In early May 1889, Deschamps was found guilty of the January 1889 murder of a twelve-year-old girl and sentenced to die. The Louisiana Supreme Court later overturned his conviction. When he was tried again in March 1890, Louisiana's highest court upheld the guilty verdict and death sentence. The governor issued a temporary reprieve in April 1892 until the Board of Pardons could act upon the findings of a self-appointed medical commission. There were some supporters of Deschamps who believed him to be insane, but in the end it made no difference.

At 5:00 A.M., Deputy Sheriff Edgar White, the death watchman, entered Deschamps's cell and found him stretched out and asleep on his mattress, with his head resting on his right arm. The condemned prisoner had woken briefly at midnight and requested a glass of lemonade for his parched throat. An hour later he woke again, staring nervously about before falling back to sleep a few minutes later.

"Deschamps," White said as he bent down and touched his shoulder. "Come, it's five o'clock," he stated in French. "Time to be up and about, Deschamps."

When Deschamps woke from his last earthly sleep, his face was "pale and wan," according to the *Daily City Item*. He spoke not a word at first. His eyes were "feverishly bright and he seemed to realize that his case was hopeless." His silvery, curly locks were unkempt, though he had received a haircut two weeks before. He bounced to his feet and used the toilet.

After emptying his bladder, Deschamps, who spoke very little English, glanced about the room before resting his head on the jail-cell bars as if meditating. Whatever thought he had at that exact moment he took to his grave, but based on his facial expression, White assumed it was about his impending doom.

If there was a set timetable that White wished to follow that morning, Deschamps wanted no part of it. As quickly as he had risen to his feet to relieve himself, he returned to the floor with his legs crossed and his face buried in his hands. White knew it was best not to disturb Deschamps at that particular moment. He had a history of verbal outbursts and tantrums while jailed, and on three occasions he had attempted suicide. On Deschamps's last day on earth, White wisely allowed him to reign over his limited dominion, if only for a little while. After some time had elapsed, he rose to his feet and breathed a heavy sigh. "It's a sad day for me," Deschamps finally uttered in French.

He then proceeded to pace around his gallery space, occasionally pausing to look down into the prison yard through the bars that ran along the third-story banister. About three feet from the end of the gallery was the gallows, a wooden scaffold with a trapdoor held in place by a series of ropes. A gangway bridged the chasm between the gallery and scaffold. Deschamps knew he would walk across it to the gallows sometime that day. Only a miracle could prevent it.

At 7:30 that morning, Rev. Louis LeBlanc, a Jesuit priest, visited the condemned man. Fluent in French, he was a natural choice as a spiritual advisor to the French-born Deschamps. On several occasions the previous day, Father LeBlanc had asked him to go to confession, but Deschamps refused. He had convinced himself, and said as much to Father LeBlanc, that God had instructed him to confess only to Him.

Etienne Deschamps (1890). (Courtesy NOLA.com/The *Times-Picayune*)

"I will not make any confessions to a man," the Frenchman defiantly remarked. But he added, "If you wish to, you may pray for me."

He admitted to Father LeBlanc that he had no time to waste in prayer himself, though he promised him that he would attend Mass and receive the sacraments later that morning, something that he had refused to do in the past.

When breakfast was announced at eight o'clock, Deschamps spoke not a word, but by his actions it was clear that he was hungry. As he continued to pace around the gallery, a number of newspaper reporters shouted questions at him. The criminal sheriff of Orleans Parish, Gabriel Villeré, had given them unfettered access to the prisoner off and on during the past three years but especially the day before, allowing them to enter his cell at will. Prior to sundown, he had conversed with some members of the press. It would have been easier for everyone, especially Deschamps, had Villeré simply banished them until just before the execution, but Deschamps's crime begged their presence. The public demanded it. Therefore, reporters literally camped out in the prison, hoping to converse with him one last time.

But by Friday morning, Deschamps held nothing but contempt for the reporters, who he believed were directly responsible for his sentence of death. A flood of negative newspaper articles written over the past thirty-nine months proved to Deschamps their bias against him, before, during, and after his various court appearances, including the various appeals by his lawyers. Unlike the evening before, when he was cordial toward the press, by morning his attitude toward them had turned 180 degrees. He wanted nothing to do with them.

When at last his breakfast was served, his appetite had waned. Nervousness had taken hold of his psyche. When he was provided with a plate of eggs, potatoes, rice, meat, and a cup of tea, he only consumed the eggs.

At 9:00 A.M., Sheriff Villeré arrived with a new set of clothes for Deschamps. He had wanted to wear his old tattered garb to the execution, but as a favor to Villeré, he acquiesced. The new clothing consisted of a grosgrain coat, white shirt, striped trousers, and slippers. A reporter from the *Daily City Item* commented after the execution that, with his long hair and whiskers freshly trimmed, "he looked like the Etienne Deschamps of three years ago, when he committed the horrible crime."

While Deschamps dressed and groomed himself, a crowd of the curious slowly gathered in the grassy neutral ground along Orleans Street. During the early years of the prison, executions were public spectacles. The gallows was situated over the first-story covered walkway that united the two halves of the prison. Standing on Orleans Street at the building's divide or atop the roofs of neighboring buildings, people could easily witness the grand event. But the state legislature put an end to that in 1858 after a public uproar over a botched execution that was observed by hundreds of spectators during a violent thunderstorm. Thereafter, all executions were performed indoors. As reported in the *Daily City Item*, the law required that "not less than four nor shall more than fifteen people, one of whom had to be a physician, shall be present" to officially witness the execution. However, scores of other spectators received passes from the prison captain or one of his custodians to enter the yard. The gallows was erected against the rear building in the whites-only section of the prison yard. It loomed high, flush with the second- or third-story gallery of the condemned prisoner's cell.

In spite of their inability to witness Deschamps hanged, throngs of onlookers gathered along Orleans Street anyway. If they could not directly witness the execution, they would not be deprived of the opportunity to hear firsthand of his demise. Surprisingly—or maybe not, given that a young girl had been murdered—the crowds that gathered in front of the prison were comprised of a disproportionate number of females, the majority of whom were African Americans. The crime committed more than three years before had undoubtedly touched the lives of many ethnic and racial groups living in the New Orleans metropolitan area. Nearly everyone who gathered in front of the prison was eager to see justice carried out for the murder of an innocent child. By 10:00 A.M., the crowds had swelled to such a degree that one or two policemen were assigned to the area to preserve the peace. Meanwhile, inside the prison, all inmates were locked up and preparations for the hanging commenced.

After donning his gallows attire, Deschamps walked the short distance to the third-floor chapel for Mass as he had promised and received the Sacraments of Communion and of the Dead. Chief Deputy Sheriff Raoul Arnoult accompanied him and sat next to him during the service. True to an earlier promise from Sheriff Villeré, no reporters intruded upon Deschamps's time in the chapel. Afterward, he returned to his cell.

Though apprehensive, Deschamps still entertained some glimmer of hope that day. On his way back to his cell, he asked a fellow prisoner if the telegraph service between Baton Rouge and the prison was defective. It was not. But even if it had been, it would have made no difference. The possibility that Deschamps would receive another gubernatorial reprieve, or for that matter a commutation of his sentence, was as remote as him flying to the moon. His legal options had finally run their course.

At 12:20 P.M., the coroner for Orleans Parish, Dr. Yves René LeMonnier,

Jr., swore in the coroner's jury. These were the gentlemen who would officially witness the execution and later attest to and certify the death by hanging of Etienne Deschamps. They included six physicians and nine newspapermen, each reporter representing one of the city's prominent tabloids of the day. Besides Dr. LeMonnier, other city or Orleans Parish officials included Sheriff Villeré; his chief deputy sheriff, Raoul Arnoult; his former chief deputy sheriff, Alcée LeBlanc, currently a bond clerk for the Second Recorder's Court; and Assistant Coroner Dr. Paul Emile Archinard.

Of all the eyewitnesses that day, Dr. LeMonnier was the most outspoken opponent to any notion that Etienne Deschamps was insane at the time of the murder and therefore not responsible for his actions. On this day he would witness justice served. Later he would comment about the autopsy findings, which involved a close examination of Etienne Deschamps's brain. For Dr. LeMonnier, the findings would definitively prove that the murderer was sane and accountable for his unspeakable crime.

Five minutes after the coroner's jury was sworn in, Deschamps was given one last opportunity to visit the chapel before walking across the gangway to the gallows. According to one source, he was not particularly interested in doing so but did it as a favor to Sheriff Villeré. Another witness disputed that notion, however, claiming Deschamps did anything and everything to delay his execution. Deschamps and Father LeBlanc entered the chapel at 12:28. A group of nuns, members of the Sisters of Mercy who had accompanied Father LeBlanc, knelt quietly on the gallery, praying earnestly for the repose of Deschamps's soul.

Nine minutes later, Father LeBlanc opened the chapel door and requested that three chairs be brought inside, along with some writing material. Deschamps wanted to dictate something—another delay, perhaps. A minute later, the chairs and materials arrived, accompanied by Sheriff Villeré and Chief Deputy Arnoult. Arnoult served as the scribe.

The foursome spoke in low voices inside the chapel. No one on the outside heard their conversation. Then at precisely 12:43, Deschamps began his dictation, "looking around indifferently," while Arnoult passed sheet after sheet of the completed manuscript to Sheriff Villeré. At 12:50, Deschamps stopped, and Arnoult and Villeré signed the document. The pair then departed, leaving Father LeBlanc and Deschamps alone in the chapel once again.

At 1:05, the chapel doors opened. Father LeBlanc called upon the nuns to say one last prayer for the condemned prisoner as Deschamps walked out into the gallery "cool and collected, followed by the others," as the *Daily Picayune* reported.

The witnesses gathered along the gallery connected to Condemned Box No. 1, awaiting the arrival of Deschamps. Once he arrived, Arnoult began to read the death warrant in English. Knowing what it was, Deschamps "interrupted in his excitable French manner," one witness recalled.

"It is only a formality. Let us dispense with it," he requested.

But Arnoult continued reading as prescribed by law while Deschamps looked upon the witnesses, paying no attention to Arnoult. When Arnoult began to recite the death warrant in French, Deschamps interrupted him again on the same grounds. But it made no difference to Arnoult, who continued.

Deschamps pointed directly at Dr. LeMonnier.

"I am innocent! LeMonnier is a murderer! Assassin! LeMonnier!" Deschamps cried out, his eyes blazing.

Alcée LeBlanc, who stood nearby, tried to calm Deschamps as his march to the gallows began. The party had scarcely walked a few yards when Deschamps cried out again. "I am innocent who am to be hung. LeMonnier is a criminal. Assassin! LeMonnier! Assassin! LeMonnier!"

They reached the gangway. The executioner placed a noose around Deschamps's neck. His hands were pinioned.

The executioner's name was not immediately known to the newspaper reporters who were present. Quietly spirited into the prison and isolated in an unidentified cell the previous night, the man had been given all the comforts of home before performing his grisly task the following day. One reporter implied that the executioner was "no other than the redoubtable Taylor," a well-known figure in the city dubbed "Hangman Taylor" by the press. Years later he was described as a tall, bearded man, "calm and most provokingly cool."

It turned out that the reporter's inclination was correct. The executioner was Hangman Taylor; one of the newspapers identified him by name the following day. Disguised "under the folds of a black domino [mask]" and undoubtedly wearing a grotesque black robe with hood and white gloves, which was his trademark costume, Hangman Taylor went about his task nameless and faceless to all but a few select prison officials.

The use of a professional hangman was still a relatively new development. In years past, the sheriff solicited help from minor criminals under his charge with the promise of a pardon if they undertook the job. But that created more problems than not for the Sheriff's Department when the hanging went badly. By the 1890s, a professional hangman was hired.

Hangman Taylor was such a person, and he was known around the country as most proficient in his trade. How Taylor—his first name was never published—acquired his skill is unknown. The circumstances surrounding his first execution are also unknown. By May 1892, he had already executed more than twenty of Louisiana's condemned prisoners. His profession would eventually cost him his marriage and alienate his son, John, who never knew his father other than by what he did for a living. Ostracized by his peers because of his father's occupation, John turned to a life of crime as a petty thief by 1904 at the age of eighteen.

By the time the old Orleans Parish Prison closed its doors in January 1895 and moved to its new location on Gravier Street, Hangman Taylor had officiated at two additional hangings there. He performed several more in the new building, before his reported death sometime during the early 1900s.

"Have you anything to say?" Sheriff Villeré asked Deschamps in French.

"Nothing. I have said all I had to say to Father LeBlanc," he replied. "He advises me to say nothing."

Father LeBlanc, standing inches from Deschamps, raised the crucifix, affording Deschamps one last opportunity to kiss the cross before being placed upon the drop door where a stool had been positioned. Taylor tied his feet, and Deschamps was then seated, "glancing about with interested unconcern," according to one reporter.

"Adieu," Deschamps muttered, looking at one of the men he recognized.

It turned out to be his last utterance—appropriate but pathetic as it was. Hangman Taylor placed a black cap firmly over his head and then retreated to a neighboring cell to await Sheriff Villeré's signal to cut the rope that held the trapdoor. The trap had been weighted from beneath to expedite its opening and to prevent it from rebounding and striking the condemned prisoner as he dangled. The time was 1:10 P.M., and Etienne Deschamps had ninety seconds left of conscious life.

At precisely 1:11 1/2 P.M., Sheriff Villeré gave the signal to Taylor, whose raised ax swung down and severed the rope with a single blow. The attached weight and Etienne's mass caused the hinged trap to swing down, making a clanging sound as the door struck the weathered prison wall. A second later, the stool hit the ground with a clatter. Deschamps's body plunged eight feet, "the upper portion leaning forward in the fall," before the rope snapped his neck, terminating his descent. "The head jerked to the right, the feet swung forward, and then the figure straightened and swayed a bit from the strain of the rope," according to one eyewitness.

A minute after Deschamps's plunge into eternity, observers noted convulsive twitches of the abdominal muscles. Lack of oxygen had triggered the beginnings of lactic acidosis, which caused widespread spasms until death. Thirty seconds later, his body hung motionless, though his "powerful lungs were yet to assert themselves," as noted by an eyewitness. A second set of strong muscular twitches then continued in regular intervals for several minutes.

At 1:16, his pulse was checked and recorded at eighty-four beats per minute. By then his breathing was much slower. Two minutes later, all muscular activity relaxed. Etienne Deschamps hanged for ten more minutes before being declared dead at precisely 1:28 P.M. From beginning to end, not a single sign of struggle had been observed by the witnesses. Hangman Taylor had done his job well.

Taylor cut down the condemned man at 1:43, and two stalwart African Americans placed the body on a wooden stretcher that had been deposited beneath the gallows. There, newspapermen and other witnesses quickly gathered. "No one [rejoiced] at Deschamps' death. The feeling [was] only one of grim satisfaction, absolutely passionless," a reporter later wrote.

A cursory examination of the body by Dr. LeMonnier showed that Etienne Deschamps had died by "a slow, but unconscious and painless strangulation." His inspection revealed that Etienne's face was badly cyanotic, and the rope had left a deep impression in his neck. "The lips were barely parted." His right eye was closed, and "the left partially open, with the eye ball in normal position." The *Daily Picayune* printed graphic details of the execution and the autopsy that followed.

A post-mortem examination of Deschamps's brain, done "in the interest of science," revealed that it was "well developed and perfectly normal," according to Dr. Archinard, who performed the autopsy at the prison thirty minutes after his death. Coroner LeMonnier was present during the operation. Archinard noted that the brain was "a little soft," but that was to be expected in a warm body. Dr. LeMonnier had previously indicated that he believed Deschamps lacked any physical or psychological signs of abnormality and therefore was not insane at the time of the murder. Of course, by today's standards, not finding any abnormalities of the brain doesn't rule out mental illness as a causative factor for the crime of murder. But in the world of 1892, in Dr. LeMonnier's mind, it had.

Deschamps's corpse remained at the prison until 4:00 P.M., when it was placed in a simple pine coffin and transported for burial to Potter's Field or Holt Cemetery, established in 1879 for the indigent. No one had claimed the body. The mostly in-ground cemetery, a rare phenomenon in New Orleans, is situated approximately three miles northwest of what was then the prison's location, along Metairie Road (now City Park Avenue) on Rosedale Drive, adjacent to present-day Delgado Community College.

The press later questioned Father LeBlanc, Sheriff Villeré, and Chief Deputy Arnoult about the content of Deschamps's dictation in the prison chapel.

"It is in no [way] relative to the crime, and is not a confession or statement," Villeré and Arnoult jointly announced. "Its nature we are bound by an oath to Father LeBlanc to keep secret." Father LeBlanc would not discuss the content of his conversations with Deschamps and also asserted that the document was not a confession or statement. As far as he was concerned, Deschamps had kissed the cross and died a Roman Catholic in good standing.

Prior to the execution, rumors had spread across the city that Deschamps was a Mason and therefore would never hang. Dr. LeMonnier was a Mason, and a Mason would never allow another Mason to hang. We do not know if Deschamps himself fueled such rumors. His membership is possible, but there's no evidence. For at least 150 years prior to the hanging, the Roman Catholic Church had been openly critical of Freemasonry, forbidding Catholic men from joining the organization. With Deschamps severing his alleged ties with "an alien Masonic body," as the *Daily Picayune* reported, all was right in the eyes of the Lord, as far as Father LeBlanc was concerned.

Etienne Deschamps now belonged to the ages and to God, his infamy forever a stain upon his family's name. For the murder of a twelve-year-old girl, there would be no forgiveness. His offense would become one of the most sensational in the crime annals of New Orleans.

Chapter Two

The Bizarre and the Lethal

Searching for truth. Doing it well, Magnetism. Dr. Etienne, professor of magnetic physiology, of Paris. All maladies cured by magnetism. Treatment at domicile.

Daily City Item, May 13, 1892

The evening before Etienne Deschamps went to the gallows, he entertained reporters' questions. From that interview, and from his last will and testament published in the newspaper the day after his death, the citizenry learned that Deschamps was born in Rennes, France, in 1830. Unfortunately, his stated birth year made no sense when he also told reporters that he was twenty-two years old when he enlisted in the French army and served during the Crimean War, fought between October 1853 and March 1856. England and France did not enter the conflict against Russia until March 1854.

Evidence suggests that Deschamps's birth year was four years later than what he told reporters on the eve of his execution. First, his name appeared on a passenger list of a German vessel that docked at New Orleans in late December 1868. The manifest indicated that the French native was thirty-four years old at the time. Second, Deschamps apparently forgot about the 1870 United States census (though census records are not infallible). In June 1870, Deschamps was living in New Orleans, a known fact, and he told the census enumerator he was thirty-six years old. So the evidence suggests that he was born sometime during the first six months of 1834. Contrary to what he said, Deschamps was probably twenty-two years old by the end of the Crimean War.

Deschamps was the eldest of eight children, born into a family described as wealthy and socially prominent but grounded by a strong sense of personal responsibility. And therein lay the rub for Deschamps, who did not share his family's philosophy. It appeared that at an early age, he believed he was entitled to a life of privilege, void of personal obligations or ambitions that could improve his life beyond the advantages of his surname. By the time

Deschamps entered his adolescent years, a rift had formed between him and his family. His parents eventually branded him the "black sheep" of the family, as did his siblings. Labeled by family members as possessing "a roving, vagabond disposition," Deschamps alienated them to such a degree that by the early 1850s, it appeared that he was either persuaded to leave the country or his parents had washed their hands of him.

Etienne Deschamps told reporters that he enlisted into the French army, fighting at some point during the siege at the port city of Sevastopol (September 1854-September 1855). During this battle, he was bayoneted by a Russian soldier and escaped "death through the shooting down of his assailant by another French soldier," according to the *Daily Picayune*. He returned to France at war's end, but the discord between him and his family continued.

What Deschamps told to reporters about his war experiences may be true, but some evidence suggests that he lived in New Orleans prior to joining the military, a point of interest he had not discussed. Exactly when this "Mr. Deschamps," as he was called, arrived in the Crescent City is not known, but by November 1853 such a person resided there and, by the following year, had begun to advertise his peculiar services in one of the local newspapers. How he earned a living by 1854 would directly connect him to the Etienne Deschamps of 1889 and the tragic death of an innocent twelve-year-old girl. It could have been two entirely different persons sharing a last name, but it's hard to imagine that there were two people called Deschamps engaged in the same shadowy business of animal magnetism.

□ □ □

The words *mesmerism* and *mesmerized* entered the English lexicon thanks to the work or experimentations of Franz Anton Mesmer, an eighteenth-century Viennese physician who dabbled in hypnosis and hypnotherapy. He was not the creator or discoverer of hypnosis or transitory states as a means of healing; the ancient Egyptians, Chinese, Greeks, and Romans experimented with this type of therapy first. Mesmer introduced his brand of therapy to Europe as an additional and/or substitute treatment for diseases, particularly those of the mind. He studied theology and law before becoming a physician, and his doctoral thesis (completed at the University of Vienna in 1766) introduced the term *animal magnetism*, though it was years before he put his theory to practice.

The work of Isaac Newton and his publication of *Mathematical Principles of Natural Philosophy* in 1687 greatly influenced Mesmer. Newton's three basic laws that governed bodies in motion—in particular, how the pull of the sun and moon created earth's tidal actions—fascinated Mesmer. In time, he came to believe that such universal forces could operate in the human body as a type of magnetism, specifically animal magnetism, as he labeled it.

After Mesmer graduated from medical school, his initial practice was quite unconventional, given that the established medical community treated an assortment of physical and psychological maladies with such crude methods as bleeding, purgatives, and heavy doses of opiates. Over time, Mesmer came to believe that a more humane approach was necessary for treating such afflictions. He eventually turned to his earlier theory of animal magnetism as a substitute.

When one of his female patients presented with a toothache and earache "followed by delirium, rage, vomiting, and swooning," Mesmer used a magnet to disrupt (as he saw it) the gravitational tides that produced such adverse symptoms. Running a magnet along her body, along with employing a series of gestures and touches known as the "mesmeric pass," Mesmer suggested to the female patient that humeral fluids flowing through her body were responsible for her condition and that his actions could drain away such negative energy. His use of the magnetic prop as an instrument, coupled with his persuasive powers of suggestion, had a miraculous effect upon the patient, whose symptoms soon disappeared.

Mesmer knew that the magnet did not directly contribute to the cure but was nevertheless a necessary tool in his practice, for it served to transfer his positive animal magnetism to the patients whose levels he believed had somehow been depleted. But his power of suggestion was the real key to his success, a fact that seemed to elude him. If the patient believed it would help, it did. Modern-day hypnosis or hypnotic suggestion was born, unbeknownst to Mesmer.

Mesmer went on to achieve similar success with patients who suffered from blindness, paralysis, convulsions, and hysterias, no doubt psychologically based, though he claimed to cure menstrual difficulties and hemorrhoids as well. As a result, Mesmer became a celebrity, touring the Continent and demonstrating his skills with all the showmanship of a circus performer. It worked for the common folks, but the medical community revolted, and over time his career suffered from unforeseen consequences. In one famous incident, he almost cured a young female pianist who suffered from hysterical blindness, but her cure would have cost her family a royal pension. Once his treatments stopped and her blindness returned, her family was much relieved. This only illustrated the power of suggestion and Mesmer's unique ability to harness it.

The public and eventually the royal court came to believe that his use of animal magnetism was a farce. He employed "magnetized" trees to achieve a cure, but when cures were also obtained using "non-magnetized" trees, Mesmer was labeled a charlatan. In spite of his difficulties, the concept of animal magnetism persisted well into the nineteenth century. In New Orleans on July 2, 1844, at the Washington Armory, a Dr. Boynton delivered a lecture on "Sympathy, Magnetic Attraction, Neurology, Phrenopathy, Music, and Clairvoyance." Dr. Boynton, a well-known lecturer on the subject of animal magnetism, magnetic sleep, and clairvoyance, enthralled his audience for fifty cents a ticket. Several months earlier, he delivered a similar lecture, labeled "Mesmerism," in Louisville, Kentucky. Like the citizens of New Orleans, the Kentucky crowd was appreciative of and receptive to Dr. Boynton. Apparently his influence never waned. Nearly a decade later, New Orleans became the site of the attempted murder of Eléonore Fouget Sage and suicide by her jilted lover. The case captivated the city and nation. The use of animal magnetism supposedly played a major part in healing the young lady. A "Mr. Deschamps" later claimed responsibility for restoring her health.

At 1:00 P.M. on Tuesday, November 15, 1853, French native and stage actress Eléonore Fouget Sage, the wife of Charles Sage, was found on the floor of her rented home at 80 Bourbon Street (now in the 400 block) in the French Quarter. She had been shot in the cheek, with the bullet exiting the other side. Although disfiguring—Madame Sage had been strikingly beautiful—the wound was hardly life threatening, as newspapers reported. Lying prostrate beside her, however, was her assailant, Jules Bettford, who upon firing his weapon at Madame Sage quickly turned a second pistol on himself. His brains were found splattered about the floor. Local and national newspapers had a field day with the attempted murder-suicide, sensationalizing it as "Love and Suicide." Madame Sage was hardly Bettford's lover. Their relationship resembled more of a stalker-victim situation than a consensual affair.

Prior to coming to New Orleans, the Sages lived in Cincinnati, where Eléonore owned a cigar store. Her youth and beauty drew a sizable number of male customers to her establishment, including Bettford, who befriended the couple. When the Sages relocated a few miles south to Latonia Springs,

Kentucky, Bettford followed them, "desperately enamored of Madame" and finding that "living out of her presence was to him a thing unsupportable," according to a Virginia newspaper. He bought a house and then mysteriously fell ill or perhaps feigned illness. No one will ever know for sure. The Sages took him in and Madame nursed him back to health. Charles was totally oblivious of Bettford's ardor toward his wife, as was Madame at that point.

When an opportunity arose for Madame Sage to act in *Vaudevilles*, a play performed at the renowned Orleans Theater, she jumped at the chance. Apparently she had some prior acting experience while living in France. She and her husband boarded the steamer *J. S. Chenoweth* and journeyed down the Mississippi River to New Orleans. Bettford was a passenger too. While aboard the vessel, Bettford finally made known his feelings toward Madame "and even went so far as to propose an elopement," according to one newspaper. She rejected him, of course, but never informed her husband, fearing that some violent encounter might ensue between the two. Once in New Orleans, Bettford continued to hound her and threatened to take her life if she did not comply with his wishes. When at last it seemed he had lost her love forever—although he never had her love—he entered the Sages' home with two pistols in hand. The husband was absent. The rest is history.

Beginning on March 26, 1854, a series of advertisements appeared in the *Daily Picayune* under the title, "Important Notice." A Mr. Deschamps, writing in third person, made it known that in large part he had restored Madame Sage's health. Exaggerating her injuries, he claimed she suffered a near-fatal gunshot wound to the neck, which left her paralyzed on one side of her body and less than fourteen hours from death. Using his homeopathic and magnetic clairvoyance, he had restored her life after just one hour of his applied therapy. "More than twenty persons present considered the cure a miracle," according to the advertisements. "It was no miracle, but the mere aiding of the efforts of nature instead of opposing them." His advertisements ended as follows: "MR. DESCHAMPS will continue, as heretofore, to give consultations for the different cases of disease. Each person as wish to be initiated to his system can find him at his office, No. 171 Royal Street, every day from 4 to 5 o'clock in the evening."

After the January 7, 1855, issue of the paper, his advertisements suddenly stopped running after appearing eighty-four times. What became of Mr. Deschamps and his business endeavor will never be known. Likely his practice went afoul, like that of Dr. Mesmer. Whatever the cause, it appeared that he simply vanished from the city—to France and then off to the war, perhaps?

With that said, Etienne Deschamps likely entered the military sometime in early 1855, time enough to fight and receive his battle wound during the waning months of the Sevastopol siege. By spring of 1856 he had returned to his native land. The Crimean War was over. Whatever his life experiences had been up to that point, it appeared they had little positive influence upon his character. In France, he reverted to his old ways of debauchery, a behavioral pattern that appears to have lasted (off and on) for the next decade or more, much to his parents' chagrin.

It is interesting to note that the October 17, 1866, edition of the *New Orleans Tribune*, ran a story that chronicled the arrest of a French actor named Deschamps who, having failed to fulfill his military duties with the army, was arrested in Dieppe, France, a small port on the English Channel. At the time of his arrest, he was acting in the town's theater. The newspaper reported that Deschamps, possessing "no ambition for military glory," attempted to elude military authorities by quickly boarding a train bound for Paris. He was stopped at one of the connecting stations "by a telegraph dispatch and sent back to Dieppe under arrest." What was peculiar about this incident was why a New Orleans newspaper would print such a story, unless it had some relevance to the Deschamps who once lived in the Crescent City. Could this be the same Deschamps of 1854? Having "cured" Madame Sage, a celebrated actress, Mr. Deschamps might have taken up acting himself when he returned to the Continent.

Regardless of what transpired in 1866 and its relevance to the Etienne Deschamps of 1889, by the late 1860s, our man in question had earned a degree in dentistry. He had also completed some coursework in medicine. One might believe that, by his early thirties, Deschamps had finally come of age, but perhaps not.

After graduating and taking up residence in Paris, Deschamps resumed a festive and irresponsible lifestyle, "practicing his profession in a desultory sort of way," according to the *Daily Picayune*. It was as if dentistry had become a means to an end. His profession allowed him to make sizable sums of money, which he spent recklessly on various pleasures. He lived for the excitement of the moment at the expense of everything else, with dentistry providing a backup source of income when needed. As a result, he never married and never had any children that he knew of.

He told reporters that he "sought diversion in national affairs, became involved in political troubles and fled the country in 1870." However, Deschamps and his twenty-eight-year-old brother, Louis, arrived in the

United States sooner than that. (At that time, he obviously still had some kind of rapport with at least one member of his family.) They booked passage aboard the German-registered vessel *Teutonia*, which departed from the port city of Hamburg, Germany bound for Le Havre, France; Havana, Cuba; and New Orleans. The brothers arrived in the Crescent City on December 31, 1868, supposedly penniless. By June 1870, the elder Deschamps was living in New Orleans, employed as a dentist. What became of his younger brother is unclear but, perhaps disheartened by his brother's behavior, Louis most likely returned to France because his name didn't appear in the 1870 U.S. Census.

Like the *Mr.* Deschamps of 1854, *Dr.* Deschamps lived in the *L*-shaped Fifth Ward of the French Quarter, bordered by the river, St. Philip Street, and St. Louis Street and extending north to Lake Pontchartrain via Bayou St. John. While living in the French Quarter, he put his dental practice to good use. Elsewhere in the U.S., being fluent in French but not in English would have created a language barrier for Deschamps when dealing with his clientele. Fortunately for him, New Orleans had a sizable French-speaking population, particularly in the French Quarter. Therefore, he was able to do quite well in the city and accumulated some wealth, which afforded him the opportunity to expand his horizons and see the world. He was forever a restless traveler. It is not known when he left the city, but according to one newspaper account, Deschamps journeyed south to Brazil, "where he again became involved in political troubles and left the country without ceremony thereby losing several thousand dollars' worth of property and personal effects."

"He returned to Europe, traveled from place to place," and, as he had done before, relied upon dentistry when his funds ran low, "living in comfort, [then] in poverty and never hearing from his family, who had long ago severed all connection with him," as reported in the *Daily Picayune*. If he had dabbled in animal magnetism in the past, as evidence suggests he did, his travels across Europe during the early 1880s must have reignited his interest in the subject.

When news began to circulate in Europe that New Orleans would host the World's Industrial and Cotton Exposition—a celebration of the 100th anniversary of America's cotton industry—Deschamps jumped at the chance to return to Louisiana. Once back in the Crescent City, he could combine dentistry with magnetism for an even greater financial yield, or so he thought. Unfortunately for Deschamps, arriving shortly before the fair's opening on December 16, 1884, his funds were exhausted (and there is little mystery why). Where he lived initially and how he earned his keep is not known.

Deschamps's only confirmed residences were on Chartres Street by 1887 and later on St. Peter Street. It appears that he established a considerable dental practice in various parishes southwest of New Orleans and in Mississippi. Deschamps spent more time in the countryside than in the city, according to Charles Serra, one of his neighbors.

Serra and his wife lived in a rented room on the second floor of a two-story brick residence at 64 (now 714) St. Peter Street, between Royal and Bourbon streets. This part of the French Quarter was considered to be a poor neighborhood. For a time, the domicile had a second entry point through one of two French doors on St. Peter Street. This entrance was designated as 66 St. Peter Street. The No. 64 main entrance (an arched doorway to the left of the French doors) led to a wide, enclosed corridor. On the right, an interior doorway led to the first-floor living quarters, which consisted of a parlor, dining room, attached kitchen, and storeroom, though for a time one of these rooms also served as a bedroom. Past the doorway, a stairway ascended to the second floor, which contained five rooms. Beyond the steps, the corridor opened into a small, side courtyard.

According to Serra's testimony at the first trial, Deschamps took up residence at No. 64 sometime in mid-1887. However, another witness claimed he and Deschamps lived at the same boardinghouse located on Chartres Street during the month of August.

The St. Peter Street house was connected to the city gas grid, but it appears that was for exterior lighting only and possibly for cooking, as the upstairs rooms were illuminated by candles, oil lamps, or direct sunlight. It also had its own cistern for water collection and an indoor commode, referred to in those days as a "water closet." A pipe ran up the wall to a flush tank filled with water. A pull of a chain or rope released the water, flushing the human waste down into the city sewer system.

The second floor was accessible via a split, twenty-three-step stairway that ran parallel to St. Peter Street. At the top of the stairs on the right was a five-foot-wide arched window, which provided a view of the side courtyard. The footprint of the house resembled a backward L. Deschamps's room was located just to the left of the top step, along an enclosed four-foot-wide inner gallery that ran parallel to the street. The next room was the Serra residence. The two rooms, each approximately twenty-two feet deep by sixteen feet across, had exterior walls up to a foot thick and shared a thinner interior wall. Each room had its own fireplace situated on the exterior wall, facing either Royal or Bourbon streets.

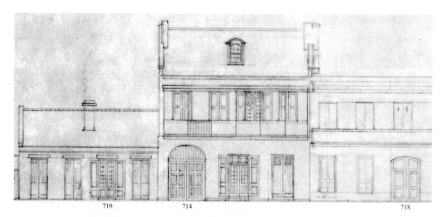

Detail of a June 1941 sketch of a portion of the 700 block of St. Peter Street, New Orleans, with Deschamps's residence in the center. (Courtesy of the Collections of the Louisiana State Museum)

Just past Serra's door was a second, narrower set of stairs that led to the third-story attic. The gable roof that created the attic space contained a centered, narrow-arched dormer visible from the street. The dormer allowed ventilation or sunlight into the upper loft.

At the time of the murder, there were at least two other tenants living on the property: Elizabeth "Lizzy" Hilroy, a widow who served as the landlady, and John P. Lewis, who apparently resided on the first floor. His address was listed as 66 St. Peter Street. His association with the property dated back to at least 1885.

Mrs. Hilroy lived on the second floor at the rear of the house, in one of the three smaller side rooms that ran perpendicular to St. Peter Street and parallel to Bourbon Street. This side of the house measured approximately twenty-nine feet across by fifteen feet deep. Beside the stairway leading to the attic was the water closet that was shared by all tenants.

The two rooms facing St. Peter Street were fairly plain. Deschamps's room, entered through what was referred to as the "rear door," was described as very simple—four basic walls. A fireplace with a very large mantel was situated along the right wall or the Royal Street side of the building. The wall fronting St. Peter Street had two four-foot-wide French doors (set four feet apart), referred to as "front doors." Each door had a pair of adjustable, louvered shutters that swung out onto a roughly three-foot-wide gallery. When the French doors were left open and the shutters were closed, the opened horizontal blinds provided ventilation for the room. When slightly or totally closed, they blocked the rain or sun's glare.

A partition door stood between Deschamps's room and the Serra family's room, though obviously when both rooms were occupied, it was kept closed and locked. During the Victorian era, bedroom doors swung out, unlike today where they swing into the room. Since this door swung open into Deschamps' room, in earlier days, his room might have been a parlor and the Serras' room a connected bedroom.

Oddly, the property was located within a block of the 1854 business establishment of one Mr. Deschamps. Its present location is 731 Royal Street. The irony doesn't stop there.

The home on St. Peter Street was built in May 1829 by Dr. Yves Julien Joseph LeMonnier, the grandfather of Dr. Yves René LeMonnier, the 1889 Orleans Parish coroner whose testimony damned Deschamps to the gallows. Like Deschamps, Dr. LeMonnier's grandfather was born in Rennes, France. He died at the age of sixty in 1832, and several years later George Raymond Lacoul, a St. Charles Parish sugar plantation owner, purchased the property. By 1860 the home was allegedly turned into a boardinghouse. One tenant was none other than Antoine Alciatore, a celebrated artist in cooking whose eatery was located at 60 St. Peter Street, at the corner of Royal Street. It then moved to 68 (now 718) St. Peter Street, the present site of Pat O'Brien's Bar. "Antoine's" relocated to St. Louis Street sometime before the end of 1866, according to the city directory. It's quite possible that his St. Peter Street restaurant was located on the lower floor of the Lacoul home, since address numbering was so chaotic at the time.

Beginning in mid-1883, the St. Peter Street property was owned by Françoise Jeanne Lobel Mahy and likely remained in her possession during Deschamps's stay. Oliver La Farge, an American Pulitzer Prize-winning author and anthropologist, rented a room there during the mid- to late 1920s. His residence served as a gathering place for other artists, writers, and scientists. As a result, the house, a restaurant today, is often referred to as the LeMonnier House, the Lacoul House, or the Oliver La Farge Home.

In 1887, Etienne Deschamps, a.k.a. Dr. Etienne, suspended "a peculiar card, inscribed in French," as reported in the *Daily City Item*, from the outer gallery railing above St. Peter Street: "Searching for truth. Doing it well, Magnetism. Dr. Etienne, professor of magnetic physiology, of Paris. All maladies cured by magnetism. Treatment at domicile." With his residence established on St. Peter Street, it appeared that Etienne Deschamps had at last taken the final plunge into the mystic realm of magnetism, legitimizing his skills with the claim of being a Parisian expert on the subject. Nevertheless, it was the same troubling, shadowy type of healing that had been offered by

"Mr. Deschamps" thirty years earlier. The only difference now was that Dr. Deschamps was using an alias: Dr. Etienne or Dr. Eugène Etienne and later Dr. Eugène Déjan. The name Eugène Déjan, a dentist residing at 64 St. Peter Street, began to appear in the *Soards' New Orleans City Directory* in 1888 and continued the following year. The puzzling question was, why the aliases? Had he defrauded someone in the city or abused his healing powers years earlier? And why did he change his name to Déjan beginning in 1888? He took the answers to his grave.

"The ignorant and superstitious poor of the neighborhood," as the *Daily Picayune* described Deschamps's French-speaking clientele, came in droves seeking cures for real or imaginary maladies. As Dr. Etienne's fee was small, he no doubt counted on volume as his chief means of turning a profit. Over the course of four and a half years, Dr. Etienne or Dr. Eugène Déjan profited off the misery of others, turning to dentistry when the need arose. By then, chloroform was the chief anesthetic agent used to render patients unconscious. And therein lies the beginning of Deschamps's fascination with the bizarre—magnetism—and the lethal—chloroform.

□ □ □

Between 1821 and 1846, only 333 surgeries were performed at Massachusetts General Hospital in Boston. That figure equated to about one surgery per month and illustrated the rarity of surgical procedures performed across the United States during the first half of the nineteenth century. Because of the intense pain suffered, most physicians and their patients opted out of performing or having surgery. Prior to the mid-1840s, there were only three principal choices of anesthesia available: opium, in the form of a powder or its liquid equivalent called laudanum; morphine, isolated from opium in 1806; and finally, alcohol. Opium and morphine were sometimes crudely injected into a wound, or morphine powder was sprinkled over the injury as a means of controlling pain. These methods were impractical in dentistry when a tooth extraction or oral surgery had to be performed.

The origins of modern surgical anesthesia are rooted in dentistry, where practitioners sought some means of relieving pain while performing various oral procedures on their patients. For a brief time during the early 1840s, carbon monoxide gas was used experimentally. The toxic substance rendered the patient unconscious, allowing the surgical procedure to be performed without inflicting pain, but the patient didn't wake up.

Ether, first synthesized around 1540 by German botanist and chemist

Valerius Cordus, was a colorless, highly flammable, and very volatile (readily vaporizable) liquid, with a slightly sweet odor and taste. Its medical applications during the sixteenth century were nonexistent. When nitrous oxide gas, a close associate of ether, was isolated in 1772 by English chemist Joseph Priestley, its vapors were used more for entertainment purposes than anything else. When the vapors were trapped in a container—a bag, for instance—and inhaled, they produced a state of euphoria, thus the term "laughing gas." Traveling salesmen eager to make a quick buck marketed the vapors to the curious. By the 1830s, American college students were staging so-called "ether frolics" (the terms "ether" and "nitrous oxide" were used interchangeably). The youngsters got high, giddy, and passed out after inhaling the substance. It would take decades before the anesthetic properties of nitrous oxide or ether were realized by the medical establishment.

In December 1844, when a showman arrived in Hartford, Connecticut, to demonstrate the effects of nitrous oxide, a large enthusiastic crowd gathered, including a local dentist named Horace Wells. Dr. Wells became fascinated with the substance after a young man inhaled it, for the amusement of the audience, then bloodied his leg in a fall. When he regained consciousness, he had no recollection of his injury. The idea of using nitrous oxide for dentistry and surgery was born. Chloroform soon followed.

The chloroform compound, a liquid, was discovered independently by three scientists, an American, German, and Frenchman, in 1831. Though it was initially used to treat asthma, by 1847 a Scottish obstetrician, James Young Simpson, was successfully using chloroform as an anesthetic to relieve labor pain. Considered superior to nitrous oxide or ether because it was easier to transport, and was nonflammable at normal temperatures and pressures, chloroform soon caught on with the medical establishment. By the Civil War, it was widely used by both sides to anesthetize soldiers suffering from battle wounds and assorted diseases requiring surgery. As a liquid, it could be easily stored in a bottle, quickly poured on a cloth, and brought to the patient's face. Inhaling it produced unconsciousness within a matter of minutes. If the patient began to arouse prematurely, the physician needed only to place the chloroform-saturated cloth back over his mouth and nose to render him unconscious again. This is not to say that chloroform was not dangerous; it was. An overdose (consumed or inhaled) could be fatal. In fact, chloroform would become the drug of choice for the despondent wanting to commit suicide.

However, the federal government did not weigh in on the problem until the passage of the Pure Food and Drug Act of 1906, which at first only regulated the labeling of foods and drugs that crossed state lines. It was years before chloroform (often an ingredient in various over-the-counter cough syrups) and similar dangerous drugs would be placed out of the reach of the buying public.

By the 1880s, a person could obtain a finite amount of chloroform at a reasonable price at their local drugstore. These shops were typically operated by or in association with a physician. There were scores of such businesses in New Orleans at that time. And so Dr. Etienne was easily able to obtain chloroform for his dental practice, though eventually his application of the drug went far beyond its intended purposes.

By all accounts, Etienne Deschamps was a competent dentist who was able to successfully combine magnetism—hypnosis, in essence—and chloroform to achieve satisfactory results for his patients. Whether his skills at magnetism were used to deliberately deceive or to legitimately heal, no one will ever know. His business nevertheless flourished and, as stated before, over time Deschamps branched out beyond the city limits. He traveled along Bayou Lafourche and into Terrebonne Parish and its parish seat of Houma, "where he attended the families of plantation owners," according to the *Daily Picayune*. His journeys also took him as far west as Morgan City in St. Mary Parish and as far east as Bay Saint Louis, Mississippi, where for a time he took up residence at the Crescent Hotel—later renamed the Pickwick Hotel. Listing the hotel as his domicile, Deschamps advertised himself as a *Surgeon Dentist* on his business cards, undoubtedly a stretch of the truth.

His frequent visits to the Louisiana bayous afforded Deschamps the opportunity to explore the many islands and inlets along the southeastern shores of the state, including the Barataria region, the home and hiding place of the famous buccaneer, Jean Lafitte. One day, he stumbled upon some old coins and trinkets buried in the sand. From that moment on, he was obsessed with finding the location of Lafitte's booty. Rumors of a buried war chest filled with plundered gold and silver had persisted for decades. The treasure probably never existed, and no trace of it was ever found, but that didn't stop adventurers like Dr. Etienne Deschamps from searching for it.

Oddly, given his peculiar nature, Deschamps had little faith in divining rods. Instead, he placed all his bets on his hypnotic-magnetic abilities to discover Lafitte's plundered fortune. In his mind, he only needed a "suitable subject," someone he could mesmerize into revealing the exact location of the treasure. Sometime after the summer of 1887, Etienne Deschamps believed he had found such a person, a young girl named Juliette Dietsh, who happened to be a native of his country, born in September 1876.

Juliette and her sister, Laurence, three years her junior, were the daughters of Jules Dietsh, born circa 1848 in Mennecy, France. He immigrated to the United States with his girls and eighty-two-year-old widowed mother, arriving in New Orleans on July 12, 1887. (The family entered the States at New York City on June 27, 1887, aboard *La Gascogne.*) Jules' wife had died in January 1881, and he moved his family to the boardinghouse of Joseph T. Michon located at 145 (now 605) Chartres Street before relocating to No. 116 (now 500), at the corner of St. Louis Street. (The three-story property is now known as the Napoleon House.) The later residence was about three blocks from Deschamps's house on St. Peter Street. Jules Dietsh was a carpenter and cabinetmaker by trade, who at times barely scraped by. Dr. Etienne entered his life either in July 1887, when they met at a local French restaurant, or a month later at Michon's boardinghouse, where Deschamps also lived for a time before he relocated to St. Peter Street.

Like Deschamps, Jules Dietsh and his family knew very little English. At first, it was fortuitous that Jules met a man with whom he could easily converse in French. In addition, when Dietsh was unable to find work for two months beginning in December 1887, Deschamps paid his expenses out of his own pocket. As a result, Dietsh, a simple man by all accounts, looked up to Dr. Etienne, admiring him as a generous, highly educated, intelligent, and trustworthy human being, with all the mannerisms of a refined French gentleman. Deschamps was able to exploit Monsieur Dietsh's belief in him, sadly to the detriment of his family. Nevertheless, the two became close friends, with Dr. Etienne visiting Jules at his home almost daily, except when he traveled for his rural practice. It was during one of those trips that Dr. Etienne discovered the coins and trinkets and then concocted his harebrained scheme to locate Lafitte's treasure. Meanwhile, during his visits with Jules, he eased the old matriarch's aches with his magnetism and lifted the spirits of his carpenter friend with tales from the Old Country, all the while instilling into both of them the notion that he could be trusted in the company of Juliette and Laurence.

The young girls, who attended Miss Adelaide M. Roux's private school at her home at 68 St. Peter Street, two doors down from Deschamps's residence, frequently passed in front of his upstairs room en route to and from their schoolroom. Miss Roux was born in France in December 1833 and immigrated to the United States in 1852. By the 1870 U.S. Census, she was earning a living in New Orleans as a teacher. Her fluency in French made her the perfect choice to educate the Dietsh children.

At the end of the summer of 1888, "Dr. Eugène Déjan"—he did not reveal his real name to Jules Dietsh until nearly the end of their friendship— made a point of visiting the girls at their home at 4:00 P.M. on schooldays. When the girls were not in school, Deschamps took them about the city and occasionally to the countryside, with the full blessing of their father. Sometimes Dietsh would join their city walks.

The threesome was spotted together so frequently that everyone assumed Deschamps was the girls' grandfather. He never corrected them. He was often seen buying them candy and trinkets. Later in their friendship, Deschamps took the girls up to his second-story room, again with their father's blessing.

Each time Deschamps departed their house on Chartres Street, the doctor made a point of kissing both girls goodnight, an act he didn't hide from their father. Later Dietsh told Juliette that she was getting to be too old to be kissed by people. When Deschamps attempted to kiss her the following day, Juliette spoke out.

"Papa don't want me to kiss anybody," she explained to the doctor.

According to Dietsh, Deschamps seemed a little put off by her comment but didn't get angry. The friendly goodnight kiss was the only impropriety that he ever witnessed between Deschamps and his older daughter.

While Jules Dietsh had nothing but implicit trust in Deschamps, that trust was not universally shared. When Deschamps's neighbors from across the street began to notice the girls going to his upstairs room, "they informed the dentist that it did not look right, but he paid no attention, and continued his course," according to the *Daily Picayune*. Sadly, the nosy neighbors would be correct.

Juliette was described as being "backward intellectually," which was not true for her younger sister. She was five feet tall, with dark auburn hair, a slim build, and by the time of her death not fully developed, nor nubile, according to the coroner. In spite of not having reached full puberty, Juliette was nevertheless a beautiful child, and her physical attractiveness drew the attention of the neighborhood boys, something that did not go unnoticed by her father. Supposedly one of the young men identified as hanging around Juliette was Charley—his last name was never mentioned—who worked at a neighborhood grocery. Allegedly the two youngsters had some type of relationship, but it was never proven. In fact, one of Juliette's friends, a fourteen-year-old girl named Anna Calamari, who lived next door to the

Dietsh family at 118 Chartres Street, categorically denied that anything ever occurred between the two. At the coroner's inquest, Anna testified that the victim barely knew who Charley was, and they never spoke to each other. Nevertheless, it may have been one of the reasons why Jules Dietsh allowed Juliette to spend so much time with the more refined French gentleman. He believed that Deschamps would be an ideal role model for both of his daughters and would naturally serve as a shield between Juliette and those unsavory boys bidding for her attention.

The date that Deschamps approached Monsieur Dietsh about his scheme to locate Jean Lafitte's treasure is not known, but it likely occurred no sooner than August 1888. According to Dietsh, Deschamps began to hypnotize Juliette that month, sometimes at his home and sometimes at the doctor's. Deschamps convinced Dietsh to lend him Juliette so that he could learn the location of the treasure. He appeared receptive to the idea after Deschamps explained that in order for the experiment to succeed, the medium had to be pure of heart and soul; in other words, a virgin. Who better to choose than an innocent twelve-year-old girl? Because he trusted Deschamps, Dietsh consented.

It was brought out in the coroner's inquest that Dietsh's mother fell ill in August 1888. This occupied his time and that of his younger daughter, Laurence, who often stayed home from school to care for her grandmother. Dietsh speculated after Juliette's death that, as a result, Juliette frequently went to school by herself and visited Deschamps alone. Laurence confirmed that her sister visited the doctor alone on one or two occasions, though she did not state when that occurred. Also during this period and continuing until her death, Juliette went to the market on a daily basis and often ran into Deschamps, according to Dietsh. He admitted that he never considered their public meetings improper. He also claimed that Juliette fell ill for a week in August 1888, though Juliette's friend Anna disputed this. Dietsh indicated that his daughter's mysterious illness had nothing to do with Deschamps, though one would naturally assume there was some connection. If not, why did Dietsh bring it up? Was Juliette being sexually abused during that time, which explained her supposed illness? Only Juliette could answer that question.

On occasion, Deschamps was able to put Juliette to sleep, but otherwise his experimentations yielded no results. The doctor briefly turned his attention to Dietsh, whom he attempted to hypnotize on six to eight occasions beginning in January 1889, without obvious success. In spite of all the failures, Deschamps pressed on with Juliette, with her father's consent. But what Dietsh could not have known at the time was the doctor's final solution for extracting the "truth" from young Juliette. Her complete willingness to follow his instructions, no matter the consequences, led to her tragic and senseless death in the midafternoon of January 30, 1889. It was a death perpetrated by a dubious practitioner who was willing to engage in the bizarre and the lethal in order to have his way with her.

Chapter Three

The Ruin and Death of
Little Juliette Dietsh

*He started to go toward the body, but the officers held him back and told him that his
daughter was dead.*
Daily Picayune, February 3, 1889

Much has been written over the years about the extent of Etienne
Deschamps's "affair" with Juliette Dietsh. Their relationship seemed to have
intensified soon after Deschamps explained his idiotic plan to Juliette's father.
She would be hypnotized using magnetism and, later, chloroform, in order
that she might reveal the burial site of Jean Lafitte's treasure. No one will ever
know with certainty if Deschamps truly believed what he was promising to
Monsieur Dietsh—treasure via magnetism—or if magnetism and chloroform
were ploys to render the young girl receptive to his sexual advances.

Seven hours after the crime, Deschamps admitted to Dr. LeMonnier
that he had been intimate with Juliette for some time. But he insisted that
in the beginning of their friendship she had strictly been his subject in his
magnetism experiments and that he had trained her in the mysteries of this
healing practice (whatever that meant). He indicated that when he returned
from his trips from the countryside, he always found young Juliette pleased to
see him, and at that time he never allowed himself to entertain any immoral
thoughts about the girl.

That changed one day when he returned to the city after visiting some
patients in Houma. The trip, which may have included a visit to Lafitte's home
base in Barataria, had taken him away from Juliette for an unusually long period
of time. When he finally returned, he discovered that she had been "ruined" by
a young man, so Deschamps claimed, possibly the mysterious "Charley" fellow.
He told Dr. LeMonnier that the girl at first denied the story. How Deschamps
learned of the affair is not known. In all likelihood, he invented the story
himself, as he sought to wash clean his revolting sins. Nevertheless, he stated
that young Juliette finally admitted to him that she had lost her virginity. It was

47

then that "he took liberties with her, which she never resented," according to the *Daily Picayune*. Her younger sister, Laurence, reportedly witnessed their sexual encounters on several occasions, but it was later explained in the newspaper that "her tender youth prevented her from understanding the gravity of the situation." Thus, their liaisons went unreported. In any event, Deschamps's version of the story changed less than twenty-four hours later—and again and again over the next three and a half years.

Not surprisingly, gossip about the cause of young Juliette's death spread like wildfire in the city and nation. The stories were eventually passed down to future generations and stated as fact or as anecdotes for the curious. One such fable indicated that Deschamps savagely beat Juliette when she was unable to conjure up the hiding place of Lafitte's treasure, ultimately murdering the girl with an overdose of chloroform in his frustration. Another story had him killing her to cover up his sexual depravity. Neither story was true, but they nevertheless persist to this day, recorded in various travel guides and articles written about the murder.

The truth surrounding the demise of young Juliette is far less dramatic. She died peacefully. She went to sleep willingly, ignorant of the dangers of the chloroform administered to her by Deschamps, and never woke up. Some people later suggested that her death was accidental. But the state in which her body was found, along with her accused murderer who lay unconscious beside her, gave everyone who witnessed the scene that day an inexplicable sense that Etienne Deschamps was strange far beyond quirky, a monster most vile, and a person who deserved to die for his actions.

On Wednesday, January 30, 1889, the Dietsh girls apparently did not attend school at Miss Roux's house. The reason is not known, but the girls—or Laurence, at least—may have been suffering from chloroform poisoning. Deschamps had made them drink the substance the day before. Laurence testified at the first trial that on January 29 while in his room, she and her sister were asked to disrobe, lie in his bed, and swallow chloroform. The drug caused Laurence to fall asleep. When she awakened, she noticed that she had vomited and had an upset stomach. She didn't know and didn't ask if Juliette had fallen asleep (she probably did). She also couldn't remember if Deschamps had disrobed, though he probably did. Either way, Deschamps and her sister were in his bed when she woke up. Laurence testified that she did not see Deschamps touch Juliette that day. But how would she have known if he had? She was asleep. According to Laurence, this was the first time that Deschamps had offered chloroform to them.

On numerous occasions in the past, Deschamps had magnetized them, with and without their father present. Laurence described a ritual where the doctor passed his hands over their faces, sometimes holding a mirror and/ or iron bar. He called the latter a "magnetizing disc." The one he owned was a five-by-three-by-one-inch piece of rosewood with a segment of highly polished, magnetized steel in the middle. Other such devices, though perhaps not like Deschamps's disc, were used by some doctors to cure all sorts of physical maladies. One Ohio physician called his instrument a "Magnetic Absorbent Disc" and claimed it could "absorb and remove all inflammation, pain, and disease by taking the real poison and matter from the blood," according to a newspaper advertisement. But on this day, Deschamps used no such hocus-pocus. Chloroform was his drug of choice, a drug he had not administered to the girls before.

Incredibly, the girls never told their father what they experienced that day. Laurence testified at the coroner's inquest that Deschamps and Juliette forbade her from saying anything. Child molesters count on that. Secrecy is critical for abusers, for their own protection as well as for controlling their victims. If the girls had told their father, the tragedy of the following day likely wouldn't have happened.

On Wednesday, Deschamps arrived at the Dietsh household sometime between 1:00 and 1:30 P.M., according to testimony given at the February 2, 1889, coroner's inquest, though Laurence testified at the first trial in May 1889 that it was closer to noon. After the children finished a late breakfast, Deschamps told them to grab their straw hats and cloaks. They were going on a walk, or so he informed their father, who remained at the house. But the threesome went directly to Deschamps's upstairs room on St. Peter Street, as they had done the previous day.

The doctor's furnishings included a four-poster, black-walnut bed with a bolster and mosquito bar, positioned to the left of the rear door. Three storage trunks and a valise or saddlebag lined the interior wall in front of the bed, blocking the partition door. (In May 1892, Deschamps claimed in his will that he owned four trunks.) One of the chests contained the doctor's clothing, clean and carefully packed, and the two others held his books, letters, business cards, and dental tools. Dr. LeMonnier later described the trunks as "very good ones."

Cater-cornered to the bed, in the outer right corner, stood a chair and rocker, with a washstand sandwiched between the corner and the fireplace. Bottles of assorted liquids used in dentistry, along with a candlestick and candle, occupied the mantelpiece. In the middle of the room was a wooden table approximately four feet long by two feet wide, bearing a gallon bottle with a small quantity of ammonia and a second bottle partially filled with alcohol. The only food in the room consisted of butter in a covered dish and a loaf of bread in a paper bag.

Upon entering his room that day, Deschamps opened the front doors and shutters overlooking St. Peter Street and lit a fire using coal and pinewood. He then realized that he needed additional kindling. It was chilly that day, with the temperature not reaching above fifty-four degrees.

Leaving the girls alone, he went to purchase some wood at a neighborhood grocery. On their own for the moment, Juliette confided to Laurence that earlier that morning, after leaving the house around seven o'clock or so to do her daily shopping for the family, she happened upon Deschamps. He told her to expect his arrival that afternoon around one o'clock and that she was going to have to undress in order for her to be put asleep again, unless her previous day's experience had been a semi-unconscious state. He divulged that this time, however, he was going to use all of the chloroform that he had. Apparently, Juliette thought nothing of it.

When Deschamps returned a short time later, he instructed both girls to disrobe and for Juliette to lie in his bed. Laurence stood or took a seat nearby. Juliette did what she was told, removing everything but her stockings. She placed her carefully folded clothes on the chair and her shoes beneath it and climbed into his bed, lying supine. While both girls disrobed, Deschamps closed and locked the French doors and shutters, locked the rear door, and lit a candle. He then turned and watched them undress as he paced about the room, saying nothing. He disrobed, placing his clothes on the rocker.

Dr. LeMonnier described Deschamps at the time of the murder as a fifty-six-year-old male (though evidence suggests he was a year younger), five feet two inches tall, about 150 pounds, muscular, and well built. He wore a sandy-white, short but full beard and had thinning dark hair that was graying. Others would describe Deschamps as "a low-sized, thick-set man with light blue eyes." The only identifiable clothing found in the room that day belonging to the accused murderer was his worsted-woven wool coat, black vest, a hat, cuffs, necktie, collar, and two red Turkish sleeping caps, though he obviously wore a collarless shirt, trousers, long johns, socks, and shoes.

Holding an open bottle of chloroform, Deschamps lay nude beside Juliette. He whispered something to her that Laurence couldn't hear and then spoke aloud, saying he was going to magnetize her using the vapors of chloroform.

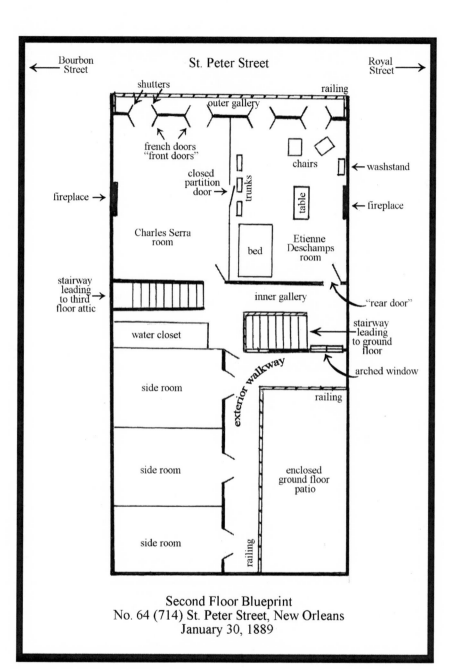

Second Floor Blueprint
No. 64 (714) St. Peter Street, New Orleans
January 30, 1889

Laurence testified that her sister had wanted to be chloroformed. Deschamps handed the bottle to Juliette, who held it to her nose, but the noxious smell caused her to turn her head away. She also complained that it made her nose itch. Deschamps straightened her head, told her that was normal, and insisted that she smell it, that it was good for her, in spite of its unpleasantness. When she did, she stated that she saw "God, [the] Holy Virgin, and Jackson Square," according to Laurence's May 1889 testimony. But during the retrial, she claimed that her sister saw the "church, God, angels, and Jackson Square." Why she had the vision of Jackson Square in the French Quarter is anyone's guess; she probably meant that she saw the visions *in* Jackson Square. Either way, as Laurence recalled, Deschamps replied that "it was good."

Placed in the bed near Juliette was one of Deschamps's tools of the trade. Described as black on the back with a white dot in the middle, the cuneiform or wedge-shaped metallic mirror had been used in the past by Deschamps to hypnotize the girls. Apparently chloroform would suffice that day. The mirror was not used, though it remained close at hand just in case.

Juliette kept her mouth open while she continued to inhale the vapors. Deschamps instructed her to do so, to allow the drug to be inhaled via two routes. Apparently that did not suffice, as she remained conscious or semi-conscious. Deschamps climbed out of bed and walked to one of his trunks to retrieve a striped handkerchief with the initials *E. D.* Pouring the remaining contents on the cloth, he returned to the bed and placed the handkerchief over her mouth and nose. Young Juliette turned her head to the side, went to sleep, and never woke up.

Since there were only two witnesses to the death of Juliette, and Deschamps never testified in open court, history recorded only Laurence's version of the story. Laurence testified at the coroner's inquest and at both trials that after her sister went to sleep, Deschamps rose from the bed, got on his knees, and said, "Dear God, let me die. I want to die." Based on her testimony, it appeared that Etienne Deschamps believed young Juliette to be dead by that point, and Dr. LeMonnier concurred. But what occurred next is subject to debate.

After chloroforming young Juliette, it appeared that Deschamps's supply of the drug was very low or depleted. He went to the table, mixed the contents of several bottles, and then got dressed. Taking two empty bottles with him—empty bottles that Laurence claimed to have seen—Deschamps told Laurence that he would return shortly. Unbeknownst to her at the time, he was off to purchase more of the drug. In the meantime, she was instructed to sit in the bed and watch over her sister but not disturb or touch her.

Prior to that, Deschamps had asked Laurence to inhale some of the chloroform he had given to her sister, but she stopped short of doing so when he turned his back. Presumably, the bad experience she had with the drug the day before had taught her a valuable lesson. She was wise enough not to repeat the mistake. As he left his room, Deschamps locked the rear door behind him and took the key.

There is debate regarding where Deschamps went during his second outing, though there is no question that he ventured out to purchase additional chloroform. According to Dr. LeMonnier's thinking, Deschamps went to two drugstores after Juliette's death. Why he needed additional chloroform when the young girl was already dead will be discussed shortly.

According to Dr. LeMonnier, at 2:00 P.M., Deschamps arrived first at the business establishment of John Mailhes, a druggist who operated his store at 105 Royal Street, at the corner of St. Louis Street. (The building no longer exists. That entire side of the street is now occupied by the Louisiana State Supreme Court and Louisiana State Court of Appeals, Fourth Circuit.) There he purchased one ounce of the drug. Mailhes testified at the first trial that Deschamps entered his establishment at about noon; at the second trial in March 1890, he amended that to sometime between 11:00 A.M. and 2:00 P.M. Why was there such a vast difference in times between trials? Was Mailhes coached the second time around? He also testified that Deschamps purchased two ounces of chloroform, not one. With that said, it's more likely that Deschamps purchased chloroform from Mailhes *before* arriving at the Dietsh household. When that quantity was depleted after Juliette's death, he went out to get more.

But assuming that he bought chloroform from Mailhes after Juliette's death, Deschamps ventured next to 195 (now 841) Bourbon Street, at the corner of Dumaine Street. Marcel Majeau, the proprietor of that drugstore, testified at the first and second trials that Deschamps arrived at 2:30 P.M. Deschamps told him that he had a girl at his home whose tooth needed to be extracted. He added that he had some chloroform that he had previously purchased, but it was no longer effective. Majeau provided a two-ounce vial, but Deschamps realized that he only had enough money to buy half that amount, prompting Majeau to remove an ounce. From start to finish, the business transaction lasted about five minutes. According to Majeau's testimony at the first trial, they had been acquainted for four to five years and he knew that Deschamps was a dentist, but this was the first time that the doctor had visited his establishment. At the second trial, he testified that Deschamps had frequently purchased chloroform from him.

Contrary to Dr. LeMonnier's assertions, it makes no sense that Deschamps ventured to two drugstores after the death of Juliette, especially when both stores offered to sell him two ounces of chloroform, which the first store did. Dr. LeMonnier claimed that Deschamps bought one ounce from each store. As previously stated, the most likely scenario was that the doctor bought two ounces of chloroform at Mailhes' business before arriving at the Dietsh residence. Rather than returning to Mailhes' establishment to purchase additional chloroform, which would have raised questions, Deschamps walked up St. Peter Street to Bourbon Street, turned right, and traveled three blocks to Majeau's drugstore.

Regarding Deschamps's need to buy additional chloroform, his supporters claimed that he was distraught over the accidental death of Juliette and that he wished to end his life by the same means. Dr. LeMonnier never offered an opinion on that subject other than to say that Deschamps had no real intention of committing suicide. It was all for show.

Once Deschamps was back in his room with the chloroform in hand, he haphazardly undressed, scattering his clothes about the floor, all the while asking Laurence if she had touched or disturbed her sister.

"No," she replied, to which he responded, "All right."

Juliette remained in the bed as Deschamps had left her: nude, motionless, with her eyes closed and mouth open. He climbed back in bed and for some unexplained reason placed the fresh, chloroform-soaked handkerchief over her mouth. If she wasn't dead already, then she died soon after. But what possessed him to reapply the cloth? The fact that he did so, according to Laurence's testimony, added credibility to Dr. LeMonnier's argument that Juliette was murdered. This was no accident.

At that point, Laurence asked Deschamps if she could go home. She was bothered that her sister was "asleep." Knowing that Juliette was dead, Deschamps got out of his bed and walked to one of his trunks. He began to gather some of his personal letters and papers and two bundles, which included a box of dental tools. He threw the papers and some of the letters into the fire and handed the bundles to Laurence, instructing her to deliver them to her father. At some previous time, Monsieur Dietsh had lent Deschamps a book on mesmerism. Perhaps it was among his personal effects, but Dietsh testified that he never got his book back from the doctor. What possessed Deschamps to think that Dietsh would want his dental tools after he accidentally killed or murdered his older daughter is a complete mystery.

Laurence proceeded to get dressed, with Deschamps (still nude) helping her into her shoes, cloak, and hat. He told her to go home quickly and tell her father that he was going to die. She left with the bundles, which she described as large and nearly too heavy to carry. Deschamps hastily closed, locked, and then latched the rear door behind her. He didn't want anyone outside to see him, according to Laurence's testimony. History can only speculate what transpired in the room after she left, based on what witnesses discovered there later. Deschamps never spoke about it, or if he did, it was never recorded.

Laurence was crying when she arrived back home at 4:00 P.M., and told her father that Deschamps was going to die and her sister was asleep on his bed. Whether or not she added that she was nude is not known. Alarmed by what he heard, Dietsh put on his overcoat and raced to the St. Peter's address. He banged on Deschamps's rear door, getting no response. He quickly returned home and got Laurence, and the pair returned to St. Peter Street sometime between 4:30 and 5:00 P.M. Monsieur Dietsh resumed banging on Deschamps's door. Charles Serra, the next-door neighbor and night watchman, who was sleeping at the time, was awakened by the commotion and asked his wife to find out what all the fuss was about. He was lying on his sofa, which was against a wall and about twenty feet from where Deschamps's bed was located in the next room.

When Mrs. Serra poked her head out the door, she saw the father-daughter team and said as much to her husband. Mr. Serra then walked out to the inner gallery, where Dietsh asked him where the watchman was. At some point Deschamps had erroneously told Dietsh that Serra was a policeman. Both men assumed that a watchman and policeman were synonymous. Serra identified himself and they went into his room.

"My little girl is in the [next] room, and Mr. Deschamps has sent me word that he was going to die," Dietsh explained to Serra.

They quickly reentered the inner gallery, where Serra knocked at Deschamps's rear door but got no better results than Dietsh did. Apparently, Serra had heard nothing unusual that day. He later testified that he had met the children and knew that they visited Deschamps almost every day, probably after school because he usually saw them carrying their schoolbags. The kids were there so often that he naturally assumed that Deschamps was a relative of the girls. Sometimes they would stay anywhere from one to three hours at a time, especially in the two weeks prior to Juliette's death. Serra often heard them talking and singing, because the partition door between the two rooms was very thin and the front doors leading to the outer gallery were frequently left open. He never suspected that the girls were in any danger or disrobing in the doctor's room. Serra admitted that he didn't know Deschamps very well, though he knew he was a dentist. On several occasions, Deschamps had extracted Mrs. Serra's teeth—without chloroform, Serra added. Prior to January 30, 1889, he thought Deschamps to be an honest man.

Getting no response to his knocking, Serra reentered his room and walked out onto the outer gallery, but he was unable to see into Deschamps's room because his shutters and doors were closed and locked. He went back into his room, where an armoire hid his side of the partition door. He reached behind it, knocked at the door, but again heard nothing. At that point, Serra didn't believe that anyone was home. It was too quiet within. Serra rejoined Dietsh on the inner gallery and told him he believed that Deschamps had gone out. But Juliette's father could not be persuaded.

"No, my daughter is in the room," Dietsh insisted.

Serra then attempted to look through the keyhole. Unfortunately, the key was still in place, preventing the watchman from seeing through the slot. He put his ear to the rear door and finally heard snoring coming from the room.

"Yes, he is there," Charles Serra confirmed.

Desperate, Dietsh wanted Serra to break down the door. He was a night watchman after all and had some police authority, Dietsh reasoned, though he later admitted he was ignorant of United States laws. Serra explained that he couldn't force open the door but suggested that he summon the police right away. The closest station, the Third Precinct, was located on the first floor of the historic Cabildo building on Jackson Square, a block and a half from the house. Serra testified that Laurence was sent, but actually it was Dietsh who went, likely taking his daughter with him, or she stayed behind with Mrs. Serra. Serra told Dietsh that he would keep an eye on Deschamps's rear door until his return.

□ □ □

George J. Legendre was assigned as the front desk clerk and operator when Dietsh arrived at the police station at 5:10 P.M. Reports of what he told the operator varied over time. Initially he indicated that his older daughter was locked up in Dr. Deschamps's room and that the doctor had expressed a desire to die. Later he said that he told Legendre that he believed that his daughter was being raped by Deschamps and no one was answering his door. Regardless of what he said, he needed help. Legendre quickly dispatched Corp. George Morris and Officers Charles Sturges and Fernand Rancé to the scene. When they arrived, Morris and Sturges were assigned to guard the building's exit points, while Rancé, the senior officer, Serra, and Dietsh went upstairs to Deschamps's room. If Laurence accompanied her father to the police station, she returned with him to St. Peter Street. She ended up with Mrs. Serra in her room while the men attempted to access Deschamps's apartment.

When knocking at the doctor's rear door received no response, Rancé secured a hatchet and broke the lock, but it was soon discovered that the door was also hooked on the inside. By then, Morris and Sturges had joined Rancé upstairs. The thought that someone might attempt to flee the scene had vanished from everyone's mind. Why they never consulted Mrs. Hilroy, the landlady (she had a master key, after all), is a complete mystery. Perhaps she was not there at the time.

Morris remained at the rear door while the rest of the men went into Serra's room and removed the armoire blocking the partition door. But they soon discovered that the door was obstructed on the other side by one of Deschamps's chests. Pushing the door partially open, they saw a girl's corset draped over the back of the chair and the doctor's hat resting on top of one of his trunks.

"Yes, they are there," Rancé said, upon observing the clothing within.

He and Serra then proceeded to the outer gallery, where Rancé broke open one of the locked shutters, then unhooked one of the front doors. Once inside, the officer immediately smelled a strange odor, later identified as chloroform. Prior to that day, Rancé was ignorant of the drug's smell. Approaching the bed, he saw Deschamps and Juliette lying supine with a sheet brought up to their waistlines. There were also two vials of chloroform, two handkerchiefs that smelled of the drug, and a sharp instrument on the bed. The instrument was later identified as a four-inch dental stick, called a "toothpicker" by dentists during that time. Deschamps had used it to stab himself. After Deschamps was transferred to Charity Hospital, his mirror and magnetized disc were also discovered in the bed. The disc was probably placed there or used by Deschamps after Laurence left, perhaps in some desperate attempt to revive young Juliette, though at some point he tried ammonia to revive her. It wasn't until after Rancé's attempt to arouse Deschamps from his stupor, without success, that he discovered both individuals were nude.

In addition, Deschamps, who was breathing heavily according to Rancé, had three self-inflicted stab wounds to his chest.

Rancé quickly unhooked the latch to the rear door, allowing the other officers to enter, with Jules Dietsh—frantic to see his daughter—close at hand. By then, the sheet had been drawn away from Juliette's body, who lay in a state of nudity. What her father saw must have been horrific.

"He started to go toward the body, but the officers held him back and told him that his daughter was dead," the *Daily Picayune* reported, based on Jules Dietsh's testimony at the coroner's inquest.

History did not document Dietsh's reaction upon seeing his nude daughter, who lay beside her accused murderer, who was also nude. It must have been a gut-wrenching moment for him and everyone else, bringing emotions that no one ever forgot. The *Daily Picayune* later described the crime scene as "a sight never paralleled in the criminal history of New Orleans." The investigation into the death of Juliette Dietsh began almost immediately.

While inspecting the room, Rancé found the charred remains of papers and letters in the fireplace and Juliette's clothes folded neatly on the chair. This was in contrast to the doctor's clothing, which was scattered about the floor. Resting on a tray in one of the trunks containing Deschamps's clothes was a four-by-three-inch white envelope containing four letters written in French and signed by Juliette Dietsh, along with three "picture cards" or postcards. One of them had *friendship, inseparable* written on it by the dead girl. In one of the letters, Juliette expressed her love for and fidelity to Deschamps, while another proclaimed that she was his mistress. According to Dr. LeMonnier, who later saw the various correspondences, they all appeared to have been strategically placed in order to be easily found. No letters written by Deschamps were found in the room. Most likely they were burned.

Jules Dietsh disputed the sincerity of Juliette's alleged love letters to the doctor, though he admitted that his daughter wrote them all, since he recognized her handwriting. To him, the emotions expressed within the letters were uncharacteristic of his daughter's level of maturity. In essence, he and everyone else believed that Juliette had been duped, the words dictated to her by Deschamps for whatever reason. Laurence confirmed that her sister had written the letters at the doctor's residence under his guidance.

Meanwhile, shortly after dispatching the officers to St. Peter Street, George Legendre was relieved of his duties at the precinct and joined them, arriving at 5:30 P.M. Officer Noel E. Delhonde and Capt. John Journeè of the Third Precinct met him. Journeè was summoned to the house from his residence on Orleans Street between Bourbon and Dauphine streets, a short walk away. The three additional officers arrived after Rancé had gained entry into Deschamps's room. Upon entering, Journeè found Juliette's nude body motionless in the bed with her head resting on Deschamps's arm. Deschamps was alive but unconscious. Attempts to revive him failed. Taking charge, Captain Journeè told Legendre to telephone Dr. LeMonnier immediately. The young girl was obviously dead, making this a coroner's case. Meanwhile, an ambulance was summoned for Deschamps.

Dr. LeMonnier received the telephone call at 6:30 P.M. All that he was told over the phone was that a rape had occurred and he needed to report to Captain Journeè at the St. Peter Street address. By the time the coroner arrived at the scene ten minutes later, Etienne Deschamps had already been placed on a stretcher and transferred by ambulance to Charity Hospital, where he was put under the care of Dr. J. D. Bloom, the assistant house surgeon. Dr. LeMonnier was met on the inner gallery by Captain Journeè, who told him about Deschamps, his suicide attempt, and the nude body of a young girl. When the coroner entered the room, he saw Juliette lying in the bed covered by a sheet, which he removed. At first he believed the body was that of a fourteen- to sixteen-year-old girl, but a cursory examination revealed that she was much younger. He also noted that Juliette's mouth (which was still open), chin, and part of her nose were bright rose in hue, as if chemically burned. There were no visible marks of violence on her body, though he concluded that she was not a virgin. He would autopsy the body the following day.

Dr. LeMonnier described the room as dirty and disorderly, "not having been scrubbed or swept for some time." The glass in the French doors was opaque from dirt, which gave "the room a dark, gloomy appearance." He made an inventory of the apartment's contents, including Deschamps's monogrammed handkerchiefs that still had faint traces of chloroform on them, and concluded that the girl had died from inhaling the drug. He also saw the letters and postcards on Deschamps's chest, along with some business cards that were off red in color. Some of the business cards declared he was a Parisian-trained dentist, like the one he distributed while living at the Crescent Hotel; others stated he healed diseases using magnetism. The latter card's information was identical to the sign he had hung overlooking St. Peter Street, except for one slight variation. The business card listed him as *Mr. Etienne* rather than *Dr. Etienne.*

Some books on medicine and magnetism were found in the drawer of the washstand as well as in two of the three trunks. On the floor behind the chests was a bottle of anisette, an anise-flavored liqueur, of which about two ounces had been consumed. Atop the mantel was an assortment of bottles containing different liquids and solids used in dentistry, along with gold foil, old lottery tickets, a set of false teeth, and some extracted teeth, kept for whatever reason. Like Rancé before him, Dr. LeMonnier saw the burned letters and papers in the fireplace.

When Dr. LeMonnier examined Juliette's clothes, which remained undisturbed on the chair, he discovered a letter in one of the pockets, which turned out to be part of a schoolwork exercise entitled, "Dictation, Dear Parents, etc." Laurence confirmed that. Later, on a closer examination of this letter's content, Dr. LeMonnier discovered it was identical to some content in the letters found in Deschamps's trunk. The only difference was that all references to *Dear Parents* had been deleted in the supposed love letters and Deschamps's name substituted in their place. In the final analysis, these were no affectionate letters written by a twelve-year-old girl to a middle-aged man, though Deschamps obviously wanted everyone to believe it.

At some point that evening, Dr. LeMonnier gathered the empty vials of chloroform and handkerchiefs as evidence, along with the letters and business cards. He then went directly to Charity Hospital. Upon his departure, Officer Delhonde was placed in charge of the body, which was to remain in the room until the following day. (There was no city morgue at that time.) Dr. LeMonnier gave Delhonde strict instructions to observe and document the progress of rigor mortis, so that the time of Juliette's death could be estimated. The officer was also placed in the room to prevent the body from being disturbed by the curious. As instructed, Delhonde sat by the bedside until the following day at 5:15 A.M., when he was relieved. He observed that the body got cold and rigid beginning at 8:00 P.M., with complete rigidity noted by 11:50 P.M. Based upon all the physical evidence, the coroner's report after the autopsy the following day, and the sworn testimony given at the coroner's inquest two days after that, Dr. LeMonnier estimated the time of Juliette's death as 4:30 P.M., which would have been after the last vial of chloroform was purchased. (Dr. LeMonnier would later amend the time of death to two hours earlier.)

At 6:15 P.M., Deschamps arrived at Charity Hospital, located approximately fifteen blocks from his residence on Tulane Avenue between Howard and Locus (now South Robertson) streets. The massive three-story brick structure was built in 1832 and served the city until 1936, when it was demolished to make room for a taller hospital. The newer structure was later destroyed from within by the effects of a levee breach from Hurricane Katrina in August 2005.

As an alleged murderer, Deschamps was placed in the reception room and put under constant surveillance, guarded that night by Officer Benjamin Shipley. By that late hour and continuing the following day, wild rumors circulated around the city that if an opportunity arose at the hospital, Deschamps would be lynched for his crime. Printed in various local newspapers, the sordid details of the crime and the actions of the accused murderer, identified incorrectly as *Eugene Dejan, alias Etienne Deschamps,* outraged the public. David C. Hennessy, the New Orleans superintendent of police, let it be known in no uncertain terms that the prisoner would be guarded until he was well enough to be safely transferred to Orleans Parish Prison.

Immediately after being admitted to the hospital, Deschamps was administered an emetic, which produced vomit containing about an ounce of chloroform. How Dr. Bloom was able to differentiate undigested chloroform from other vomited gastric fluids was never explained. Deschamps regained consciousness at 11:15 P.M. By then, Dr. LeMonnier had completed his physical examination of the accused, which included the discovery of three distinct stab wounds to the left chest, between the third and fourth ribs. At the beginning of their examination, Drs. Bloom and LeMonnier "thought they were scratches made by the dead child," according to the *Daily Picayune.* But it was later determined that the four-inch toothpicker used by Deschamps had punctured his left lung, producing internal hemorrhage, the degree and severity of which was undetermined. The other two wounds were considered superficial. In addition, it appeared that he had swallowed at least an ounce of chloroform, though hardly enough to be lethal. If Deschamps's goal was to kill himself, he had done a poor job given his supposed medical knowledge and experience in dentistry.

Once Deschamps regained consciousness, Dr. LeMonnier informed him of young Juliette's death. The accused expressed a surprising degree of bewilderment, as if her death was unexpected. He told the doctor that he had wished to die, had tried to do so, but was discovered too soon. He failed to mention, however, that he had instructed Laurence to go tell her father of his plans. He then described his relationship with Juliette as platonic at first, then intimate.

■ ■ ■

The following morning between ten and eleven o'clock, Dr. Albert B. Miles, house surgeon at Charity Hospital, examined Deschamps and found that he was stable enough to be discharged. He could recuperate from his wounds and chloroform poisoning at the prison infirmary. The police were notified, and Officer Rancé and Corp. John B. Cooper were assigned to pick him up. Rancé knew that Deschamps had been transferred to Charity Hospital without benefit of clothing, so he and Cooper went to his room on St. Peter Street to retrieve some form of garment. When they arrived, they were met by a large crowd of people in the street, described in the *Daily Picayune* as being "of all grades and colors." Though it was a peaceful gathering, the officers had great difficulty accessing Deschamps's room. Meanwhile, Captain Journeè appeared before Judge Guy Dreux of the Second Recorder's Court, whose courtroom shared the first floor of the Cabildo with the Third Precinct police station. There he swore out an affidavit for the arrest of Deschamps for the murder of Juliette Dietsh. Dr. LeMonnier had completed his autopsy of the young victim by then.

In spite of Dr. Miles' pronouncement that the prisoner could be discharged, when Rancé and Cooper arrived at the hospital, Deschamps complained to them that his chest hurt and he feared for his health if his feet got wet. It had been raining off and on since the night before and wouldn't stop until 4:00 P.M. that day. It was also quite chilly. Since Deschamps had attempted suicide the day before, the officers asked him if he still wanted to die. If he did, what would it matter if his feet got wet? But Deschamps told them no. Apparently, what Rancé had brought him to wear was insufficient for the current weather. Deschamps suggested that they stop at his room en route to Judge Dreux's chambers, where he was to be arraigned, so that he might retrieve his flannel shirt and some warm clothing. He must have known that he was headed to Orleans Parish Prison after his court appearance.

It's unclear if Rancé consented to his request or if he alone returned to Deschamps's room to retrieve the clothing. In any case, during Deschamps's short trip from Charity Hospital to the Cabildo, he appeared unruffled at first. His attitude changed, however, as the police van passed in front of his residence, where scores of people still gathered in the street. Deschamps and his police escort anticipated the same when the accused murderer stepped out of the vehicle in front of the Cabildo and walked into Judge Dreux's courtroom. Fortunately for the prisoner, nothing unruly transpired that afternoon.

Appearing before Judge Dreux, Deschamps was read the charge against him—the murder of Juliette Dietsh—and asked to enter a plea, to which he answered "not guilty." He was then remanded to the criminal sheriff's department and transported to Orleans Parish Prison without benefit of bail.

At some point that day, Deschamps spoke to someone, but who that was—a reporter or some other person—is unclear. According to the February 1, 1889, edition of the *Daily Picayune*, Deschamps refused at first to discuss his problems and then later pled ignorance to the circumstances surrounding Juliette's death. Finally, he admitted that he had been magnetizing the young girl for a period of time in order to develop her into a "beautiful subject." Was this part of his Jean Lafitte scheme? History will probably never know. Whatever his goal, he admitted that he failed, but not because of anything he did. He discovered that Juliette was not of pure heart and body; in other words, she had lost her virginity.

So far, Deschamps's version of the truth sounded like the same fable he had spun for Dr. LeMonnier the night before. But then he added that because of her impurity, he became disheartened. When young Juliette came to visit him that day in his room, he told her that he was going to kill himself. Deschamps claimed that upon hearing his plans, Juliette wanted to do the same. Did she decide to end her life because of her lost virginity or because she knew she could never live without Deschamps? The murderer left those intriguing questions for others to ponder.

According to Deschamps, he approved of Juliette's decision to kill herself. She disrobed, walked to the table, inhaled some chloroform from a bottle, saturated a handkerchief, and then lay down in his bed, holding the cloth a short distance from her face.

"Oh, how pleasant! Oh, how nice it smells," Juliette said, according to Deschamps.

Shortly afterward, she fell into a slumber, never to awake. Deschamps said that he followed suit by inhaling, then drinking some of the chloroform before going to bed. He ended his story by stating that when he discovered Juliette was truly dead, he "stabbed himself and laid down to die." The rest is history, but his version of the truth was pure fiction, uncorroborated by Laurence's statement and later court testimony.

Young Juliette was dead, and her father was without the financial means to bury his older daughter. When the news of this compounded tragedy reached the streets of New Orleans, an overwhelming response came from its citizens, who were determined to give the girl a proper funeral and burial, no matter the cost. One of the first gentlemen to come to the aid of Monsieur Dietsh was an acquaintance of his, J. Julius Weinfurter, a jeweler who operated his business at 46 (now 618) Conti Street, at the corner of

Exchange Alley (now Exchange Place). Within twenty-four hours of Juliette's death, Weinfurter had raised fifty-four dollars, collected from thirty-two individuals including himself, eight of whom remained anonymous. When their names and the amounts they contributed toward the funeral fund were published in the *Daily Picayune* on February 1, 1889, it triggered an even bigger outpouring of financial support from the community. By the time of the funeral, all expenses were paid, with money to spare. These surplus funds were specifically allocated toward future prosecution expenditures. The public wanted justice for young Juliette Dietsh.

Sometime during the midafternoon of January 31, Juliette's body was transferred to John Bonnot's funeral parlor, located at 45 (now 625) St. Ann Street, between Royal and Chartres streets. (The funeral parlor vacated the building long ago.) There the body was laid out in a rear room with two entry doors, the room draped with lace curtains. On a table at the head of her coffin were three bouquets of flowers, "the tribute of some stranger who wished to express pity for the poor little victim," according to the *Daily Picayune*. Near the coffin was also placed a contribution box with a slit in the lid. By the following day, the box was filled with coins.

The public viewing began shortly after 4:00 P.M. The coffin was covered with a white cloth and studded with silver nails and its interior lined with white satin silk. Juliette's body was dressed in a white satin robe, and resting on her forehead was a crown of white flowers that blended with her pale skin, which was described as white as marble. According to the *Daily Picayune*, "She bore a sweet expression on her face, and in the coffin had the appearance of a wax doll. Her large black eyes and ringlets of dark auburn hair on the forehead augmented her beauty."

Every imaginable type of person came to view the body that day. It was a crush of humanity, black and white, young and old, rich and poor, and both genders. In fact, there were so many visitors that two police officers were assigned at the parlor to keep order. All told, over two thousand people reportedly viewed the body that first day, with a long line slowly moving through one door and out the other. The parade of people continued uninterrupted until long past midnight, with nearly everyone a stranger to the Dietsh family. The funeral was set for ten o'clock the following morning.

As day broke on February 1, 1889, scores of people gathered once again at the funeral parlor of John Bonnot. By the time the service began, hundreds of people lined the block to pay their final respects. Visitors continued to pass in and out of the establishment to view the body.

At 9:45 A.M., Rev. Jean M. Bérronet, the assistant pastor of St. Louis Cathedral, along with three of his acolytes or altar boys, entered the room to perform the Sacrament of the Dead. That morning he had only a short distance to walk from his home base, located on Jackson Square and flanked by the Cabildo and the Presbytère. The latter building, part of which functioned as a civil district courthouse, was located at the corner of Chartres and St. Ann streets, a half-block from the funeral parlor.

By the time Father Bérronet and his acolytes arrived, Jules Dietsh and his daughter, Laurence, had already taken their seats at the head of the coffin. With his eyes fixed and staring and his forehead wrinkled with sorrow, Dietsh shed no tears that morning for his lost daughter, though his face projected both anger and horror, according to one eyewitness. No doubt, he felt responsible in some way for his daughter's death. As for little Laurence, she sat quietly, thankfully not realizing "the full meaning of all that was transpiring and which had taken place," the *Daily Picayune* reported.

Promptly at 10:00, after Father Bérronet had completed his religious duties, the lid of Juliette's coffin was closed and screwed down. It was then placed in a waiting hearse by six pallbearers, including J. Jules Weinfurter; the hearse was described as being "profusely draped with white crape." Father Bérronet and his three attendants preceded the death carriage, which was followed by six other carriages, the first containing Jules and Laurence Dietsh. The funeral train proceeded along Royal Street to Canal Street, up to North Rampart Street, then right to St. Louis Street. The procession headed up St. Louis Street to St. Louis Cemetery No. 2., a three-block-long, aboveground cemetery bordered by St. Louis, North Claiborne, Custom House (now Iberville), and North Robertson streets. Each city block in the burial ground is a numbered square.

Those who had gathered around the funeral parlor made a mad dash to the cemetery, though many proceeded in error to St. Louis Cemetery No. 1, located at the corner of St. Louis and North Basin streets—four blocks below No. 2. It wasn't until after the funeral procession passed them by that some of the weary spectators changed course. By then, a large crowd had already gathered around Juliette's allotted space in Square No. 1, situated between St. Louis and Conti streets.

Once the parties arrived at the St. Louis Street entrance (there was a second entrance on Conti Street), the coffin was lifted out of the hearse by the pallbearers and solemnly walked to Oven No. 12, Row 2. This is located along St. Louis Alley, an inner pathway parallel to St. Louis Street. (The vault is closer to the North Robertson Street side of the alley.) Father Bérronet said a few prayers in Latin before the coffin was slipped into the vault. A sexton stood nearby with a trowel, mortar, and bricks, to seal "the aperture and shut out from the sight of the hundreds there the casket which contained the victim," one eyewitness sadly reported.

For several more minutes, the massive crowd lingered near the tomb and then "appeared to turn away in regret." By then, the possibility that Etienne Deschamps would be set "free as air" was on everyone's mind. Already, there was talk that he would claim insanity to avoid the hangman's noose. The legal and emotional battle lines pitting one side against the other were beginning to be drawn.

The unmarked tomb of Juliette Dietsh (beneath the tomb of François and Adelaide Theard), in St. Louis Cemetery No. 2, Square No. 1, St. Louis Alley, Oven No. 12, Row 2, June 2015. (Courtesy of Gerard Peña)

Chapter Four

The Investigation and First Trial

Did sodomy and carnal intercourse exist between Deschamps and that child? And if so, did this cause him to kill her?

Dr. Yves René LeMonnier, June 1889

Within twenty-four hours of Juliette Dietsh's death, the city of New Orleans was awash with stories fed to them by the press that the twelve-year-old girl had been the victim of a grotesque rape and murder. How else could one explain her nude body lying in the bed of her accused killer, who was also found nude but alive? It did not help Etienne Deschamps when he freely admitted to Dr. LeMonnier that he had been in a consensual affair with young Juliette for some weeks prior to her death. But any sane person knew better. No one believed that such a relationship could exist between a middle-aged man and a prepubescent girl. Deschamps's version of the story only got worse after he accused the victim of losing her virginity prior to their affair, casting aspersions upon her character and family name.

The fact that Deschamps was never charged with rape made no difference to the general public. Because Juliette Dietsh had died under such senseless and abhorrent conditions while under the influences of a grown man who should have known better, it was nothing less than capital murder. Leading the charge calling for a rope around Deschamps's neck was none other than the forty-six-year-old Orleans Parish coroner, Dr. Yves René LeMonnier, Jr.

Dr. LeMonnier had paternal roots in a long line of distinguished gentlemen, many of whom were doctors and surgeons. His great-great-grandfather Louis-Guillaume LeMonnier served as a member of the Academy of the Sciences and First Physician of the king. He attended to King Louis XV's medical needs during a portion of his reign (1715-74) and, beginning in 1788, during the reign of his grandson, King Louis XVI (1774-92). But unlike Louis XVI and his queen, Marie Antoinette, the doctor was spared the wrath of the French citizenry during the French Revolution of 1789. This was due

Dr. Yves R. LeMonnier. (Courtesy NOLA.
com/The *Times-Picayune*)

in no small measure to the generous medical services he provided to the poor
during his fourteen-year absence between royal families. In September 1799,
he died of natural causes at the age of eighty-two.

Dr. LeMonnier's grandfather Yves Julian Joseph LeMonnier was also a
physician. He and his older brother immigrated to the white-minority, French,
slave-based colony of Saint-Domingue (Haiti) in 1791, where they operated
a coffee plantation while Yves continued to practice medicine. In August
of that same year, a slave revolt began, which ultimately led to the creation
of an independent, black-majority government. In 1803, when Napoleon
Bonaparte attempted to reconquer the country (without success), the Haitian
government ordered the execution of remaining whites. Dr. Yves LeMonnier
was forced to flee the island and settled in the Spanish colony of Cuba. His
misfortunes didn't end there, however. In 1808, Napoleon invaded Spain and
placed his brother on the throne, which caused a backlash in Cuba against
any French natives living on the island. In May 1809, Dr. Yves LeMonnier
again uprooted himself and settled in New Orleans, which at the time had a

large and robust French-speaking population. Thus, he easily assimilated into the culture of the city and became a well-respected doctor. Eventually he would serve as chief surgeon in Plauche's Battalion, Louisiana Militia, under Gen. Andrew Jackson during the Battle of New Orleans (January 1815).

In 1811, prior to the war, he purchased a lot and unfinished building at 156 (now 640) Royal Street, at the corner of St. Peter Street, where he commissioned the construction of a three-story building, New Orleans' first skyscraper. Until then, no one believed that the soil could accommodate anything higher than two stories. Dr. Yves LeMonnier's medical practice was located on the third floor; the lower floors were made into apartments. (A fourth floor was added to the building in 1876.) A half-block from the "skyscraper," Dr. Yves Julian Joseph LeMonnier constructed the famous, or infamous, 64/66 St. Peter Street property three years prior to his death.

In 1814, Dr. Yves LeMonnier married Marie Charlotte Aimée Bouclet Saint-Martin of Des Allemands in St. Charles Parish, and the couple would have three daughters and a son, Yves René LeMonnier, Sr., who was born in 1817. Like his father, Yves René became a highly respected physician in New Orleans. In 1838, he married Adele Marie Communy, and the couple would have at least seven children, though it may have been as many as eleven, the others dying at an early age. Yves René LeMonnier, Jr., was their third child and first son. He was the couple's only child born outside the United States. His parents, both United States citizens, were visiting Paris, France, when the future Orleans Parish coroner was born on January 29, 1843.

Nicknamed Paul, LeMonnier was formally schooled at Jesuits' College in New Orleans and later St. Thomas' Hall Military Academy in Holly Springs, Mississippi. When the Civil War broke out, he returned to New Orleans and in July 1861 enlisted as a private in Company B, Crescent Rifles, which by March 1862 became Company B, Twenty-Fourth Louisiana "Crescent" Regiment. His regiment participated in the Battle of Shiloh (April 6-7, 1862) and the military operations at Corinth and Tupelo, Mississippi. In July 1862, Pvt. Paul LeMonnier was transferred to the Orleans Light Horse Company and participated in the Kentucky-Tennessee campaign in late 1862, where he saw action at Perryville, Kentucky, and then Murfreesboro, Tennessee. he fought at Chickamauga in September 1863 and during the Atlanta campaign in the summer of 1864. Later that year, he saw action at Jonesboro, Franklin, and Nashville, Tennessee, before surrendering with the Army of Tennessee under Gen. Joseph E. Johnston at Bentonville, North Carolina, in April 1865.

After the war, LeMonnier studied medicine at the Medical Department of the University of Louisiana (now School of Medicine, Tulane University Health Sciences Center) in New Orleans, where he graduated in the spring of 1868. He then traveled to Paris, France, to further his medical education. When his father died unexpectedly in June 1870, the doctor returned to New Orleans and assumed his practice with distinction, serving also as a visiting surgeon to Charity Hospital between 1871 and 1881, as well as secretary and treasurer of the Louisiana State Board of Health from 1875 until 1877.

By all accounts, he was a skilled surgeon and very knowledgeable about the use of chloroform. On April 23, 1884, an Austrian named John Pastorek, who resided at 99 St. Peter Street, one block up from Deschamps's later residence, accidentally shot himself in the abdomen. The 38-calibre bullet perforated the right lobe of his liver and right kidney before it lodged near the eleventh rib, about two inches to the left of his spine. When Dr. LeMonnier was summoned, Mr. Pastorek was pronounced in critical condition; his survival was very doubtful. Dr. LeMonnier induced unconsciousness with chloroform and, with the assistance of Dr. Archinard, successfully extracted the bullet. According to the *Daily Picayune*, Mr. Pastorek was one of only a handful of people to survive a bullet to the liver and kidney. After his near-fatal accident, the gentleman lived thirty-one more years. Ironically, he died from a second accident on July 1, 1915, at the age of fifty-one, when he drowned in Lake Pontchartrain near Spanish Fort. At the time of his death, he still resided at his old address; the number eventually changed to 811 St. Peter Street.

On February 5, 1873, Dr. LeMonnier married Marie Eulalie LeBreton Deschapelles—born in April 1850—and the couple would have two children, though by the time of the 1900 U.S. Census, both children had died. In late October 1881, when the Orleans Parish coroner's position became available, Gov. Samuel D. McEnery appointed Dr. LeMonnier to fill that vacancy until 1884. He was subsequently elected coroner in April 1888 and served in that capacity until June 1892.

By the time of Deschamps's execution, Dr. LeMonnier was an advocate for the mentally ill, dealing with city officials over a host of related issues. Under the Louisiana Constitution of its day, as parish coroner LeMonnier also served as ex-officio city physician, whose responsibilities included examining all persons declared insane. Often these individuals were transferred to the city prison, where they were all but forgotten. Dr. LeMonnier fought to send them to various insane asylums in the city and state where proper treatment, crude as it was in those days, could be administered. His almost daily contact with these patients made Dr. LeMonnier a leading authority on the diagnosis and treatment of the insane, valuable expertise he would later use to determine the mental state of Etienne Deschamps.

Standing five feet eight inches tall, with hazel eyes and a fair complexion, Dr. LeMonnier was compassionate enough toward his fellow man but not a person to be crossed. Such an instance occurred on March 6, 1882, a few months after his appointment as coroner. His October 1881 appointment stemmed from the criminal indictment of the current Orleans Parish coroner, Dr. Joseph G. Beard. One Orleans Parish doctor who had lobbied for Beard's position was Dr. William Riley. Apparently bad blood developed between him and LeMonnier, especially after the governor chose LeMonnier as interim coroner. When the two men crossed paths in early March and Dr. Riley failed to apologize after stepping on LeMonnier's foot, heated words were exchanged, followed by blows initiated by Dr. Riley. The ensuing fight left both men on the ground with Dr. LeMonnier in the inferior position, or so it seemed at first. According to the *Galveston Daily News*, "When an attempt was made to separate them it was found that Riley's nose was in LeMonnier's mouth. The latter held on with bulldog tenacity, and it was only after strong efforts that he could be made to loose his hold." Dr. Riley was left with a badly lacerated nose for his efforts. On the other hand, Dr. LeMonnier walked away satisfied that he had extracted his ounce of flesh for his troubles. This was the type of man that Etienne Deschamps and those who rallied around him would have to deal with. For Dr. LeMonnier, there was right and there was wrong and there was nothing in between.

On Thursday, January 31, 1889, after being charged with the murder of Juliette Dietsh, Etienne Deschamps was brought to Orleans Parish Prison, where he was assigned to the second-floor infirmary. He remained there for the next three days, recovering from the effects of chloroform poisoning and his self-inflicted chest wounds. Dr. LeMonnier indicated that the accused had bloodshot eyes, an inequality of the size of the pupils, and a flushed face that precluded him from being sent into the general prison population. Within twenty-four hours of his admission, however, Deschamps was lucid enough to attempt suicide for the second time.

Deschamps was apparently given permission to relieve himself unescorted. After a short time, a guard discovered that Deschamps had somehow climbed atop the water closet, on a ridge about seven feet above the floor. His intention, so he claimed, was to dive headfirst and end his life, but a guard compelled him to come down and return to his bed. Upon his discharge from the infirmary, he was placed in the whites-only section of the prison, where he shared a cell on the first floor with other prisoners.

During this period, Dr. LeMonnier wasted little time investigating the death of Juliette Dietsh. Having completed an inventory of Deschamps's room, Dr. LeMonnier performed an autopsy in the early afternoon of January 31 in Deschamps's old room, in the presence of another doctor and five resident students from Charity Hospital who had been sworn in as members of his official coroner's inquest. After an extensive examination of the head (brain and upper spinal cord), chest (lungs and heart), and abdomen (stomach, uterus, fallopian tubes, and ovaries, including the exterior genitalia and anus), no traces of chloroform were found in the tissues or stomach. Thus, Juliette had not swallowed chloroform, as later corroborated by Laurence's testimony. In addition, the interior organs lacked the smell of chloroform by then, which would not have been the case, according to Dr. LeMonnier, had the body been properly stored beforehand. Nevertheless, the death was later determined consistent with the inhalation of chloroform, based on Laurence's testimony, Juliette's chemically burned mouth and nose, the chloroform-laced handkerchiefs, and the two empty bottles of chloroform retrieved at Deschamps's apartment. According to LeMonnier, Juliette's death was rapid, with undigested food and fluids still in her stomach. Had she died over several hours, the amount of solids and fluids would have been appreciably less than what the coroner observed.

It was what Dr. LeMonnier added to his findings, unrelated to her immediate cause of death, that sparked the most controversy among those who wished Deschamps to swing for his crime and those who wished justice only for the criminal charge filed by the district attorney—the murder of Juliette Dietsh by chloroform inhalation.

Dr. LeMonnier noted that Juliette's "genitals were bathed with a profuse viscid and milky white fluid," similar to that of semen, "the result of a recent copulation." Though he didn't say it, the implications were clear: Etienne Deschamps had mounted Juliette Dietsh postmortem. All other times that afternoon were accounted for by Laurence. A large quantity of fluid, at least a teaspoonful, was noted on the floor of the vagina and smeared over the exterior vulva. Dr. LeMonnier had gathered it on January 30 at 7:00 P.M., or about three hours after Juliette's death and before rigor mortis began. The coroner admitted that when he collected the fluid, it didn't smell like semen, but he claimed that the elapsed time and the temperature of the day could explain this. He also found no spermatozoa under the microscope, though he explained there were numerous reasons for this. One was that Deschamps was most likely sterile.

Making matters even worse for the defendant, Dr. LeMonnier found "the anus dilated, admitting easily the introduction of the first joint of the index finger, and funnel shaped, in a word, symptons [*sic*], characteristic of sodomy." He went further.

"Did sodomy and carnal intercourse exist between Deschamps and that child? And if so, did this cause him to kill her?" He posed these questions to a group of colleagues when he spoke of the murder case at the International Medico-Legal Congress held in New York City in June 1889. By then, Deschamps's first trial was over.

With the autopsy complete, its findings recorded, and all physical evidence gathered from Deschamps's room, all that remained for Dr. LeMonnier to do was call upon the various witnesses of January 30. A total of eight people were called to testify before the coroner's inquest, held on February 2, 1889. The proceedings took about nine hours and ended just before midnight. The findings were never in doubt, especially after Laurence Dietsh testified. Juliette's death was caused by the inhalation of chloroform administered by Etienne Deschamps on January 30, 1889. Impressed with the thoroughness of Dr. LeMonnier's inquest, Charles H. Luzenberg, the district attorney, presented the coroner's pronouncements to the grand jury on February 16, which indicted Deschamps for murder two days later. Meanwhile, a rumor circulated in town that a secret meeting had occurred to dispense with Deschamps either on his way to the courthouse or in the courtroom, though nothing came of the planned assassination.

□ □ □

With the indictment handed down, the case was assigned by lottery to Section A of the Louisiana Criminal District Court in New Orleans, presided over by Judge Robert H. Marr, a former jurist on the Louisiana Supreme Court. Determining who would defend Deschamps became one of Marr's first priorities. The courthouse (located on Camp Street at the southeast corner of Lafayette Street, directly across from Lafayette Square) became the site of a three-month-long legal battle to find a suitable defense lawyer who wanted the case. (The courthouse was torn down during the early 1900s to make room for an elaborate, three-story, Italian Renaissance Revival-style structure built between 1909 and 1915. The new building included a courthouse and post office. The post office vacated the building in 1961. It is currently the home of the U.S. Fifth Circuit Court of Appeals—John Minor Wisdom U.S. Court of Appeals Building.)

On February 23, after Deschamps made an application for the appointment of an attorney, Judge Marr selected Charles J. Theard to defend the accused. That same day, Deschamps appeared in Judge Marr's chambers for the first time. Before the court, he again pled not guilty to the charge of murder. Three days later, on February 26, Theard informed the court that he declined the appointment. He provided no specifics, though clearly he was at odds with the defendant. The following day, the court appointed Henry C. Castellanos, but at some later date Deschamps refused his legal services. Castellanos was far from being upset over his decision. He clearly believed Deschamps was guilty of at least manslaughter, though that had nothing to do with Deschamps's choice not to retain him. From the beginning, Deschamps had desired a defense attorney who spoke French, as he claimed it was difficult to receive a fair trial when he couldn't understand what was said in the courtroom. This was in spite of the fact that Judge Marr had assigned Deschamps an interpreter. In the end, however, it appeared that Deschamps manufactured the language barrier as a tactic to disrupt or delay the opening of his trial.

As a case in point, sometime in March the deputy sheriff at the prison went to Alfred Roman's law office at 26 (then 200) Carondelet Street and told him that Deschamps wished to see him. (That building no longer exists.) Roman was a former state judge and the predecessor of Robert Marr's judgeship. He also spoke fluent French. When Judge Roman met with Deschamps, the defendant asked him to represent him. Deschamps claimed that he had 2,000 francs waiting for him in France, which was his part of the inheritance from his deceased mother. Apparently he had a document to prove the claim. He assured the judge that if that wasn't enough money, he had at least two siblings back home who would compensate him for any legal fees incurred (though he admitted in a subsequent visit that he had not heard from his family in some time). In spite of that, all would be forgiven (as if his siblings were at fault) once Deschamps received his portion of the inheritance.

It's not known if Judge Roman ever agreed to become his defense attorney, but in the end it made no difference. He was promptly released or fired some days later, with Deschamps ranting that everyone, both friend and foe, was conspiring against him. Years later, attorney Henry Castellanos wrote that Deschamps was "one of the most disagreeable prisoners that the Parish Prison ever held." He described him as a morose, fretful, and dictatorial man who found fault with everyone, including his counsel, keepers, members of the press, and even friends who rallied around him. Though Castellanos didn't say so, he was probably pleased when Deschamps refused his services after Judge Marr assigned him to the case.

Following Castellanos's rejection, Judge Marr appointed attorney Ferdinand B. Earhart to defend Deschamps, but Deschamps refused him as well. This appeared to be one of Deschamps's many clever moves to paint himself as insane, something that Judge Roman eventually came to believe. He would represent Deschamps at his second trial, claiming the defendant was innocent by reason of insanity.

Deschamps wasn't satisfied with only verbal outbursts and mood swings as proof of his psychosis. He continued his attempts to kill himself, though he strictly followed Dr. LeMonnier's instructions regarding the proper care of his self-inflicted chest wounds. After he failed to dive headfirst off the water closet, prison guards found him trying to hang himself in his cell. He would now be more closely watched.

His next suicide attempt was much more theatrical. On Wednesday, March 27, 1889, shortly after 7:00 A.M., the captain of the watch, James Burke, and a prison trustee, "Tug" Wilson, walked up to the second floor on the St. Ann Street side of the building and began to release the prisoners from their cells. This was customary each morning; after breakfast, the inmates were free to mingle in the prison yard below. On the second floor, the cells opened onto an eight-foot-wide gallery that overlooked the yard. The gallery's edge was protected by a railing about three feet above the floor, with no bars between the railing and the floor.

Prior to this particular day, Deschamps consistently complained of the harsh treatment he received while confined to his ground-floor cell. He stated on numerous occasions that he could not shake the feeling of dampness he felt related to his cell's location. He complained that such moisture caused chronic pain in his hips. In reality, his objective was to be transferred back to the prison infirmary. This it would afford him a temporary respite from the general prison population and the chores he was required to do as an inmate, such as sweeping and cleaning the prison yard. Dr. LeMonnier saw through his motives, however, and instead had him transferred to the second floor to cell No. 6, where he shared a stall with three other prisoners.

Beginning with cell No. 8, Burke and Wilson proceeded down the gallery, releasing the prisoners until they reached Deschamps's cell. Upon his release, Deschamps, still identified in the *Daily Picayune* in late March as "Etienne

Dejan, alias Deschamps, the dentist and magnetic healer," nonchalantly walked over to the railing, quickly stooped under it, and plunged ten to twelve feet to the brick-lined ground below. He struck his right shoulder, then the right side of his head. The prison warden, Capt. Lemuel Davis, and the captain of the yard, Thomas Casey, rushed to the aid of the unconscious prisoner. A nasty laceration on his forehead bled profusely. The tissues around his right eye were swollen and the eyelid was closed tight. His nose was bloodied, with extensive ecchymosis to the conjunctivae of both eyes, and his right shoulder was dislocated. An ambulance was called and Dr. LeMonnier was notified immediately. After receiving medical attention, Deschamps was carried upstairs to the prison infirmary to recuperate. Dr. LeMonnier also diagnosed a slight depression of right frontal bone, but the *Daily Picayune* reported that Deschamps's injuries did "not appear to be fatal." More importantly, according to Dr. LeMonnier, the magnetic healer had not injured his "intellectual faculties." He added, "If he had really intended to kill himself . . . all he had to do was to plunge head foremost over the railing and he would surely have fractured his skull and pulverized his brain." Legal proceedings would go on as planned.

Deschamps's verbal outbursts and suicidal antics were not his only attempts to thwart justice. From the beginning of his prison confinement, he was very much aware that his fate was in the hands of the Orleans Parish coroner. He attempted to win Dr. LeMonnier over by offering him his three trunks as a gift, one of which contained a number of anatomical plates and medical books. How better to obtain the goodwill and protection of his chief antagonist than by offering the doctor a quasi-bribe? Besides, Deschamps knew that his medical wares were of little use to him while he was incarcerated. Dr. LeMonnier refused his bequests, of course, citing the obvious conflict of interest, but he did want Deschamps to designate in writing to whom the keys of his trunks should be handed over. The coroner had taken charge of the personal possessions.

In requesting a written note from Deschamps, Dr. LeMonnier was actually seeking to obtain a sample of his handwriting, to compare it to Juliette's letters and the five words the defendant appeared to have written on some business cards found in his room: *No. 64 Rue St. Pierre*. Except for an older business card listing the Crescent Hotel as Deschamps's previous domicile, Dr. LeMonnier had discovered no other correspondences in his St. Peter Street residence written by the defendant. Deschamps had burned them in his fireplace.

Deschamps was far too clever to fall for Dr. LeMonnier's trick. He consented to the doctor's request, but he never followed through. The day before his fall, Deschamps had asked Captain Davis to allow him to go to the clerk's office. He wanted to write a letter and requested a pen, some ink, and paper. Davis complied, but when Deschamps arrived in the office, he refused to write anything and proceeded out to the yard, where he encountered a fellow prisoner whom he enticed to write the letter in his stead. The letter turned out to be a note requesting the French consul to come see him. Dr. LeMonnier never got a sample of Deschamps's penmanship.

Deschamps apparently relished his time in the prison infirmary on both occasions, as Dr. LeMonnier suspected, though he continued to play his insanity card when it suited him. He refused to take medicines that Dr. LeMonnier prescribed, stating that the coroner was trying to poison him. When the doctor stopped his medicines, Deschamps then complained that the food was poisoned, and yet he ate it. When the French consul and Judge Roman visited him at his request, he feigned insanity. Once they departed, however, he appeared rational in the presence of Dr. LeMonnier.

Though Deschamps had been charged with murder, he had yet to go to trial. On April 18, the defendant was finally ordered to appear for trial, scheduled for April 29. Once he was out of the infirmary for the second time, Deschamps was placed with prisoners who were also awaiting trial or serving time without a capital sentence. His endless complaining about the prison, personnel, food, and other prisoners only stopped when he slept, which was often most of the day, since he also complained that he couldn't sleep at night. Dr. LeMonnier concluded right away that Deschamps was not insane, nor did he know how to properly feign insanity. In the coroner's mind, Deschamps was an actor, and a very poor one indeed, who later blamed the doctor for not allowing him to die from chloroform poisoning.

On Monday, April 29, 1889, almost three months to the day of the murder of Juliette Dietsh, the case of the *State v. Deschamps*, alias Déjan, at last began in Judge Marr's chambers. Orleans Parish District Attorney Luzenberg and Special Counsel Lionel Adams, the former district attorney, represented the State. The defendant was still without legal representation. In spite of that, Deschamps was ushered into Marr's courtroom, still bearing evidence of his last suicide attempt, "walking slowly and with a slouching, unsteady gait," as the *Daily Picayune* described him. His gray hair had been cut short, and he was now clean-shaven except for a thick gray mustache. When his name was called, a low hum of voices was heard among the court spectators. This was quickly silenced by one of the deputies, who commanded, "Order in court!" Chief Deputy Sheriff Alcée LeBlanc was then sworn in as Deschamps's interpreter.

When Judge Marr asked if the defendant was ready for trial, Deschamps responded, through LeBlanc's translation, that he had yet to be provided with a lawyer of his liking. The district attorney informed the judge that he did not oppose delaying the trial for forty-eight hours, as long as the proceedings could then begin without further objections. Even as he spoke those words, he had little hope in seeing that scenario played out, knowing Deschamps's history of rejecting qualified counselors. Deschamps then reiterated his request to the court that he be provided with a competent lawyer who spoke French.

His request seemed easier said than done, for Judge Marr next appointed Edward S. Whitaker, who apparently spoke French; however, Whitaker refused to take the case. The judge then sent several of the deputy sheriffs out to Judge Guy Dreux's courtroom in the Cabildo to round up three attorneys known to be in the building: J. J. A. Blancharge, John E. Staes, and Eugene Luscy. Staes and Luscy were law partners. The trio arrived at 12:30 P.M. and Deschamps was once again brought before the bar, but when asked if any of them would represent him, they politely declined.

James Dowling, described in the *Daily Picayune* as "a young and rising lawyer," and apparently close at hand in the courthouse, was then assigned as Deschamps's attorney. After consulting with Judge Marr privately, Dowling consented to the task, though he was given little option. At that late stage of the proceedings, the judge told Dowling that if he didn't take the case, he would be held in contempt of court. The fact that Dowling spoke not a word of French became irrelevant by that time.

Dowling immediately asked for a continuance until Wednesday, May 1, at 10:30 A.M., which Judge Marr granted. To ensure that the accused child murderer received a fair trial, he was provided with not one but two interpreters, one who would sit between him and Mr. Dowling and one who would stand near the witness box to provide immediate translations of all English-spoken testimony. A call of witnesses was then entered into the record and appropriate notices sent, informing them of the time and date of the trial. For Judge Marr, the Deschamps murder trial would proceed as planned, no matter what.

◻ ◻ ◻

In spite of the inclement weather—nearly half an inch of rain fell that day—on Wednesday morning, May 1, 1889, a large crowd of the curious gathered in Lafayette Square opposite the courthouse, eagerly awaiting its opening. Everyone was keen to enter Judge Marr's courtroom and witness the trial of Etienne Deschamps, the "French 'magnetic' doctor and dentist" charged with the murder of young Juliette Dietsh. When the doors finally opened, the courtroom quickly filled to capacity. At least a dozen of the spectators were women who took their seats, with another seventy-five people forced to stand along the walls for lack of space. "As a rule the most sensational cases have failed to attract the presence of the fair sex," the *Daily Picayune* noted, but apparently those ladies overcame their modesty in the courtroom that day. The matter pending before the court was too important.

The first half-hour of the court's time was taken up with routine matters among Judge Marr, District Attorney Luzenberg, Lionel Adams, and James Dowling. At 11:30 A.M., the names of the potential jurors were called, and all were present. Deschamps was then ushered into court. Wearing a collarless shirt and looking "generally neglected in attire, and rather careworn," according to the *Daily Picayune*, Deschamps bowed to the court and joined Dowling at the defense table. Luzenberg then stood and announced that the State was ready.

Judge Marr asked the defense, "Are you ready?"

The answer was negative; Mr. Dowling filed a motion for a continuance. He reminded the court that he had been assigned as counsel for the defendant less than forty-eight hours before and was entitled to a reasonable time to prepare. This was a capital murder trial after all, and he needed to research the prosecution's case.

"How long will it take you to get ready?" Judge Marr asked Mr. Dowling.

"At least a month," he stated.

Judge Marr pondered the situation for a few minutes and then asked the district attorney if he had any open dates available on his calendar. Mr. Luzenberg said no, and after reviewing Dowling's motion he indicated to the court that the defense had no plans to prove any point of the case or even a desire to do so.

Judge Marr then stated that unless the defense needed time to ascertain facts of importance, the motion for a continuance would be denied. Mr. Dowling responded again that he had only assumed the defense on Monday afternoon and needed time to familiarize himself with the case, but Mr. Luzenberg would have none of it. The district attorney reminded the court that when Judge Marr granted the defense a forty-eight-hour continuance on Monday, the State was assured the trial would go on as scheduled. He also pointed out that it was not unusual for an attorney to be appointed as defense counselor on the first day of trial. He appreciated Mr. Dowling's predicament, but if the case was postponed again, the district attorney feared that Deschamps would later fire Dowling in open court, again delaying the start of the trial. Besides, the district attorney assured the defense that there were no surprises waiting in the wings. Every detail of the case had been printed in the local newspapers. In addition, as far as Mr. Luzenberg was concerned, the defense had no favorable witnesses planned nor any strategy needing a month to devise.

Judge Marr again asked the district attorney if a day in the near future could be assigned for the case, but Mr. Luzenberg fired back that he wanted to enlighten Deschamps that he was a ward of the court, accused of murder, and must stand trial. Mr. Dowling assured the court that it was he who desired a continuance, not his client. Finally, Judge Marr denied his motion, basically citing these reasons: (1) the defendant (repeatedly over the past three months) refused to accept counsels appointed to him by the court; (2) the continuance granted on April 29, 1889, provided sufficient time to ascertain a defense; (3) the defendant never indicated that he had any defense or any fact he expected or desired to prove, and he never asked the court for a continuance; (4) Dowling's affidavit asking for a continuance didn't indicate any line of defense or facts he wished to prove, nor did he request time to summon witnesses; and finally (5) with the court on vacation between June 1 and September 1, a month's continuance would in reality grant the defense a four-month continuance, an unacceptable option. Mr. Dowling, of course, wisely presented the court with a bill of exception, which the judge noted. The call of prospective jurors then commenced.

A total of thirty-eight potential jurors were questioned (all men—state law prohibited women from serving as jurors). The defense and/or the defendant challenged without cause twelve of the prospective jurors, their court limit. In virtually all of the cases, they were excluded because they were married with children. Deschamps excused with cause only one juror—a man who was a carpenter by trade with a wife and children, almost identical circumstances as those of Jules Dietsh. However, at least five of the jurors ultimately chosen were married fathers.

Throughout the jury process, the defendant constantly read faces, whispering his wishes to the interpreter, who then transmitted the information to Mr. Dowling. It appeared that Deschamps sought to select a jury of young, even-tempered men who he believed would give him the benefit of the doubt. As the *Daily Picayune* implied, Etienne Deschamps's calculated behavior in the courtroom that day removed any doubt that he was sane.

The State's major objection to a potential juror was his conscientious objection to capital punishment, though one gentleman stated that he could never sentence a "crazy man" to the gallows. At least two of the men were mutually excused because of their limited knowledge of the English language.

The final jury consisted of: four clerks (one of whom was unemployed), two laborers, a bookkeeper, a shoemaker, an engraver, a salesman, a business owner, and a "weigher," a clerk who weighed shipping cargo at the Port of New Orleans. The chosen jurors had all read about the case in the newspaper, but some were unsure if that information was factual. Several had even seen the coroner's findings and testimony of witnesses in the paper. In addition, some of the men admitted that they had formed an opinion on the guilt or innocence of Deschamps but promised to base their verdict on the evidence presented in court.

With the jury complete, Minute Clerk Thomas A. Marshall, Jr., read the grand jury's indictment signed by John J. Finney, assistant district attorney. Then Judge Marr called a recess until 6:00 P.M. The jury selection had been a grueling process, and now a difficult trial was about to begin.

The court reconvened at 6:15 P.M., with Jules Dietsh taking the stand for the State. Testifying in French, with Sheriff Gabriel Villeré translating, Dietsh explained that he was the father of the deceased child, who lived at 116 Chartres Street. He enlightened the jury as to how long he had known the defendant, the particulars of their former friendship, the doctor's supposed magnetic and hypnotic abilities practiced on himself and his children, and his children's relationship with the defendant. He then recalled the specifics of January 30, 1889, starting when Laurence arrived home crying at 4:00 P.M. He identified Juliette's clothing found in Deschamps's room, which was later placed in evidence. He described his deceased daughter as intelligent but childish and simple, who went to church on Sundays but at no other times. He admitted that he consented to the magnetic experiments Deschamps performed on his daughters.

On cross-examination, Dietsh conceded that he did not know how his daughter had died, but he suspected it was from poison. He testified that Deschamps had tried to magnetize him on seven or eight occasions, but the results were only a clouding of his mind. He recalled that Juliette had been magnetized twice, once at his home and once at Deschamps's residence, but was unaware of any other times. As far as Dietsh knew, Dr. Deschamps had only magnetized his family and no one else. He described his daughter's appearance—tall and strong but not well developed—then stated the age of his younger daughter. The defense was clearly trying to establish Laurence's immaturity based upon her age alone. Mr. Dowling knew that she would take the stand sooner or later.

In closing, the defense asked Dietsh to identify one of Deschamps's business cards printed in French, claiming he could cure diseases with magnetism. This he did. Perhaps Dowling was attempting to show the jury the lunacy of his own client's business venture.

Capt. John Journeè was sworn in next and testified that he was in command of the Third Precinct, which included 64 St. Peter Street. He recalled arriving at the second-floor room sometime between 5:00 and 6:00 P.M. on the day in question. There he was met by Charles Serra, Officers Sturges and Rancé (identified in the *Daily Picayune* as "DeRance"), and Corporal Morris. He further testified that he saw the nude body of young Juliette, with chemical burns to her face, and the naked and unconscious Deschamps lying beside her before he was removed to an ambulance. In addition, he recalled observing assorted items in the room, including the victim's clothing, chloroform-saturated handkerchiefs, the toothpicker used by Deschamps, a bottle of anisette, several other bottles, the girl's letters conveniently placed in one of the defendant's clothing trunks, and ashes in the fireplace.

On cross-examination, Journeè clarified that Serra was a commissioned officer, though Serra refined that when he took the stand, and that Jules Dietsh was also present when he arrived. Journeè admitted that Dietsh remained in the room for some time thereafter. Perhaps Mr. Dowling was trying to insinuate that Dietsh had contaminated the evidence or been given facts related to the police and coroner's investigation that he later shared with his daughter. Journeè also testified that when the coroner arrived, he drew the witness's attention to the magnetized disc found in the bed, which the district attorney entered into evidence.

George J. Legendre testified that he was the clerk in charge on the afternoon in question and joined the other police officers when he was relieved of duty at 5:30 P.M. He was present when the coroner arrived and testified that Officer Delhonde was left in charge of the body. Dowling chose not to cross-examine him.

Fernand Rancé was then called and testified how he and the other men gained entrance into Deschamps's room, where he found the nude body of Juliette Dietsh and Deschamps, also nude and unconscious beside her in his bed. He recalled seeing Juliette's folded clothes, the handkerchiefs, and empty vials and some letters in a trunk. He also stated that he detected the odor of chloroform in the room. Again, Dowling chose not to cross-examine.

Charles Serra then testified that he lived next door to Deschamps and was employed as a private officer; he was a commissioned night watchman in reality. He had known the defendant for some time, nearly two years. He knew that Deschamps was a dentist; he had worked on his wife's teeth on several occasions, without chloroform. Serra knew about the children's visits and recalled that "Juliette was a pretty good-sized girl for her age," as noted in the *Daily Picayune*. He then described the events of that day. Some of his testimony contradicted prior testimony, though that didn't seem to alarm the defense. On cross-examination, Serra stated that he heard snoring that sounded like someone was trying to catch their breath, but it may have been moaning; he wasn't clear. He did not see the girl's head resting on Deschamps's chest, as Dr. LeMonnier would later testify. He recalled that the girls came to visit the doctor about five times a week and that their visits were pleasant. He often heard them singing and playing, as the partition door between their rooms was thin. Mr. Dowling was clearly trying to establish that Deschamps was not a coldblooded killer, that Juliette's death was instead a tragic accident.

Officer Delhonde was then called to the stand to establish for the State the timeframe of postmortem rigidity, as he was assigned to observe the body during the night of January 30-31, 1889. On cross-examination, he testified that he did not search the room during the night and did not know the defendant, the victim, or her family. He stated that he left the room the following morning at a 5:15 and that the coroner was there during the night, which was clearly not the case.

The next two witnesses were the druggists, Marcel Majeau, followed by John Mailhes. As noted before, Majeau indicated that the defendant entered his establishment at 2:30 P.M. to purchase some chloroform, because he had a girl at his home whose tooth needed extraction and his supply of the drug was no longer potent. Majeau offered to sell him a two-ounce vial, but Deschamps bought only one ounce, two ounces being too much. He stated that Deschamps had never purchased chloroform from him before. On cross-examination, Majeau testified that he heard Deschamps was a dentist and had known the defendant for four to five years.

When Mailhes took the stand, he testified that Deschamps bought two ounces of chloroform from him at about noon. The witness stated that Deschamps was in the habit of purchasing chloroform from him. However, on cross-examination, Mailhes indicated that he had known Deschamps or rather saw him around town for the past three or four years and didn't remember selling him chloroform prior to January 30, though he had sold him other drugs in the past.

◻ ◻ ◻

Finally, the State called Laurence Dietsh forward to testify. By that late hour, she was the only female left in the still-overflowing courtroom. She was clothed in a mourner's black dress. Judge Marr asked the nine-year-old girl if she understood the nature of an oath, and she responded in the affirmative. She was then sworn in in French, with Chief Deputy Sheriff Alcée LeBlanc serving as her interpreter.

Even before Laurence began to testify, Mr. Dowling objected to any testimony she might give, citing her extreme youth and her inability to understand the true nature of a solemn oath. But Judge Marr was satisfied that the young girl was mature enough to know the difference between a falsehood and the truth. He could recall no legal obstacles that would preclude her sworn testimony. Mr. Luzenberg then read a legislative act passed in 1886 that stated, "A competent witness shall be a person of proper understanding." Mr. Dowling filed a bill of exception, which was noted by the court, and Laurence began her testimony.

Laurence started by introducing herself, stating her relationship to the victim, and testifying that her sister had died in Deschamps's room. She identified the doctor in the courtroom. She explained how she and her sister met Deschamps and that they had known him for some time. She then described what occurred on the afternoon of January 30, 1889, beginning with the doctor's arrival at her house and ending with her departure from his room, including their disrobements. She testified that Deschamps administered the chloroform to Juliette before his second departure, whereupon he fell to his knees and expressed those pathetic words about wanting to die, and then about his final return to his room. She observed him burning papers taken from one of his trunks. She testified that Deschamps handed her two bundles and told her to go to her father and say that he wished to die. She added that this was not the first time Juliette had been put to sleep with chloroform; it had occurred the day before. Lawrence also indicated that on the day her sister died, she too was offered chloroform, which she did not take.

"Did you ever see Juliette strip and go into the doctor's bed before?" the district attorney asked the witness.

Mr. Dowling immediately objected on the grounds that it was irrelevant.

Deschamps had been charged with murder and nothing else. He argued that, in the final analysis, what difference did it make whether she went to bed once or a dozen times with the defendant? Mr. Luzenberg didn't press the issue. Laurence then identified the magnetic disc used upon them and recognized the bottle of anisette. Mr. Luzenberg asked the court's permission to withdraw the witness and put Dr. LeMonnier on the stand. The coroner had not been present when the trial began earlier that morning and apparently had just shown up.

Dr. LeMonnier testified that he was the coroner of Orleans Parish who visited the house where Juliette Dietsh had been murdered. He made an inventory of the room's contents, including the business cards and some letters found in one of the defendant's trunks that appeared to have been strategically placed there for easy discovery. He also found another letter in the pocket of the victim's dress. The district attorney then temporarily withdrew Dr. LeMonnier from the witness box.

Mr. Luzenberg offered the mentioned letters and two business cards as evidence, which Mr. Dowling objected to, based on their lack of relevance to the charge of murder. Judge Marr could not rule either way until he examined the letters' contents. In the meantime, because of the late hour (10:30 P.M.), he adjourned until the following day at 10:30 A.M.

During the course of the first day's trial, the reporter's table was continuously surrounded by a mass of spectators who occupied the chairs and space provided for the press. It was hoped that by the following day, a more accommodating setting would be afforded the newspapermen covering the proceedings. That apparently didn't happen.

The weather front that had blown through the day before ushered in a beautiful, cloudless day for the start of the second day of trial. When the court reconvened, curious spectators again filled every available seat and spilled out into the aisles, making it almost impossible to maneuver in and out of the courtroom. Even before the proceedings got under way, a rumor began to circulate that Deschamps had pled guilty without capital punishment. Mr. Dowling and the defendant were questioned privately as to the merits of this rumor, which both denied. Deschamps went even further by indicating he had no desire to plead guilty to any charge.

Chief Deputy LeBlanc then signaled for the jurors to be brought into the courtroom, and at precisely 11:00 A.M., Etienne Deschamps was escorted back in. The names of that day's witnesses for the State were then called, which included only Laurence Dietsh and Dr. LeMonnier. Those remaining witnesses who had testified the day before were therefore excused, though Jules Dietsh likely remained and took a seat among the other spectators.

With Mr. LeBlanc still acting as her interpreter, little Laurence once again entered the witness box. She testified that she was in the defendant's room and saw the doctor take a bottle of chloroform from his mantelpiece, the contents of which he eventually gave to her sister. She then identified for the State Juliette's clothing and those belonging to Deschamps.

On cross-examination, she described in great detail what had transpired between the time Deschamps arrived at her house and when she exited his room approximately three to four hours later. During her testimony, the defense placed a bottle near Laurence's nostrils and asked if it smelled like chloroform; she said no. To Mr. Dowling's chagrin, when a second bottle was presented, she said yes, it was chloroform. The latter bottle contained a more potent dose of the drug. In other damning testimony, Laurence told the court that the defendant applied another chloroform-laced handkerchief to her sister's face after his second trip outdoors, while Juliette's eyes remained closed, her body motionless, and her mouth open.

At this point in her testimony, Deschamps asked Sheriff Villeré, who sat between the defendant and Mr. Dowling, what Laurence had just said. Apparently he couldn't hear her testimony spoken in French. When he was told what she had said, the defendant shook his head as if in denial. Though it was never known for sure, his body language suggested that, contrary to Laurence's testimony, he didn't reapply chloroform to Juliette's face when he returned to his room the second time.

With that testimony introduced, Mr. Dowling apparently allowed the floodgates to open even further. Laurence went on to describe what transpired on January 29, 1889, when she and her sister disrobed and drank chloroform at the request of Dr. Deschamps, though she did not know why the drug was administered to them at the time. Laurence testified that the doctor never provided a reason.

On redirect, the district attorney jumped at the chance to question her further about the particulars of January 29. Laurence reaffirmed that Deschamps had given them chloroform to drink after she and her sister disrobed at his request. She testified that the doctor also took off his clothes, but she never saw Deschamps touch her sister inappropriately that day, though she was asleep a part of the time. She also admitted that upon awakening, she discovered that she had vomited. She remembered that Deschamps was still in his bed, undressed, with her sister.

Of course, Mr. Dowling had no choice but to re-cross-examine the witness at this juncture. When he pressed her about whether Dr. Deschamps disrobed on January 29, Laurence recanted, stating that she couldn't remember exactly. With that, the witness concluded her testimony, having been on the stand for a little over an hour. The time was 12:05 P.M. At this juncture, Mr. Dowling must have known it was hopeless, though nudity had nothing to do with the cause of Juliette's death nor had his client been charged with rape. Perception was everything for the jury, and Dowling knew it.

With Laurence's testimony complete, the State called their last witness to the stand, Dr. Yves R. LeMonnier, Jr. As he stepped into the witness box, the silence in the courtroom was deafening as everyone wanted to listen intently to his testimony. He began by stating that he was called to the St. Peter Street house on January 30 to investigate an alleged rape. Upon his arrival, he discovered that Deschamps had already been taken to Charity Hospital and Juliette's nude body remained. He again recalled what he found in the room, its general untidiness and dirtiness, the victim's clothing folded neatly as opposed to Deschamps's clothes strewn about floor, the fresh ashes in the fireplace, and, in particular, two vials of chloroform, which had been recently used. At that point, the defense objected to Dr. LeMonnier's chloroform reference as drawing conclusions, rather than simply stating the facts. But Mr. Luzenberg responded that the coroner was only giving his expert testimony. Mr. Dowling fired back by saying that Dr. LeMonnier appeared to be arguing the case for the district attorney.

Dr. LeMonnier continued his testimony by recalling what he found in the personal trunks of Etienne Deschamps: the business card that advertised his peculiar services and, specifically, the books on medicine and magnetism. But Mr. Dowling objected again, citing that these had no relevance to the charge of murder. The district attorney explained to the court that the purpose of this line of questioning and the coroner's testimony was to prove that Dr. Deschamps had a thorough knowledge of the effects of chloroform, and the condition of the room in which the murdered child was found was most definitely relevant to the case. Dowling's objection was overruled.

The business card with the handwritten address that Mr. Luzenberg had been submitted to the court the night before was at last entered into evidence and shown to the witness, who identified it. It was then shown to the jury. Dr. LeMonnier told the court of his other discoveries in the room: the magnetizing disc, the toothpicker, and handkerchiefs with the odor of chloroform. He then described the corpse of the nude victim, including

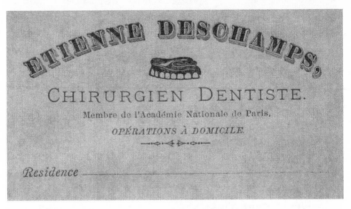

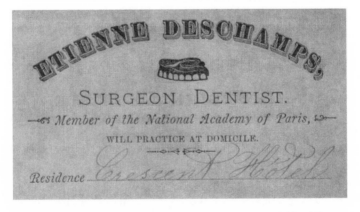

Etienne Deschamps's business cards. (Courtesy Louisiana Division/City Archives, New Orleans Public Library)

the slight discoloration on her face like a chemical burn. He provided great detail about the victim's external genitalia, the fluid found within, her dilated anus, and the implications. Mr. Dowling vigorously objected to this, on the grounds that the defendant had not been charged with rape or any crime other than murder. Of course, Mr. Luzenberg stated that the coroner's testimony established a motive for the crime, which Judge Marr ruled was a legitimate part of the State's case. The defense then offered a bill of exception to the admission of Dr. LeMonnier's testimony related to his sexual findings. Judge Marr took a short recess to allow Mr. Dowling to write up the bill.

When the court resumed, Dr. LeMonnier repeated the orders he gave Officer Delhonde to guard the body and document the stages of postmortem rigidity. He was satisfied that Juliette Dietsh died from the inhalation of chloroform sometime between 2:00 and 3:00 P.M. on January 30. He then cited his reasons. This time of death conflicted with what he had written in his January 31 coroner report—4:30 P.M.—something that Mr. Dowling obviously missed due to his unfamiliarity with the case. He made other objections to parts of Dr. LeMonnier's testimony, of course, but the court overruled them all and he filed more bills of exception.

The cross-examination was brief, with the defense asking only two questions: what was the distance between Majeau's drugstore and Deschamps's residence—1,127 feet—and was he positive that the victim died of inhalation of chloroform? Regarding the first question, perhaps the defense was trying to establish if there was time enough for the defendant to purchase the chloroform and administer it to the victim, given that she died between 2:00 and 3:00 P.M. If she was already dead and Deschamps purchased the chloroform at 2:30 P.M., did it make any sense that he reapplied the cloth to her face upon his return? But because Dowling called no witnesses, nor did he offer a closing argument, any possible rationale for that question remained unheard by the jury. Dr. LeMonnier answered yes to the latter question, and so ended Dowling's cross-examination. At 1:15 P.M., Dr. LeMonnier left the witness box and Mr. Dowling asked the court for some time to privately consult with his client. Judge Marr gave him until 2:00 P.M.

At 2:05 P.M., Mr. Dowling informed the court that he had no witnesses to call and proposed to submit the case to the jury without a closing argument. He must have known his case was lost and gambled that the Louisiana Supreme Court would overturn the conviction based on any number of bills of exception he filed during the two-day trial. Mr. Luzenberg advised that the State was willing to submit the case to the jury without closing arguments.

With that portion of the trial concluded, Judge Marr delivered his charge to the jury. The defense asked the judge to instruct the jury that if they harbored any doubt about Deschamps's guilt, they must find him innocent; if they thought him guilty of manslaughter, they were bound to convict him on the lesser charge. Judge Marr did so.

On behalf of the State, Judge Marr informed the jury that if they were satisfied the death occurred under special circumstances, and also if the death was accidental after the defendant rendered her unconscious for the purpose of committing any sexual or unnatural acts, such a crime was murder. At 2:58 P.M., having understood such instructions, the jury retired upstairs to deliberate.

Their decision came almost immediately. At 3:16 P.M., the jury sent a message to Mr. LeBlanc indicating that they had reached a verdict. The defendant was brought back into the courtroom as the jury reentered. The verdict was handed over to Clerk Marshall: "Guilty. Robert Brooks, Foreman, New Orleans, May 2, 1889."

Mr. Dowling asked Judge Marr to poll the jury, which he did, and then the jury was discharged. According to the *Daily Picayune*, "The accused took the verdict stolidly, not even winking his eyes or twitching his body when he comprehended its meaning." The large group of spectators heard the decision with "seeming satisfaction." The sentencing for Etienne Deschamps came eleven days later. His appeal process began almost at the same time.

Chapter Five

The War of Words

No one, however criminal he may be, should be condemned without having been defended in Court.

Dr. John Havá, June 4, 1899

On April 30, 1889, the day after James Dowling was assigned to defend Etienne Deschamps, Jacques "J." Maximé Queyrouze penned a short letter to him in French—a curious thing to do since Dowling spoke only English. He informed Dowling that he was an attorney in the city, of French descent who also spoke English, and that he had taken an interest in the Deschamps case. Queyrouze proposed that they meet to discuss the possibility of him taking over the defense. At the very least, he would offer his expertise to Mr. Dowling. Why Queyrouze never directly petitioned the court on behalf of Deschamps will never be known; he had three months to do so. It was probably his older sister, Marie Léona Queyrouze, who persuaded him to write at the eleventh hour. Seldom using her first name and using an assortment of pseudonyms—Constant Beauvais being one of the best known—Léona wasn't afraid of controversy.

The siblings were part of a wealthy Creole family. Their father, Léon Queyrouze, was born in February 1818 in Beaumont, a village in southwestern France within present-day Dordogne Department. Léon was the son of Simon Queyrouze, an officer and trusted friend of Napoleon. For some reason, at twelve years of age, young Léon left his native country and came to New Orleans. He arrived with few resources, but that didn't discourage him. Possessing a singular focus and endless ambition, Léon was determined to be successful in the United States. He quickly made friends.

He soon moved on to study English at a school in Lexington, Kentucky, but returned to the Crescent City in 1833. He then set his eyes on his next target, the island of Cuba, where he hoped to gain knowledge of the business world and learn Spanish as well. By 1835, he was back in New Orleans, where he found work as a clerk with Carriere, Daran & Company, an importer of French wines, brandies, and other liquors. Within five years, he was made a junior partner. After that, he branched out on his own, establishing the House of Queyrouze and Langsdorf, which became Queyrouze & Bois until the Civil War interrupted his business venture.

In 1857, Léon married Anne Marie Clara Tertrou, a twenty-one-year-old Creole lady from St. Martinville, Louisiana, and they would have two children. Miss Tertrou's ancestors were from France, and some settled in Beauvais, the capital of Oise Department in the north. She was related to Armand Julie Beauvais, who briefly served as governor of Louisiana after Gov. Pierre Derbigny was killed in a carriage accident in October 1829.

In the spring of 1861, Léon answered the call to serve in the Louisiana state army, becoming the commanding officer of the Thirteenth (Orleans Guard) Battalion in March 1862 when it was incorporated into the Confederate army. His battalion participated in the Battle of Shiloh in April, where Major Queyrouze sustained a serious knee wound, which caused him to be sent home to recuperate for ninety days. As a Confederate officer, he was eventually arrested as a registered enemy of the United States by Union general Benjamin Butler, who took formal possession of New Orleans on May 1, 1862.

During Butler's occupation of the city that year, it was Anne Marie Queyrouze who allegedly got the general to issue General Order No. 32, on May 27, forbidding his soldiers from unwarranted seizure of private property. Butler's original General Order No. 15 issued on May 1 apparently had gone unheeded by his men.

After two months in prison, Léon was given a choice to swear allegiance to the United States or leave the country. He chose the latter and returned to Cuba, where, in Havana, he engaged in a brokerage business. From Cuba he moved to Matamoras, eventually associating and winning favor with the French occupiers of Mexico under Emperor Maximilian's rule. When the Civil War ended, Queyrouze returned to New Orleans, signing an oath of allegiance to the Union in August 1865 but definitely remaining "unreconstructed" until his death in January 1895. After the war, he resumed his business as a commission merchant under various names, the last being Léon Queyrouze Company, Limited.

Léon Queyrouze took a very active role in literary, social, and political circles in the city after the war, serving as the president of the Fifth Ward Democratic Club and one of the founding members of L'Athénée Louisianais, a society that studied and promoted the French language and its literature. He was also involved with the Union Française and the Casaforas Association, French-based benevolent organizations whose memberships were open only to the most prominent French citizens of New Orleans.

Léona Queyrouze was born in New Orleans on March 23, 1861. She became a celebrated poet, essayist, composer, pianist, the only female member of L'Athénée Louisianais, and, beginning in the spring of 1889, a tireless advocate for the defendant and later convicted child murderer, Etienne Deschamps. (It will never be known for sure, but she was probably among the ladies in the courtroom that first day of the trial, though no female spectator stayed for the entire day.) Schooled in Paris, France, Léona was fluent in seven languages and the first female New Orleanian to give a speech and read her own work in public. At five feet four inches tall, with dark hair and brown eyes, Léona was described as being a petite woman with muscular arms due to her mastery of fencing, another passion of hers, and "big mystical eyes and a masculine mouth." She inherited from her father ambition and purpose, qualities that she did not squander. Though she was unable to prevent the execution of Etienne Deschamps, she, her brother, and a third ally, Dr. Juan (John) G. Havá, delayed the inevitable for more than three years. That alone was a great accomplishment, given that most executions during that time occurred within a year or less of the sentence.

Léona's younger brother, J. Maximé Queyrouze, at age seventeen became the winner of the L'Athénée Louisianais society's best philosophical essay and a graduate of the University of Louisiana (Tulane) law department in New Orleans. Over the years, he became a well-respected and influential attorney in the city. For his part in the defense of Etienne Deschamps, he, among other things, would assist in writing the legal brief that was presented to the Louisiana Supreme Court in the fall of 1889. It called upon the High Court to overturn the May 2, 1889, murder conviction of Deschamps.

Mr. Dowling probably didn't receive Mr. Queyrouze's offer of help until after the trial's conclusion. He naturally assumed that Dowling would be granted a continuance, time enough for both men to meet and plan a defense strategy. J. Maximé Queyrouze was wrong.

On Monday, May 13, 1889, Etienne Deschamps and Mr. Dowling appeared in Judge Marr's courtroom for sentencing. Dowling moved for a new trial, based upon the judge's refusal to grant a continuance, but Judge Marr denied the motion. For Dowling it was only a formality. The case would be appealed directly to the Louisiana Supreme Court.

Léona Queyrouze, oil on canvas by John Genin, 1880. (Courtesy the Collection of the Louisiana State Museum)

There were no surprises when it came time to sentence the defendant. Judge Marr sentenced Etienne Deschamps, who had been found guilty of murder by a jury of his peers, to death by hanging, the time and date to be fixed by Gov. Francis R. T. Nicholls at a later date. Before the sentence was read, Deschamps was asked if he had anything to say to the court. He replied that if he had been given the time and ordinary means of defending himself, he would have proved his innocence.

Léona Queyrouze might have taken issue with Deschamps's claim of total innocence, but she stoutly believed that he had been deprived of due process by the court's refusal to grant a continuance and for allowing evidence to be entered that was irrelevant to the murder charge; specifically, Dr. LeMonnier's testimony about the sexual history between the defendant and young Juliette Dietsh.

On May 16, 1889, in one of many post-trial letters written to the editor of the *New Orleans Times-Democrat* under her pseudonym, Constant Beauvais, Léona expressed her belief that among the more "serious thinkers and analysts" in the city, a "gradual and salutary change" had occurred since the trial in favor of Etienne Deschamps. She and other likeminded persons across the nation believed that Deschamps had been unjustly convicted in a rush to judgment. With the entire trial lasting less than thirty-six hours and the verdict being reached in fifteen minutes, Léona believed that the jury was part of a mass of "untutored, unlearned, and passionate" people who were governed by their emotions, rather than facts. Had the jurors done their job correctly, according to Léona, they wouldn't have reached their verdict in such haste. In her mind, these kinds of people were "slaves to sentimentalism," for they believed that Deschamps got what he deserved, based on irrelevant testimony allowed during the trial. It was the opening salvo of her "A Desirer of Justice" campaign for the convicted child murderer. Aiding her was Dr. Havá.

It appeared that Léona Queyrouze and Dr. Havá first met shortly after the May 2 guilty verdict, perhaps after Dr. Havá read one of her letters to the editor. They quickly recognized that they shared one goal: to rectify the injustice of Deschamps's trial. Like Léona, Dr. Havá had closely followed the case since its inception in late January. For the next three years, they would work tirelessly together against impossible odds.

Dr. Havá was born on July 12, 1833, in Guines, Cuba, and came from a family of physicians. His father was Dr. Francisco Havá, a very prominent physician on the island. John earned a bachelor of arts degree from the University of Havana at the age of fourteen. He then traveled to Philadelphia, where he earned a degree in dentistry in 1854, and then returned to Cuba. Not content to remain a dentist, Havá decided to study medicine in Paris, graduating as a physician in 1859. He returned to his native island and practiced medicine with great success. In the early 1860s, he married Francisca Balbin, a native Cuban of German descent, and from the couple would have three sons. The first two boys were born on the island, and their last child was born in New Orleans in 1870.

Dr. Havá and his family would have stayed in Cuba if not for the outbreak of the Cuban Revolution of 1868 and his political associations with the revolutionaries. With Cuban natives seeking their independence from Spain, Havá wielded his formidable writing talents on behalf of the revolution, editing a newspaper in opposition of Spanish rule. His political activities forced him to flee the country the following year. The revolution eventually burned itself out nine years later, and Spain retained its control of the island for a time.

Dr. Havá planned to take his family to Philadelphia, where he had been educated during the 1850s, but while passing through New Orleans, he found the city more hospitable and decided to stay. (Another way that Dr. Havá possibly knew Léona was through her father. It's conceivable that the doctor knew Léon Queyrouze when he lived briefly in Cuba during the Civil War and their friendship renewed when both came to New Orleans. This may be one of the reasons why Dr. Havá stayed in the city rather than moving north to Pennsylvania.)

Over the years, his medical practice flourished and he became an authority on medical jurisprudence and the treatment of yellow fever; he was in the city during the epidemic of 1878. Beginning in 1877, Dr. Havá also owned a large drugstore at 99 and 101 (then 415) Chartres Street, between Conti and St. Louis streets, though that address no longer exists. (The entire city block bordered by Chartres, Conti, Royal, and St. Louis streets is now occupied by the Louisiana Supreme Court, Louisiana Fourth Circuit Court of Appeals, Law Library of Louisiana, and Judicial Administrator's Office, with its main entrance at 400 Royal Street.) As a physician and druggist, whose business was in close proximity to Etienne Deschamps's various residences in the French Quarter, Dr. Havá quite possibly knew Deschamps prior to January 1889. Over the years, the Frenchman could have easily bought drugs and other chemicals from Dr. Havá, since the doctor was fluent in Spanish, English, and French.

Whether the two met prior to Juliette Dietsh's death is immaterial.

Dr. John G. Havá. (Courtesy NOLA.com/The
Times-Picayune)

Nevertheless, as a medical expert, Dr. Havá took a keen interest in
Deschamps, before and after his trial, and particularly in Dr. LeMonnier's
autopsy findings and later court testimony. On May 29, 1889, he wrote to the
coroner and enclosed a copy of a paper he had written entitled "Medico-Legal
Considerations on the Case of Etienne Deschamps." (He self-published his
letter and paper—fourteen typed pages in all—as a pamphlet on June 3, 1889.)
Dr. Havá's intentions were very clear. In writing his "Considerations," he set
out to refute the sexual allegations set forth by Dr. LeMonnier and thereby
make them irrelevant in any future court action.

In his letter, Dr. Havá stated that, after a close examination of all the
evidence, newspaper articles (erroneous and slanted as he believed they
were), sworn testimonies given in criminal court, and autopsy findings, he
firmly believed that Deschamps was not the "vulgar criminal" that everyone,
including the press, portrayed him to be. It was clear that as a medico-legal

expert, he meant to fight to overturn Deschamps's conviction in the court of public opinion.

Dr. Havá's interest in setting the record straight intensified after he received an article printed in the May 3, 1889, *Courrier des Etats-Unis*, from his friend, "Constant Beauvais." The *Courrier* was a famous New York City-based, international, French-language newspaper (published between 1828 and 1938), which had gotten word of the Deschamps murder trial, undoubtedly from Léona. In that issue, with its headline, *"Une Condamnation à mort"* or "A Death Sentence," the paper reported, among other things, that the French defendant had "offended," implying raped, Juliette Dietsh. On May 9, Dr. Havá wrote to the editor that no such crime had been committed on the day in question. He let it be known that the young girl had died from "an imprudent administration of chloroform" and that no sexual intercourse had occurred within forty-eight hours of her death, according to Dr. LeMonnier's autopsy report.

On May 14, days after receiving Dr. Havá's letter, the *Courrier* printed "La condamnation d'Etienne Deschamps," stating that, according to Dr. Havá and Constant Beauvais, Deschamps's recent death sentence had caused "painful emotions" among the French population of Louisiana. It went on to correct its earlier report regarding Juliette's alleged rape and her cause of death. It added that the letters received from Constant Beauvais and Dr. Havá were "proof that there still exists in New Orleans generous people who were not afraid of compromising their principles when it [came] to the defense of an unfortunate man deemed guilty by all."

Not everyone saw Deschamps as an "unfortunate" soul who had been unjustly deprived of his liberties by a rush to judgment. A writer from Jackson, Louisiana using the pseudonym "Fair Play" lashed out at Constant Beauvais and others who defended the Frenchman. "How any man or woman, after reading the particulars of this most horrible and revolting crime, can raise a voice in defense of Etienne Deschamps is something deplorable and beyond my comprehension," Fair Play expressed to the editor of the *Times-Democrat*. Regarding the trial lasting less than thirty-six hours, Fair Play posed this question to the readership: "How many hours, let us ask, did Etienne Deschamps spend in disposing of the life of his fair young victim?"

Fair Play went on to assert that Deschamps had been given every opportunity to present a defense and ample time to prepare, if it had not been for his continuous refusal to accept a court-appointed attorney. For the sake of argument, "giving every doubt to the prisoner," he admitted that Juliette Dietsh's death could have been due to a "careless handling of chloroform," but Fair Play could never excuse Deschamps's crime of rape, "one of the most awful crimes known to mankind."

And therein lies the quandary that pitted one side against the other; the crime that he was actually charged with and the sexual relations between the defendant and the young girl that the jury—and a sizable portion of the New Orleans population—couldn't erase from their minds.

At the time, the age of sexual consent in Louisiana was twelve. But many people felt that because there was such a vast age difference between the two people, and because Deschamps had used chloroform as a supposed means to an end, he was guilty of rape—a capital offense—whether he was ever charged with the crime or not. With that prevailing attitude, Léona Queyrouze firmly believed that the jury had convicted Deschamps based upon their prejudices, not the crime that he was charged with. She may have been right. In Léona's mind, the jury elected to convict a middle-aged rapist but used chloroform poisoning, accidental or not, as a convenient pretense for their decision. The war of words continued.

Not to be outdone, on June 4, 1889, Dr. Havá fired a salvo at Fair Play with a letter to the *Times-Democrat*. He declared that Constant Beauvais, who he proclaimed as "one of Louisiana's fairest and most amiable daughters," cared little for the man personally but rather based her desire for a new trial on a principle afforded to any accused person in a civilized society. "No one, however criminal he may be, should be condemned without having been defended in Court," he wrote. Regarding those who sided with the defendant, he added, "*It is not Deschamps* whom they are defending; it is a *principle* and the honor of Louisiana, above all."

At least one other gentleman vented his frustration and downright anger toward Fair Play: Charles O. Roome of Palmetto, Louisiana. The *Times-Democrat* rejected his June 3, 1889, letter for its supposedly incendiary tone and his suggestion that Fair Play was a member of the jury that convicted Deschamps. Roome then forwarded a copy of the letter to Constant Beauvais, to show her that other citizens in the state wished to rally around her cause. With his letter rejected, he was convinced that the press in New Orleans was as prejudiced against Deschamps as the jury had been, but he was not to be deterred.

In a follow-up letter to the *Times-Democrat* printed on June 26, Roome added that the Frenchman was quite insane. "Deschamps and myself boarded at the same restaurant and hotel in the town of Morgan City, La., and I can say truthfully that in my opinion the man's sanity was to be questioned at any time." It was signed, *Desirer of Justice*. Léona believed that the entirety of Roome's letter was an "honest, impartial and forcible argument." She too, in short order, would be convinced that Deschamps was a lunatic.

With the temperatures rising into the upper eighties by the second week of June 1889, New Orleans was not only feeling the heat from the approaching summer season but also from the tense exchanges between those who either opposed or supported Deschamps's efforts to seek a new trial. Truth be told, Etienne Deschamps probably had little to do with the campaign pursuing this goal. Immediately after being sentenced to death by Judge Marr, he was placed in the condemned section of Orleans Parish Prison, where he remained confined until the legal process ran its course. What to do next was a perplexing question for Léona Queyrouze, for writing letters to various editors in the city and elsewhere could only get her so far. She needed some legal advice.

In March 1889, the Medico-Legal Society of New York announced that it would sponsor the First International Congress of Medical Jurisprudence in New York City, the four-day event to begin on the first Tuesday of June. As a member of the National Medico-Legal Society, the New York branch invited active, honorary, or corresponding members to submit papers to be presented at the Congress. One of the New York members was Edward W. Chamberlain, a New York City attorney. In March 1889, Chamberlain, the chairman of an ad-hoc committee looking into what proportion of the insane in the United States was the result of sexual causes, sent out a one-page questionnaire to medical and legal professionals across the country. One of the copies undoubtedly ended up in the hands of Dr. Havá, who shared it at some point with Léona Queyrouze. She later learned that Mr. Chamberlain was of the opinion that repression of one's sexuality had a negative effect upon the individual and the nation at large. He firmly believed that society needed to begin a frank and open dialogue about sexual matters. As he put it, "more light and broader knowledge" was a positive thing. This was at a time when sexual repression was at its zenith.

It's not known if Léona shared his views, but she did seek his legal advice in early June 1889 regarding what to do next for Etienne Deschamps. In a letter he wrote to her on June 16, 1889, he simply told her to do nothing while the appeal was pending. He added, "If the appeal is decided adversely then an appeal must be made to the people of the whole country, in an effort to procure pardon."

There is little doubt that Dr. LeMonnier received the same questionnaire from Chamberlain and the information about the upcoming Congress. But unlike Dr. Havá, the coroner was invited to speak, though he was not a member, nor was Dr. Havá. His talk would be the recitation of his controversial paper, "Medico-Legal History of the Deschamps Case," in which he graphically detailed the autopsy findings and gynecological evidence he gathered at the crime scene. His paper also provided numerous other facts about the case and his explanation for why Deschamps was not insane, nor Juliette Dietsh suicidal at the time of her death, contrary to what Deschamps had confessed to him.

In mid-May 1889, when the local newspapers announced Dr. LeMonnier's upcoming talk, the coroner took an opportunity to take a swipe at Deschamps's defenders, particularly Constant Beauvais. In one article that appeared in the *Times-Democrat* on May 22, 1889, Dr. LeMonnier stated that he had read Beauvais's May 16, 1889, letter to the editor. He scoffed at her assertions that Deschamps had not received a fair trial and even brought up her gender. When the New Orleans-based *Le Franco-Louisianais* refused to publish her comments that she had also forwarded to the *Courrier*, Dr. LeMonnier indicated that it was based "on the grounds that it was a subject of which a lady should tread lightly, if at all." It was clear he was insinuating that as a woman, Léona Queyrouze, a.k.a. Constant Beauvais, didn't know what she was talking about, or it was a subject no *lady* should ponder.

Of course, Léona had to reply to Dr. LeMonnier's comments. Her father had engrained that into her psyche. She claimed in a follow-up letter to the *Times-Democrat* that the French-language paper's refusal to run her Deschamps-related story had nothing to do with her gender and everything to do with its concerns that such a story would run afoul of the American press. In other words, according to Léona, it was too controversial to print regardless of who wrote it—male or female. She seemed to have been satisfied with the paper's explanation. But it will never be known if the newspaper was truthful with Léona.

When Dr. LeMonnier finally spoke before the sparsely attended First International Congress of Medical Jurisprudence in New York during its late-afternoon session of June 4, 1889, Edward Chamberlain wasn't surprised that his topic was received negatively by some of the audience. One highly esteemed member of the society told Chamberlain, who did not attend the coroner's talk, that Dr. LeMonnier's presentation was "very nasty" and should not have been read to the audience, which included some ladies.

Though Chamberlain took issue with the method of Deschamps's prosecution, he also believed that the jury had convicted him based on the sexual evidence presented. He defended Dr. LeMonnier's usage of explicit sexual terms during his talk. He said in his June 18 letter to Léona Queyrouze, as "long as superstition bars the way to knowledge of sexual matters, so long will there continue to be these Deschamps cases." He even speculated, "Had Juliette Dietsch [*sic*] possessed such knowledge she might by means thereof have saved her life."

It wasn't until sometime after Dr. LeMonnier's return to New Orleans that he had an opportunity to read Dr. Havá's letter of May 29, 1889, and the enclosed copy of his rebuttal. And it wasn't until the middle of August that he wrote back to Dr. Havá, stating that he needed to read or reread Dr. LeMonnier's publication. Apparently every point Dr. Havá raised, especially related to the autopsy findings, had been addressed in the coroner's delivered speech.

□ □ □

With that said, one of the most striking examples to illustrate Dr. LeMonnier's point was the difference between what he found and what Dr. Havá believed regarding the "viscid and milky white fluid" that bathed the victim's genitals. As stated before, Dr. LeMonnier found the fluid characteristic of semen, though it was void of spermatozoa. Even without the evidence of sperm, which Dr. LeMonnier could account for, he held to the belief that recent copulation had occurred between the defendant and victim. Dr. Havá, on the other hand, believed that this substance was nothing more than the various fluids found in the uterus and vulva, especially in females afflicted with leucorrhea. He also quoted the coroner's own official autopsy report, which stated he had "found no trace indicating that sexual intercourse had taken place within 48 hours before the young girl's death."

Dr. LeMonnier obviously amended that portion of his report upon closer examination of other physical evidence, such as the victim's clothing. He ruled out leucorrhea by indicating that the vast quantity of fluid retrieved from the victim's vagina on the day of her death would, by gravity alone, have soiled her undergarments while she walked about the city prior to her arrival at Deschamps's residence. Yet no such bodily fluid was found on her clothing, neatly folded on the chair in Deschamps's room the day she died.

Dr. Havá also took issue with Dr. LeMonnier's implications that Deschamps was not only guilty of vaginal intercourse but sodomy, after the coroner discovered that the victim's anus was dilated and "funnel shaped," allowing him to easily insert two fingers. Dr. Havá explained that there was nothing unusual in that finding, especially twenty-four hours after death when the autopsy was performed. "These [rectal and vulvar] orifices which are susceptible of considerable dilation during life, become much more so after death," the doctor wrote. "Rigor-mortis, instead of closing them has the contrary effect." But Dr. Havá failed to consider Dr. LeMonnier's timeline. His examination of the victim's anus occurred before the onset of postmortem rigidity.

There were other differences of opinion, especially regarding how Juliette Dietsh came to her death. Dr. LeMonnier saw it as premeditated murder when Deschamps placed a second chloroform-soaked cloth over her mouth while she remained unconscious. Dr. Havá saw it as "a rash imprudence," an accident that occurs from time to time with the best of surgeons and physicians. Dr. LeMonnier probably took issue with that, believing that skilled practitioners (he being one) knew what they were doing with chloroform.

Dr. Havá admitted that Deschamps had no legal right to administer chloroform in the first place, since he was neither a physician nor dentist, in spite of what the defendant claimed. Simply stated, Dr. Havá saw Deschamps as "nothing but a *mesmerizer* and *hypnotizer* anxious to possess a *clairvoyant.*" Such practices he viewed as science for "quack doctors." He saw the defendant as an unhappy, demented individual, "notwithstanding his more or less lucid way of reasoning in regard to other matters." On the other hand, Dr. LeMonnier saw Deschamps's behavior as calculating, as when he burned possibly incriminating papers the day of Juliette's murder. He believed that Deschamps was far from insane. But Dr. Havá reasoned, "Do the insane lose their instincts of preservation through insanity?"

In the final analysis, Dr. Havá was most disturbed by the singular actions taken by the Orleans Parish coroner, which the district attorney or court should never have allowed. According to Dr. Havá, Dr. LeMonnier was the sole physician to view the body within hours of her death. He was the one to hold an inquest, not the district attorney. He was the one who heard the accused's declarations of guilt. And finally, he was the one who interrogated the witnesses and the sole person to decide the mental state of the suspect.

Dr. Havá especially took issue with the testimony of Laurence Dietsh, whom he saw as having no legal responsibility to tell the truth given her age and having been "allowed to remain under the immediate influence of both her father and grandmother." (Did he expect the young girl to be placed in solitary confinement until the end of the trial?) And finally, according to Dr.

Havá, Dr. LeMonnier was the sole individual who pled the State's case before the judge and jury while in the witness box, "with a view of establishing and proving the guilt of the accused; thus overstepping the limits of the functions assigned to him."

After Dr. Havá's pamphlet was published in early June 1889, Léona Queyrouze sought, with the doctor's permission, to have it printed in the *Times-Democrat*. It was obvious what their strategy was—to enlighten the vast majority of New Orleanians who believed that Etienne Deschamps was a vile murderer. But the newspaper responded that the editor and manager, Page M. Baker, respectfully declined her request. Mr. Baker believed that the article was more suited for a medical journal than a secular newspaper such as his. It was clear that the language used in Dr. Havá's pamphlet, as was the case in Dr. LeMonnier's paper, was too graphic for the delicate eyes of the female readership and likely would have sent shock waves across the nation had it been published. During this time, the 1873 Comstock Law, a federal law prohibiting the circulation of obscene literature, remained in effect. There was little doubt that some aspects of this pamphlet would have fallen under the purview of the law, or at least made things complicated for the *Times-Democrat* had they chosen to print it.

Of all the writers who sent letters to the editor about the Deschamps case, pro and con, the Frenchman was especially struck by the sympathetic and supportive tone of Constant Beauvais. Obviously, someone in the prison had alerted Deschamps that he had an ally on the outside. During the latter part of June 1889, Deschamps requested a meeting with this person. He expected the individual to be a man and was surprised when Léona arrived at the prison.

Léona Queyrouze was immediately struck by the Frenchman's apparent mental peculiarities. To her, he was a person "whose mind was anything but well-balanced." He still bore the physical signs of his March 1889 suicide attempt when he had plunged to the prison yard from the second-story gallery. He complained to her of dizziness and an inability to collect his thoughts, but he believed that his disorder was the result of poisoning by prison officials. He knew how hated he was. Léona told him that his symptoms were more likely related to his fall than poison, but he shrugged his shoulders in disagreement. He went on to inform Léona that he had not attempted suicide that day but rather "had been pushed from behind, as he was looking [down] into the yard," which was a physical impossibility. Whether Léona knew that is not known.

Somehow Deschamps received a copy of Dr. Havá's pamphlet, and his reaction, among other things, placed into question his mental capacities. In this first meeting with Léona, he expressed his displeasure at the doctor for his "theory of insanity therein exposed." He told her that it was unfair of Dr. Havá to refer of him as "crazy," especially since he had never seen or spoken to him. Léona found it useless to argue with the Frenchman as he went from subject to subject in a disconnected manner. By the end of their meeting, she was convinced that Etienne Deschamps was mentally imbalanced and could not possibly feign insanity, which she believed was beyond his "limited intellectual faculties." Apparently, his insistence that he was not insane convinced Léona that he was.

It wasn't until she rose and was about to leave his cell that Deschamps admitted why he had sent for Constant Beauvais in the first place. "My French name had pleased him," she later wrote, citing that as one of the reasons for the requested visit. The other reason was that he wished to talk to her about securing the services of another attorney. Should he be given a second chance to prove his innocence, he wanted someone other than Mr. Dowling to represent him. He had been condemned once. He was afraid it would happen again unless he got someone else. Léona thought otherwise; no attorney could have done any better than Mr. Dowling, given the same circumstances. "[But] Deschamps seemed to entertain a sort of superstitious fear in that respect," she noted. She left his cell promising to return.

When they met again, Léona asked Deschamps if he had a particular gentleman in mind among the attorneys he knew. She could contact this man if he so desired. He named a few lawyers who had visited him. Undoubtedly, Henry Castellanos was among those mentioned. But of all the attorneys he named, he was especially opposed to retaining Judge Alfred Roman.

"I will take anybody else for my counsel but never *Roman*, never!" Deschamps strongly insisted. "I prefer to have nobody!"

After considerable time "and much useless talk," according to Léona, Deschamps chose John MacMahon as his legal counsel, of the law practice MacMahon & Pratt. He was not among his previous lawyer acquaintances, and how he became aware of this man is not known. He may have learned about MacMahon's unsuccessful attempt to petition the Louisiana Supreme Court in late March 1889. MacMahon sought an injunction against the Deschamps murder trial, undoubtedly based upon his belief that the defendant was insane.

Léona knew nothing of this gentleman, and had two other lawyers in mind, but she acquiesced to Deschamps's choice. She insisted, however, that he put his choice for legal counsel in writing and have it verified by witnesses. By then, Léona was unquestioningly convinced, erroneous as she was, that Deschamps possessed "a complete lack of mental equilibrium, of a most subtle disconcerting type," and "queer disconnected, vacillating and rather contradictory ways regarding his peculiar notions about occult sciences." Because of that, she thought it was best for all concerned that he did what she asked. The witnesses were procured from the prison staff, with Deschamps dictating in French his wish to retain MacMahon as his counsel, which was precisely translated into English. The English translation was then read back to Deschamps in French, with the bilingual witnesses, all Creoles, attesting to the accuracy of the translation. Deschamps then signed the paper in front of the same parties.

Two days later, Léona returned to inform the Frenchman that MacMahon had agreed to represent him. He was anxious to take on the appeal and offered his services pro bono, though she forwarded $100 to his office as a retainer, just to be sure. But according to Léona, Deschamps had a complete change of mind. When she and the prison guard entered his cell, they found him "prostrate, sobbing bitterly." His tears quickly turned to anger when he accused Léona of deceiving him, though he gave no specifics, and of being the cause that would eventual lead to his hanging.

"I know what paper you have made me sign!" he protested. "I can trust no one in the world."

If Léona needed any further proof to validate her belief that Deschamps was insane, she had it then. Only madness could explain his rejecting her after everything she had done for him, or so she thought. She was more determined than ever to aid in his defense.

As the fall season brought welcome relief from the heat, the appeal process went on as planned, in spite of Etienne Deschamps's change of mind. His signature affixed to that paper requesting MacMahon's representation meant the case would proceed. His earlier emotional outburst was apparently for the sole benefit of Léona Queyrouze. Had he been serious, he would have informed the High Court of his wishes.

With the legal assistance of J. Maximé Queyrouze in writing the brief (he played no other part in the legal proceedings), MacMahon and his law partner, James M. Pratt, went before the Louisiana Supreme Court on Saturday, November 9, 1889. At that time, the court resided in the Sala Capitular, or meeting room, on the second floor of the Cabildo.

As a point of curiosity, it appeared that John Dowling, the counsel of record for the convicted murderer, was left in the dark. When he arrived to argue the case, MacMahon and Pratt informed the court that Deschamps had engaged them to defend him instead. Their legal brief had already been filed some weeks before. Mr. Dowling asked the court for a continuance so that he might confer with the gentlemen to determine the validity of their claims, but the court decided to hear the case instead. The justices allowed Mr. Dowling three days to file an affidavit and brief, if he so chose. In the end, it made no difference. When the court rendered its opinion in early December, Dowling, MacMahon, and Pratt were cited as the defendant's co-counselors.

The filed brief essentially identified two major problems with the May 1889 trial of Etienne Deschamps. First, Mr. Dowling had insufficient time to prepare a defense, forty hours to be precise, and therefore the court erred in refusing him a continuance. Second, in charging the jury, Judge Marr erred by innuendo or deduction that Deschamps not taking the stand on his behalf equated to his "fear of a rigid cross-examination." In other words, Judge Marr did not press upon the jury that "no imputation of guilt could flow from him not exercising his right" to testify. Deschamps's "silence can never be worked into guilt under the law," the brief reminded the High Court.

The brief went to great lengths to explain the legal history of this case, Deschamps's communication barriers with his defense attorney, and his state of mind. By that date, his counselors firmly believed that the defendant was an unfortunate, demented spiritualist who unlawfully used chloroform, not as a weapon of murder but to develop a medium, the tragic results being that Juliette Dietsh died of asphyxia.

Their brief went on to explain that from the time that Etienne Deschamps was found alongside the young girl's body until the jury rendered its guilty verdict, the defendant was a target of the press and "the curses of an unthinkable populace," his weak mind "horrified at the universality of his accusers." These gentleman lawyers painted him as if he was a martyr, who lived "in a strange land, among unknown tongues," and who endured the "angry glares of prejudice and passion" until, having nothing more to live for, he attempted to take his life on three occasions while jailed.

Fortunately for Deschamps, according to his attorneys, he had friends among "distinguished scientists," a reference to Dr. Havá (his pamphlet was included with the brief), "as well as literary talent, of both sexes, from the bearded sage to the young, lovely and educated girl," a reference to Léona Queyrouze. "Their hope is not the acquittal of Etienne Deschamps, if he be guilty; but that he have an opportunity to present fully his defense to a petit jury."

The appeal asserted that Judge Marr had legally erred in four instances: (1) refusing a continuance, (2) hearing an incompetent witness—Laurence Dietsh, (3) admitting certain testimony (Dr. LeMonnier's sexual allegations), and (4) giving an improper charge to the jury related to Deschamps not taking the stand.

Representing the State in court that day was the assistant attorney general of Louisiana, William W. Vance, with Atty. Gen. Walter H. Rogers filing the State's brief beforehand. The State's case was straightforward and rested solely on the assertions that the defendant had been given adequate time to prepare a defense and that he shared some responsibility when he repeatedly refused the counselors appointed to him prior to April 29, 1889. It was also reiterated that the defendant never intimated that he had any defense, facts he wished to prove, or witnesses to call on his behalf. Thus, two days were adequate time to prepare for trial.

On Monday, December 2, 1889, the Louisiana Supreme Court rendered its opinion regarding the *State v. Deschamps*, Case No. 10,414. While sidestepping the defendant's claim that an incompetent witness had testified, certain testimony had been erroneously allowed, and the judge had erred in his charge to the jury, in a three-to-two split decision, Chief Justice Edward Bermudez, speaking for the majority, stated that the motion for a continuance ought to have been granted in a capital case when supported by the lawyer's affidavit that he did not have sufficient time to prepare a suitable and valid defense. The verdict was therefore quashed, the sentence set aside, and the case remanded to Judge Marr's court.

Of specific interest, the High Court was of the opinion, based on Louisiana statute, that the defendant was under no legal obligation to accept any court-appointed attorney or to give a reason for refusing. In addition, when seeking a continuance via an affidavit, the defendant was not bound to divulge a line of defense or disclose a list of witnesses to call. If the counselor was so obligated, he wouldn't have been able to do so without being given sufficient time.

When the opinion was rendered, there was a collective sigh of relief among Etienne Deschamps's supporters. They had won their first legal battle in what they knew would be a protracted war. The State was not about to set Deschamps free, though by month's end he was removed from the prison's condemned section, as he was no longer under a sentence of death. He would be placed back into the general population of Orleans Parish Prison until his fate was known after the second trial.

Though the State had lost this particular battle, Attorney General Rogers was not quite ready to set aside the district attorney's efforts at the May trial. He erroneously saw a glimmer of hope in the dissenting opinion issued by Associate Justice Samuel D. McEnery. According to Justice McEnery, in refusing a continuance, the trial judge had not erred, nor had he abused his powers as a judge. Louisiana statute and legal precedent gave the court discretion regarding requests for a continuance.

On December 21, 1889, the attorney general filed a brief with the High Court asking for a rehearing. He believed that since there was "much divergence and conflict" within the High Court on this case, its members should reconsider it. Associate Justice Lynn B. Watkins, who sided with the majority, thought otherwise. In his opinion rendered on December 31, 1889, Justice Watkins essentially admonished the attorney general for his attempt to undermine majority rule. "Justice has been done," he wrote. The rehearing was refused.

For many New Orleanians, December 1889 was an emotional time, and not just for those who had sought justice for little Juliette Dietsh. Four days after the High Court's opinion was read, news came of the death of the former Confederate president, Jefferson Davis. He died in New Orleans at the home of Associate Justice Charles E. Fenner, a former Confederate officer and current member of the Louisiana Supreme Court. Businesses closed, schools were dismissed, and courts adjourned following the news. The city went into mourning. Davis's body lay in state at City Hall (now Gallier Hall) until his burial on December 11, in the Army of Northern Virginia tomb in Metairie Cemetery. His body remained there until late May 1893, when he was reinterred in the Hollywood Cemetery in Richmond, Virginia.

As New Year's Day 1890 dawned, both sides in the Deschamps legal battle readied for what they knew was coming. Their hope was that the next trial, scheduled for March, would forever establish the guilt or innocence of Etienne Deschamps.

Chapter Six

Swift Justice

Have you anything to say in arrest of judgment or why sentence should not now be pronounced upon you?
Judge Robert H. Marr, April 5, 1890

Even before the Louisiana Supreme Court rendered its majority opinion, the Frenchman was having second thoughts about his earlier dismissal of Judge Roman as his counselor. Deschamps asked for Roman to see him in his cell, but the learned counselor declined and wrote him a letter instead. In his reply, Deschamps begged Roman's pardon for his rude behavior toward him earlier that year. Deschamps then asked the judge to take charge of his case, which he agreed to do if the court granted a new trial. Apparently it made no difference to Deschamps that MacMahon and Pratt, along with J. Maximé Queyrouze, had done all of the groundwork for the appeal and MacMahon expected to represent the defendant at retrial. For Deschamps, the choice between Judge Roman and Mr. MacMahon was simple. Judge Roman spoke French; MacMahon did not.

Alfred Roman was born on May 24, 1824, in St. James Parish, the son of Louisiana governor André B. Roman. He attended school in New Orleans and at Jefferson College (now Manresa Retreat) in Convent, Louisiana, before beginning his three-year study of law in New Orleans. He was admitted to the bar there in 1845. After practicing for a year in the city, he moved back to his native parish and entered into a law practice with his cousin. He would remain there for the next three to four years. In 1849, he married nineteen-year-old Rose Felicité Aime of St. James Parish and they would have three children. Beginning in 1851, he broke free of the partnership and practiced law alone until 1853 when he took a two-year sabbatical, much to his father's disappointment. He resumed his law practice in 1855, until health issues with one of the children forced the family to move to France in 1858. Ironically, while living in Paris, his wife passed away in late January 1859. Their sickly child survived but died four years later.

111

Alfred Roman. (Courtesy NOLA.com/The *Times-Picayune*)

When the Civil War broke out, Roman returned with his children to his native state and offered to serve in the Louisiana army, where he initially wanted to be a cavalry officer. But Louisiana needed infantrymen more, so he formed the Chasseurs of St. James, a company later designated as Company E, Eighteenth Louisiana Infantry Regiment. Alfred Mouton served as its colonel, and Lt. Col. Alfred Roman was his second in command. In one of the oddest coincidences in this story, Alfred Roman fought at the Battle of Shiloh in April 1862, along with the future coroner of Orleans Parish, Dr. Yves R. LeMonnier, and Léona's father, Léon Queyrouze, all members of Gen. Albert Sidney Johnston's Army of Mississippi.

After the horrific battle in which General Johnston was killed and the Eighteenth Louisiana Regiment lost 200 men, killed or wounded, Mouton was promoted to brigadier general and Roman to colonel. Roman was soon sidelined by illness. He later became a staff officer under Gen. P. G. T. Beauregard and served in that capacity until the war's closure. In 1863, while stationed in Charleston, South Carolina, he married nineteen-year-old Sarah Taylor Rhett, the daughter of Robert Barnwell Rhett, a well-known politician of his time and a leading secessionist from the state. The couple had twelve children over a twenty-three-year period.

During Gov. Francis Nicholls' first administration, Roman served as a clerk in the Louisiana Supreme Court from January 1877 until April 1879. Gov. Louis A. Wiltz appointed him in 1880 to the Orleans Parish Criminal District Court, Section A, where he served until the expiration of his term in 1888.

Known as a cultivated gentleman, Roman enjoyed the advantages of his education and travel. He became a French and English scholar and acquired some skill in music, painting, and writing. While serving as a judge in 1884, he published *The Military Operations of General Beauregard in the War Between the States, 1861-1865, Volumes I and II.*

Many viewed Alfred Roman as a fair judge who presided from the bench in a caring and distinguished manner. It appeared that Etienne Deschamps was now in the hands of a seasoned jurist.

Soon after the verdict was quashed, Léona Queyrouze asked Dr. Havá to see Deschamps at Orleans Parish Prison. After he berated her during the summer, she knew she couldn't return but thought it was safe for the doctor to visit instead. As far as she knew, Deschamps had not yet personally pointed an accusatory finger at him, though he was upset that the doctor had questioned his mental capacities. Léona wanted Dr. Havá to tell the Frenchman that he still had a chance to escape capital punishment now that he had been granted a new trial.

When Dr. Havá spoke to him in his cell, Deschamps thanked him for the news and asked him to take a seat, but the doctor had other things on his mind. This was not going to be a social visit consisting of idle chatter but a rebuke of the Frenchman's prior conduct toward his allies, who had done everything in their power to help him.

"Listen, now," Dr. Havá scolded Deschamps. "If you are going to change your mind and treat your attorney as you have those who did so much in your behalf, you will deserve to be hung and I rather think you will be. Remember that if you act in such a way, those who have helped you until now shall certainly abandon you to your sad fate."

Stunned by his comments, the Frenchman responded, "No, Doctor, I give you *ma parole d'honneur* [my word of honor] that I shall not in any way go against that which has been done for me. I am too happy that my attorney has secured a new trial."

Satisfied that he had accomplished what he had set out to do, Dr. Havá departed, only to encounter Judge Roman on his way out of the cell. The judge informed him that Deschamps had requested his legal services and that this was his twelfth or thirteenth visit since taking over the case. Deschamps later claimed that he had been pressured into signing the paper designating MacMahon as his lawyer, "the meaning of which he had no knowledge of," Léona Queyrouze wrote.

Sensing that John MacMahon harbored some animosity toward him, Judge Roman penned a letter to the learned counselor on Saturday, December 7, 1889, suggesting that they go tell Deschamps that they would both represent him at the retrial. The judge also informed MacMahon that the prisoner felt he had been put in a difficult position having to choose between the two. The judge felt confident that the Frenchman would be relieved if he knew that both gentlemen were working on his behalf.

MacMahon had yet to meet Deschamps; the language barrier may have been one reason why. Judge Roman offered to introduce him and thereafter begin to plan the defense strategy. "I think we can save the poor creature's neck, if nothing more," Judge Roman wrote. In addition, he informed MacMahon that by Monday he would have "the names of three or four parties who knew him well, and who may [throw] important light upon many of the phases of his life here during the last six or seven years." The judge was curious to know MacMahon's opinion on this matter.

His letter must have reached MacMahon's hands the day it was written, because MacMahon penned a letter to Léona Queyrouze on the same date, informing her of the judge's correspondence and enclosing the judge's letter with his. It appeared to MacMahon that Deschamps was not yet comfortable with Judge Roman going solo with his case. MacMahon explained to Léona that in the past he hadn't refused to go with the judge to see Deschamps, but apparently his inaction amounted to the same thing. MacMahon clearly wanted to assume total control of the defense, and having Judge Roman as a partner seemed to him an unnecessary burden. If the two men ever met, they did not plan a single defense strategy. This lack of a coordinated effort was evident on the first day of the retrial.

Friday, March 28, 1890, dawned clear in New Orleans, with the temperature rising no higher than seventy-six degrees. It was a perfect day for the start of the retrial of the infamous Etienne Deschamps. Appearing again before Judge Robert Marr, District Attorney Charles Luzenberg represented the prosecution, aided by the Honorable Lionel Adams. The Honorable (former)

Judge Alfred Roman and Mr. John MacMahon replaced the former counsel for the accused, James Dowling.

When Deschamps was escorted into the courtroom, he looked as he had at the first trial. Described as looking healthy, his eyes clear and keen, he appeared to have survived prison life quite well. There was no perceivable loss in weight, though his mustache (and now regrown beard) had grayed significantly since his last court appearance. He listened attentively to the proceedings but spoke very little to his counsel.

When the call of witnesses was announced, several of the people were unaccounted for, prompting Judge Marr to attend to other court business pending before him. During the trial's recess, information was filed with the court regarding a defendant accused of "shooting with intent to murder, inflicting a wound less than mayhem." Judge Marr then deposed an assault charge in which the suspect pleaded guilty, and fined two individuals, one for assault and one for assault and battery. With that concluded, and the absent witnesses now present, the case of the *State v. Deschamps* resumed at 11:30 A.M.

MacMahon immediately made two motions before the court, one asking that a medical commission be impaneled to investigate the sanity of the accused, and the other for a change of venue. He obviously believed that the pool of prospective jurors was poisoned by the unprecedented amount of publicity surrounding the case. He was unquestionably right about that point, but surprisingly his co-counsel immediately objected to both of MacMahon's motions, stating that this was not his plan of defense. Both counselors then began to argue with one another as to who best represented their client. Judge Roman reminded everyone that the court had assigned him to defend the accused, that he had planned the defense, and that Deschamps had accepted his services. MacMahon stated that friends and relatives of the accused had paid him $500 to defend Deschamps. He made it known that Judge Roman had not received a dime for his services and the only reason that Deschamps had requested him was that both gentlemen spoke French. (Regarding MacMahon's reference to money contributed to the defense, there's no question who Deschamps' "friends" in the city were. The "relatives" were his siblings living in France, as reported by the *Daily City Item* in April 1892, though it's not known if they all participated or shared equally in the funds they contributed toward their brother's defense.)

Judge Marr ruled that he would allow Deschamps to speak for himself as to which of the two counselors he wished to represent him. But MacMahon immediately objected, reiterating that his first line of defense was to question the sanity of the accused. According to the counselor, if Etienne Deschamps were insane, how could he rationally choose between them? He went on to cite the *State v. Patten:* "Whenever a prisoner's sanity at the time of the offense alleged is in question, the rule that he may control or discharge his counsel at pleasure should be so far relaxed as to permit them to offer evidence on these points, even against his will."

Judge Marr wasn't impressed. He would leave it to Etienne Deschamps to decide; Judge Roman did not object. MacMahon then reserved a bill of exception and told the court that he would take his case before the Louisiana Supreme Court if need be. Apparently not impressed with that either, Judge Marr then put the question to Deschamps, using Marcel Margeau as his interpreter. The Frenchman replied that Roman was his attorney. MacMahon responded that he would seek an immediate writ of mandamus (a writ of mandate, in more modern terms) from the Louisiana Supreme Court. He retired from the courtroom hoping the High Court would stop the proceedings, pending a medical examination of the accused.

Counselor MacMahon never got his writ from the Louisiana Supreme Court, and it appeared that Léona Queyrouze and others who had paid MacMahon to represent Deschamps had wasted their money. Still, even after this incident, Léona staunchly remained in the Frenchman's corner. By then, she was obsessed with the case. She obviously believed that his defiance was further evidence of his madness.

Now that the MacMahon drama had subsided, the process of selecting a jury commenced. From among sixty-six potential jurors, the prosecution vetted some, but not all, regarding their views on capital punishment and whether they had a fixed opinion and/or knowledge of the case. There were no challenges by the State. The defense added queries regarding the status of their families or lack thereof, then dismissed ten men without reason and ten more for cause. At 3:40 P.M., after four hours' work, the jury was chosen and consisted of a blacksmith, secretary, and merchant, two business owners, two cashiers, and five clerks. The court recessed at 3:45 p.m. until 6:00 P.M.

◻ ◻ ◻

At 6:15 P.M., the evening court convened. The indictment was read, and the first witness, Jules Dietsh, was called to the stand. Since Dietsh didn't speak English, Judge Marr appointed Chief Deputy Sheriff Alcée LeBlanc to be sworn in as his interpreter; this was approved by the State and the defense. Speaking in French, Dietsh told the court that he was the father of the murdered child. He went on to tell where he lived, how he came to know the accused, and how the accused came to know his children. Dietsh testified that he was aware that Deschamps was a dentist but that the defendant also spoke of himself as being a magnetic doctor. Dietsh added that the defendant experimented with magnetism on the witness and his two girls, without success.

Dietsh then detailed the events of January 30, 1889, starting with Deschamps's arrival at his home, his departure with the children at 12:30 P.M., Laurence's tearful arrival back home at 4:00 P.M., and Dietsh's subsequent movements. He recalled that the police stopped him from going to the bedside of his dead daughter, but he saw her lying beside Deschamps, who he thought was dying at the time. The witness described Deschamps as looking as though he was in agony.

Dietsh then identified Juliette's clothing and testified that her body was transported to the undertaker the day following her death and buried the day after that. He then gave the court a history of when he arrived in the United States from France and how old Juliette was when she met Etienne Deschamps—ten years old. He ended his testimony by claiming that he never saw Deschamps's business cards indicating that he was a dentist but did see those indicating that he was a mesmerist.

On cross-examination, Dietsh admitted that he didn't know the defendant as anything but a dentist and that he had once had Deschamps remove one of his teeth. The witness was aware that Deschamps had business cards that stated that he was also a "Professor of mesmerizing and magnetism, of Paris," but he testified that Deschamps told him he never practiced mesmerism for a living. In fact, Dietsh told the court that he didn't think Deschamps ever distributed or used those particular cards. Dietsh continued that in spite of this, he allowed Deschamps to mesmerize his daughters, with neither one being mesmerized more than the other, as far as he knew. He knew of only two occasions when it occurred, and both times were at his home, though his daughters told him later that they were also mesmerized in Deschamps's room. Even when done outside his home, Dietsh consented to this practice, though he admitted that he never knew that Deschamps was using chloroform in conjunction with hypnotism.

All in all, Dietsh considered Deschamps a friend. Dietsh noted that when Laurence returned home after the death of her sister—though she didn't know Juliette was dead at the time—she carried a box of Deschamps's dental tools that he gave to her father. He ended by stating that Juliette was twelve years, five months old at the time of her death, though St. Louis Cathedral burial records noted her death age as twelve years, four months old.

Judge Roman's line of questioning was clearly intended to illustrate to the jury that there was nothing premeditated about Juliette's death and that Deschamps had the full blessings of their father at all times. If the jury was inclined to convict, Judge Roman was attempting to sway them to the lesser charge of manslaughter versus murder.

On redirect, Dietsh admitted that Deschamps had never been successful in putting him or his daughters to sleep and told the court that the defendant never spoke about attempting to mesmerize anyone with chloroform. He ended by stating that he had lent the defendant a book on mesmerism, which Deschamps never returned. The prosecutor was clearly trying to show that Deschamps was a fraud as a mesmerist, ultimately using chloroform without Dietsh's consent to take advantage of the girls, particularly Juliette. He was laying the groundwork for Dr. LeMonnier's later testimony.

Charles Serra was the second witness for the prosecution. He gave his name and address and then stated that Deschamps was his next-door neighbor and a dentist who had done some dental work on his wife. He then recalled the events of January 30, 1889, starting when he heard knocking at his rear door, which was a slight variation of what he said during the first trial, and continuing with the police successfully entering the defendant's room. He recalled seeing the nude, dead body of Juliette Dietsh lying in the bed, still warm, her mouth red and raw in appearance, and Deschamps lying beside her, also nude, gasping for air.

Serra testified that he was present in the room when Deschamps was taken to the ambulance and that he never observed the girls in Deschamps's room before. He had heard them from time to time because the two gallery doors facing St. Peter Street were partially open when they visited.

On cross-examination, Serra was asked if he saw any marks on Deschamps's body at the time the police officers burst into the room. He replied no, but he later observed a single stab wound to his chest. On redirect, Serra testified that he saw no sign of violence on Juliette's body, except what he testified to earlier, related to her mouth. He also stated that he had no knowledge that Deschamps was a doctor of magnetism. One of the jurors then asked if Dr. LeMonnier came after Deschamps was taken away; Serra confirmed he did. (It appeared that, at the time, jurors could ask questions.)

Officer Fernand Rancé then took the stand, testifying that Jules Dietsh arrived at the station worried that his daughter was locked up in Etienne Deschamps's room. Rancé recalled how he and two other officers broke into the room and discovered the defendant in bed with the dead girl. Rancé stated that he found two handkerchiefs saturated with chloroform in the bed, two vials that contained chloroform, and a sharp instrument. The girl's clothing was neatly folded on the chair, and Deschamps's clothing was thrown about in disorder. Rancé recalled seeing the open trunk, the letters within, and a number of burned letters and papers in the fireplace. He further stated that Deschamps looked no different that day than he did when he first saw him in his room. He indicated that his beard and hair had not changed, which was a curious thing to say given that Deschamps had grayed considerably since his arrest. Rancé ended by stating that he was present when the coroner arrived and had handed him the handkerchiefs, vials, and a bottle of anisette that he had found. Judge Roman chose not to cross-examine.

The clerk and operator of the Third Precinct police station, George J. Legendre, was the next witness to take the stand. He recalled Jules Dietsh coming to the station in the late afternoon saying that he was afraid that his daughter was being raped. Surprisingly, Judge Roman offered no objection to that statement. Legendre testified as to what occurred next, including his dispatching Corp. George Morris and Officers Charles Sturges and Rancé to the Deschamps residence and then later meeting Capt. John Journeè in the room. Legendre stated that he summoned Dr. LeMonnier on Journeè's orders and that he was there when LeMonnier arrived. He also confirmed that Officer Noel E. Delhonde was left in charge of the girl's body.

On cross-examination, Legendre testified that he thought Deschamps had been taken away from the room before Dr. LeMonnier's arrival. The State then offered into evidence the clothes that the victim had worn the day of her death, which Jules Dietsh had talked about earlier.

Legendre was followed by Captain Journeè, who testified that he arrived at Deschamps's room at about 6:00 P.M., where he met the aforementioned police officers, Serra, and Jules Dietsh. He summoned Dr. LeMonnier, who arrived after Deschamps was taken to Charity Hospital. Like Officer Rancé had before, he confirmed seeing the two handkerchiefs, vials, burnt papers in the fireplace, and a bottle of anisette, which he claimed was three-quarters full. In addition, he found a glass and a magnetizing disk in the bed. He then identified the clothing found in the room. He stated he gave the victim's clothing to the coroner later.

Like Serra, Journeè stated that Juliette's mouth appeared as if it had been burned. He also corroborated Legendre's statement by testifying that Delhonde was left in charge of the body and, per Dr. LeMonnier's instructions, was to observe for the onset of postmortem rigidity.

Judge Roman's cross-examination consisted of determining if Deschamps had any bodily injuries prior to his departure to Charity Hospital. Captain Journeè stated that he saw what appeared to be a scratch on Deschamps's left chest.

The State's final witness that evening was Corp. George Morris, who corroborated what the other officers had testified to previously. Judge Roman saw no need to cross-examine. At 10:00 P.M., the court adjourned until 10:00 the following morning.

It was another beautiful day in New Orleans when the retrial resumed at 10:25 A.M. The two druggists took the stand first—John Mailhes followed by Marcel Majeau. Mailhes reiterated what he had testified to at the previous trial. He sold Deschamps two ounces of chloroform on January 30, but the timeframe of the purchase had expanded from noon to between 11:00 A.M. and 2:00 P.M.; neither side caught the discrepancy. Judge Roman chose not to cross-examine.

When Majeau took the stand, he was consistent with his prior testimony regarding the amount of chloroform that Deschamps purchased—one ounce, but he further explained that the defendant only had enough money to purchase one ounce, not two; the time—2:30 P.M.; and why he needed it— to extract a tooth from a young girl. The only inconsistency in his testimony was that he had previously told the court that he never sold chloroform to the defendant prior to January 30, 1889. At the retrial, he said that he often sold the drug to Deschamps. The vials in question from both witnesses were offered in evidence. Again, Judge Roman chose not to cross-examine the witness.

Officer Delhonde then took the stand and corroborated prior testimony as to his role in observing the onset of postmortem rigidity. Reading from his notes taken the evening of January 30, 1889, he testified that the corpse began to stiffen at 7:55 P.M., with the victim's arms stiffening by 10:53 P.M. and complete rigidity observed by 11:50 P.M. As with the previous witnesses, Judge Roman saw no need to cross-examine Officer Delhonde.

At long last, Laurence Dietsh was called to testify. A reporter from the *Daily Picayune* wrote that she, dressed in black, appeared pale in the witness box "but bravely bore the close examination." As she was not able to speak

English, LeBlanc served as her interpreter. She began by telling the court that she was ten years old as of November 23 and that she remembered well the death of her older sister, Juliette, in the room of Etienne Deschamps. She went on to describe their friendship with the accused, including taking walks with him along the Mississippi River levee and visiting him in his room. There he would magnetize them by passing his hands in front of their faces. She testified that they were never able to be put to sleep using this method.

Laurence then recalled what occurred the day of Juliette's death, from their departure from their home with Deschamps to their disrobing after Deschamps returned to his room carrying some firewood. She remembered that Deschamps had two handkerchiefs, wet with chloroform; he placed one over Juliette's mouth and the other on her abdomen. When the prosecutor asked her to describe the condition of Juliette's mouth prior to having the handkerchief placed over it, Laurence replied that there was nothing wrong with her mouth when she entered Deschamps's room. Obviously, this line of questioning was to establish that the chloroformed handkerchief caused the facial burns. The witness then identified a vial used by the defendant.

Laurence added that before Deschamps placed the handkerchief over Juliette's mouth, he handed her the vial of chloroform sister and made her smell it. Laurence remembered that Juliette turned her head away after a quick whiff of the drug, but Deschamps insisted that she smell it again and moved her head. After she inhaled a second time, Juliette said she experienced visions of the church and so forth, which Deschamps said was a good sign. Laurence further testified that Deschamps also gave chloroform to her before he left the room a second time, and he told her to lie beside her sister and not disturb her until he returned. (She obviously did not inhale the drug.) She testified that upon his return, Juliette was still unconscious, Laurence hadn't touched her, and Laurence told Deschamps that she wanted to go home.

If there was a single statement given by Laurence that sealed the fate of Etienne Deschamps, it was what she said next in the witness box. As she had done in the first trial, Laurence testified that upon his return, Deschamps placed a second chloroformed handkerchief over Juliette's mouth. In addition, she stated that he offered her the drug too, which she pretended to inhale. For the prosecutor, this testimony amounted to proof positive that Deschamps was guilty of the premeditated murder of Juliette Dietsh.

Laurence also recalled the other particulars of that day—the Frenchman's spoken desire to die, the burning of his papers, the bundles he gave to Laurence, and the message he told her to repeat to her father.

Laurence was asked if this was the first time Deschamps had given chloroform to her and her sister. She replied no and described what had occurred in his room the day before Juliette's death. She ended by stating that Juliette never referred to Deschamps as "doctor." Judge Roman chose not to cross-examine.

The prosecution's last witness was Dr. Yves LeMonnier, the coroner. He testified that he had received a message about a possible rape at 64 St. Peter Street. He then described what he found when he arrived: the nude body of the victim, furniture and personal items found in the room, and the ashes discovered in the fireplace. He testified that on closer examination, he determined that the young girl was not a virgin and had not been so for a number of weeks.

Judge Roman immediately objected to this line of testimony, stating that it was irrelevant to the charge of murder. He reminded the court that Etienne Deschamps had not been charged with rape and that bringing up the sexual history of the victim could only prejudice the jury. Luzenberg, on the other hand, stated the prosecution's theory was that the victim had died from chloroform inhalation administered by the defendant, whose sole purpose in using the drug was to perform unlawful acts upon her. The State wanted all the facts surrounding the incident to be brought out in the open for the jury's benefit and understanding.

Knowing that the prosecution had used this particular tactic successfully in the first trial, Judge Roman again reminded the court that Deschamps had only been charged with murder, and no crimes—such as rape (and sodomy, which Dr. LeMonnier later brought up)—not necessarily included in murder should be referenced in testimony. Such crimes were not included in the original indictment.

Judge Marr overruled the objection, stating that it was important to show whether the killing was done while the defendant was engaged in a lawful or unlawful act. The condition of the victim's body when found could shed some light on that question. He stated that he would instruct the jury on that fact. Judge Roman then asked the court's indulgence while he wrote a bill of exception to the ruling. Judge Marr granted his request, taking a thirty-minute recess.

When Dr. LeMonnier's testimony resumed, he again brought up the "viscid and milky-white fluid" discovery, void of sperm or the characteristic smell of semen, and the evidence (by inference) of sodomy perpetrated upon the young victim. After the rectal and gynecological findings were introduced, Dr. LeMonnier discussed the chemical burns he found on the victim's mouth, chin, and lower part of her nose. He then testified about the alleged love letters discovered in the room, which brought another immediate objection from Judge Roman on grounds of irrelevancy. This time, however, his objection was sustained and the witness was instructed to omit all references to the letters. The State did not object. After the court allowed the anatomical findings, the omission of the love letters was a minor setback for the prosecution.

Dr. LeMonnier continued with the chloroformed handkerchief evidence—monogrammed with the initials *E. D.* He also discussed the magnetizing disk and dental probe he found and concluded that Juliette Dietsh had died from chloroform inhalation. It was evident to him that the young girl had died quickly, and he explained why. He also discussed other physiological evidence found during the autopsy.

Dr. LeMonnier testified that after leaving the defendant's room, he went to Charity Hospital to examine Deschamps. The doctor found the defendant to be suffering from chloroform poisoning. He informed the court that Deschamps was given an emetic as part of his treatment. On closer examination, the coroner discovered three apparently self-inflicted wounds on the defendant's left chest, caused by his dental probe. One of Deschamps's business cards stating he was a dentist was then offered into evidence. The State rested.

□ □ □

Contrary to what Judge Roman had written in his December 1889 letter to Mr. MacMahon stating that he had three or four potential witnesses for the defense, only two witnesses were called.

Elizabeth Hilroy, a middle-aged widow, took the stand first and testified that she lived in the house where the defendant resided. She indicated that she lived in the rear of the house and the defendant, Serra, and his wife lived in the front. Hilroy admitted that she seldom saw the defendant; sometimes it was months between sightings. When she did spot him, he was often seen with the Dietsh children. She testified that he was a quiet person who never bothered anyone at the house and who always locked his door when he was in or out of his room. She concluded by admitting that she seldom spoke to him or him to her.

There were probably three reasons why she was brought to testify. First, she could establish that Deschamps was not a vile person or a premeditated murderer. Second, Laurence earlier testified that, on the day in question, Deschamps locked his door upon both of his departures and Laurence was allowed to leave afterward. Hilroy's testimony proved that was not an unusual thing for the defendant to do. And third, Hilroy's testimony, along with that of Serra and Jules Dietsh, showed that Deschamps made no secret about his meetings with the girls in his room. The defendant was not having clandestine meetings with two underage girls that were about to be exposed; thus, he had no need to kill Juliette or perhaps her sister.

Judge Alfred Roman was then sworn in as a witness. He described his first encounter with Deschamps in March 1889 and the defendant's complete lack of understanding regarding his predicament. Judge Roman was attempting to paint his client as a person not totally in charge of his mental capacities. He spoke of Deschamps's paranoia and his own abrupt firing by Deschamps without real cause prior to the first trial, even though Deschamps told him that everyone was persecuting him, including the judge.

By June 1889, Deschamps again retained Judge Roman before the first verdict was thrown out. Roman said that during his visits with Deschamps, his client entertained him with information not irrelevant to his case. He described Deschamps as dull, sullen, and taking little interest in anything, except the subject of hypnotism. At times his eyes became glassy and his face flushed as he uttered bizarre statements that were entertaining but totally inappropriate given the possible death sentence hanging over his head.

The State, in its cross-examination of the witness, was going to quash from the outset the notion that Etienne Deschamps was a lunatic, as Judge Roman implied. Judge Roman was asked about the previous day's proceedings regarding whom Deschamps wanted as his counsel—and the fact that he was allowed to choose without objections from Judge Roman. In this manner, the State proved its case that Deschamps was neither incompetent nor insane that day nor the day that Juliette Dietsh was murdered. The defense rested.

The State called Dr. LeMonnier as a rebuttal witness. He testified that Deschamps was as sane a man that day as he was on the day in question and that he could distinguish between right and wrong. Both sides then rested, with the State proposing that the case be submitted to the jury without closing arguments. Judge Roman insisted otherwise. Judge Marr called for a recess at 3:00 P.M., with arguments to begin at 5:00 P.M.

Adams spoke for the State for an hour and fifteen minutes, detailing the horrid nature of the crime and rehashing Dr. LeMonnier's prior testimony.

The question he asked the jury was simple and to the point. How did a twelve-year-old girl die in a state of nudity in Etienne Deschamps's bed, her corpse bearing traces of a recent sexual encounter? Did she commit suicide using chloroform, or was she murdered? Laurence's testimony excluded suicide, and the defendant's deliberate actions of placing a second chloroformed handkerchief over the unconscious victim's mouth, chloroform that he specifically purchased during his second outing, proved that his actions and the subsequent murder were premeditated. The burning of any incriminating evidence further proved that Deschamps's behavior was calculated and planned. From the outset, he intended to use chloroform to render Juliette unconscious in order to have his way with her, as he had done the day before she died. The fact that she died as a result of his deliberate and premeditated actions made him guilty of murder, not manslaughter. He deserved to be executed by hanging, according to the prosecution.

At 6:15 P.M., Judge Roman rose from his seat and addressed the jury. His subtle and analytical study of the case, his arguments written and delivered as an essay, lasted for three hours and twenty minutes. He began by declaring Deschamps insane, by the actions he took on the day in question and his crazed actions and bizarre thought processes noted thereafter. His ill-placed devotion to mesmerism had clouded his mind, so Judge Roman believed, and made him oblivious to everything, except that eccentric subject. Because of his insanity, he could not be held responsible for his actions that day, particularly his own suicide attempt when he could have easily fled the scene or held Laurence captive. Only insanity could explain the illogical actions he took that day.

Thereafter, in great detail, Judge Roman discussed the charge of murder lodged against his client. Judge Roman declared that the State had not proved malice. Without it, there could be no premeditated murder. They also didn't provide a motive. Nothing in the evidence showed a necessity for Deschamps to intentionally murder the young girl that day. The fact that he allowed the only witness to leave proved that. Judge Roman then provided the jury with copious extracts from the best legal minds regarding criminal law. The *Daily Picayune* described his presentation as thorough and brilliant, something that had not "been delivered in the criminal court for a very long time." At 9:35 P.M., having completed his closing argument, Judge Roman sat down.

District Attorney Luzenberg had the last word, reminding the jury that the defense had not produced a single witness to refute Dr. LeMonnier's testimony that Etienne Deschamps was sane at the time of the young girl's death. He also stressed that the jury not confuse "diseased morality" with insanity, the latter of which no medical testimony had proved. He reminded the jury that some people believe that anyone who committed a murder is insane, but he explained that common law was clear on this point. Luzenberg also stated that, though there were clearly depraved individuals who gravitated toward crime, the greater portion of society had an even stronger duty to punish such criminal behavior.

At 10:00 P.M., the district attorney concluded his remarks, and Judge Marr excused the jury for five minutes to refresh themselves. Upon their return, Judge Marr took ten minutes to deliver his charge to the jury, in which the State added another clause regarding motive. The jury was instructed that the motive of the crime was the fact that an unlawful act had been perpetrated in the commission of the murder. Judge Roman then offered the judge three charges that he asked to be included in the jury's deliberation instructions. One, that Etienne Deschamps was charged with murder and nothing else, and no other offense should be considered in forming their verdict. Two, if the jury found the defendant guilty of negligence or gross imprudence, but not premeditation, he was guilty of manslaughter, not murder. And three, if the jury found that the defendant was insane at the time of the murder, their verdict should read not guilty by reason of insanity.

Judge Marr refused his first and third charge. In the latter charge in particular, no testimony had provided authoritative proof of Deschamps's insanity. Regarding Roman's second charge, the judge only agreed to clarify the legal definition of manslaughter to the jury and nothing else. In his charge, Judge Marr instructed the jury that manslaughter was the next grade of homicide below murder, committed without malice. For example, he stated, the "killing was done upon a sudden quarrel or provocation, in the heat of blood, without premeditation." It was far short of what Judge Roman had requested.

At 10:40 P.M., Chief Deputy Sheriff LeBlanc handed the indictment over to the jury foreman, and the jury retired to begin their deliberations. Fifteen minutes after leaving the courtroom, the gentlemen notified Judge Marr that they had reached their verdict. As in the first trial, swift justice prevailed. By then, the courtroom was packed with lawyers, doctors, and the curious, though an "oppressive stillness" permeated the room, according to the *Daily Picayune*. Moments later, Etienne Deschamps was escorted back into the courtroom as the jury filed in. Crier Louis S. Boisdore then called the jury roll. Minute Clerk Thomas A. Marshall, Jr., received the verdict from the foreman. He paused before holding the paper up for Judge Marr to view. The judge adjusted his eyeglasses as he read the verdict, then Marshall stopped at the front of the bench and read it aloud in a clear voice. By then, the tension in the courtroom was unbearable.

Marshall read on the charge of murder, "New Orleans, March 29, 1890. Guilty. Henry C. Clause, Foreman."

Deschamps barely moved when Judge Roman delivered the translation to him, though many of the spectators were more deeply affected by the verdict, one way or another. It's not known if Léona Queyrouze was present in the courtroom at that late hour, but her brother was probably there, along with Dr. Havá.

"Etienne Deschamps, you are remanded," Crier Boisdore declared.

Deschamps was then escorted to the sheriff's office located on the same floor, walking with "a dull, heavy, wallowing step," according to one reporter. It wasn't until the Frenchman was locked into a temporary cell and began pacing its length that he finally broke down sobbing. Five minutes later, he was taken downstairs to the first floor, placed in a van, and driven back to Orleans Parish Prison. By midnight, he was back in the condemned section, most likely on the second floor. He would be moved to Condemned Box No. 1 on the third floor sometime after mid-March 1891, where he remained until May 1892.

On Saturday, April 5, Etienne Deschamps and Judge Roman appeared once again in Judge Marr's courtroom to hear either the fate of a motion filed three days before or, if unsuccessful, the judge's sentence imposed. Judge Roman's motion asked the judge to grant a new trial, citing four reasons. The *Daily Picayune* printed the particulars of his motion on April 3: "First— The verdict was contrary to law and against the weight of evidence adduced on the trial. Second—Because the jury disregarded their oaths and allowed themselves to be governed by the actions of the jury on the former trial. Third—Because the jury was swayed by the theories of the coroner of the parish of Orleans, ostensibly an expert, but in reality the main witness for the State, who against the defendant's protest was allowed to testify upon matters extraneous to and not necessarily connected with the charge recorded and filed in this case. Fourth—Because no malice, no evil intent, no premeditation of any kind was established against the defendant, who if sane, as contended by the prosecution, was guilty of manslaughter at the upmost and not murder as charged."

Judge Marr asked Judge Roman if he wanted to speak further about this matter before he ruled on his motion, but he declined. He probably knew it had no chance of being affirmed.

"The motion for a new trial in this case does not present any grounds for which, in my mind, a new trial should be granted," Judge Marr declared. He gave no reasons for overruling the motion. Judge Roman reserved a bill of exception, which he hoped to cite when taking his appeal forward.

Judge Marr then spoke directly to Deschamps, which was translated into French. "Do you understand the English language sufficiently to comprehend what is said to you?"

"I do not," Deschamps responded in French.

"Have you anything to say in arrest of judgment or why sentence should not now be pronounced upon you?" the judge asked.

"I have not," Deschamps answered, still speaking in French.

Citing the verdict of the jury and the 1870 Louisiana statute that governed the sentence for murder, Judge Marr ordered the defendant back to Orleans Parish Prison.

"There you shall remain until such day as the governor shall appoint for the execution of this sentence, and on that day you shall be hanged by the neck until dead," Judge Marr declared. "I sincerely trust that God shall have mercy upon your soul."

According to the *Daily Picayune*, when Judge Marr's death sentence was translated into French, Deschamps looked indifferent, "showing no sign of agitation or distress." He undoubtedly knew what his fate was prior to the pronouncement. As he waited in front of the court building for a carriage to take him back to prison, he sat at one end of a bench and "went fast asleep." Once returned to his cell, Etienne Deschamps would never again see the outside of those prison walls.

Chapter Seven

The Long Appeal

I have heard people say, "I don't believe he killed Juliette Dietsh and don't care to know if he did. He ought to be hung for his nastiness."

Léona Queyrouze, August 25, 1890

On Monday, April 7, 1890, two days after Etienne Deschamps was sentenced to death, Judge Alfred Roman appeared before Judge Marr at the criminal court building. He sought and was granted an opportunity to appeal his client's conviction to the Louisiana Supreme Court. The object was to seek a new trial. Judge Roman wasted little time once his request was granted.

His legal brief, divided into two sections totaling twenty-eight typed pages, was presented to the High Court. The first section consisted of a two-page syllabus that addressed twenty-two points of law, with the remaining section chronicling the arguments raised and the bills of exception filed during the retrial. Many of the points of law raised by Judge Roman were supported by legal precedent or referenced from scholarly books on jurisprudence. The judge had done his homework—or so he thought.

In his first point, Judge Roman reminded the High Court that the essential feature of premeditated murder was malice. "There can be no murder without it," he wrote. His intent was to sway the High Court toward a lesser charge in the absence of malice. "Where a homicide is unintentionally committed when in the performance of an unlawful act," he continued in point six, "the offence is manslaughter."

Also, since Dr. LeMonnier was allowed by the lower court to introduce the sexual history between the victim and defendant, Judge Roman wrote in point seven, "A man who, in order to have sexual intercourse with a girl uses artificial means [i.e., chloroform], with her consent, to make such intercourse practicable, in consequence of which she dies, is guilty of manslaughter." The judge was obviously incorrect when comparing this point of law to the facts surrounding the Dietsh murder. Nothing in the record indicated that the

129

victim consented to using chloroform in order to have sex with Deschamps. Nevertheless, Judge Roman was attempting to take the death penalty off the table, as tenuous as his argument was.

Judge Roman's point eight focused on the indictment issued against his client. "The indictment must contain an allegation of every fact essential to the punishment of the crime charged," he wrote. And referring directly to what had occurred at the first and second trials, the judge added point nine: "The crime the indictment speaks of must be well defined, and the court and jury can take into consideration nothing except what is specifically charged in the indictment." In addition, in point thirteen he wrote, "What is not charged in an indictment does not exist." His point twenty best summarized his argument against the indictment: "A defendant ought not to be convicted of the offense charged simply because he has been guilty of *another offense.*"

Four issues were raised in the defendant's bills of exception and Judge Roman's arguments thereof. First, the coroner's testimony went far beyond what his official expertise allowed. According to Judge Roman and the evidence presented at the retrial, Juliette Dietsh died of asphyxia by chloroform, period. The trial judge should never have allowed Dr. LeMonnier's sexual theories, articulated in court as allegedly connected to the death (in his opinion). Judge Roman claimed that Judge Marr's based his rationale upon Deschamps's killing of Juliette Dietsh, intentionally or unintentionally, "while he was engaged in the doing of some other unlawful act or [felonious] act." Yet there was no concrete evidence presented in court that the defendant engaged in sexual intercourse or any other act with the victim while she was under the influence of chloroform the day she died. Only Dr. LeMonnier theorized as much.

Second, the judge refused the defendant's three charges to the jury, merely reciting an elementary definition of manslaughter to the jury.

Third, the verdict was reached in a haphazard and quick fashion. Judge Roman believed that the jury was more interested in going home on Saturday evening than rendering a just decision, fearing they would be sequestered until Monday morning if a unanimous verdict was not reached that night. He also thought that the jury was swayed by the action of the last jury—both juries reached their verdicts in about the same time—and by the whole nature of the case, regardless of the evidence. Judge Roman believed that the trial judge erred when he refused to grant a new trial based upon the jury's callous actions and other cited reasons.

Fourth and finally, Etienne Deschamps was not only a dentist but a magnetizer who sought a medium in order to discover buried treasure. The defendant had the consent of Juliette Dietsh and her father. Her death, though tragic, was not brought about by malice or premeditation. It was a crime that clearly lacked motive.

Atty. Gen. Walter Rogers, along with Lionel Adams, represented the State. Their arguments essentially countered the defendant's.

On Wednesday, May 21, 1890, the Louisiana Supreme Court announced its opinion regarding the *State v. Deschamps*, Case No. 10,629. In a unanimous decision, with Associate Justice Lynn B. Watkins handing down the opinion, the court affirmed the lower court's decision and sentenced Etienne Deschamps to death for the murder of Juliette Dietsh. The High Court found nothing improper in the lower court's decision to allow certain testimony (i.e., Dr. LeMonnier's), or its refusal to allow the defendant's special charges delivered to the jury, or the lower court's refusal to grant a new trial.

Regarding the defendant's alleged lack of malice, the High Court stated, "Since malice cannot usually be directly proved, and the evidence of it, therefore, being circumstantial, any facts which go to afford an influence of its existence are admissible."

The High Court also saw no legal problem with the State introducing subsequent crimes (i.e., rape and/or sodomy), along with the original indictment of murder by chloroform inhalation, when such offenses were linked to the crime and constituted parts thereof and for purposes of showing intent. In this case, according to the High Court, further proof of premeditation was unnecessary.

Finally, regarding questions of law alone, the High Court was of the opinion that its judicial power rested in appellate decision making. Therefore, it would not tamper in the lower court's refusal to grant a new trial based purely on what the defendant claimed were improper acts done by the jury or their motivations or prejudices when they reached their verdict. The lower court's judgment was affirmed.

Judge Roman wasted little time regarding his next move. On June 3, 1890, acting as a private citizen, he filed a petition with Judge Frank A. Monroe, Division C, Civil District Court for Orleans Parish. He sought the interdiction of Etienne Deschamps; in other words, declare him insane. If successful, Judge Roman believed that his former client's sentence could be commuted to life or some lesser sentence; anything but capital punishment.

In his petition, Judge Roman stated that Deschamps, undeniably insane, was not responsible for the consequences of his actions and that his mind was already diseased on the day of the offense, of which he was later found guilty and sentenced to death. He further explained in his petition that if Deschamps was not insane the day that Juliette Dietsh died, he was certainly insane now. Therefore, he was a proper subject for judicial intervention, "to say nothing of executive clemency." With the defendant having no blood relatives living in the country and no wife, and now deprived of all further legal avenues, Judge Roman asked the court to appoint "a commission of two or three physicians to inquire into Deschamps' sanity and report to the court."

Surprisingly, Judge Monroe accepted Judge Roman's petition. On June 18, 1890, he appointed George H. Theard to represent Deschamps in the matter of interdiction, and Deschamps was declared a pauper. George was the brother and law partner of Charles J. Theard, whom Judge Marr had appointed to represent Deschamps at his first trial. Theard had removed himself after three days.

If there was any chance that George Theard would assume his court-appointed duties with all the energy and devotion they required, and that he would not be influenced by his brother's previous actions and dealings with Deschamps, it presumably evaporated soon after his appointment. On Thursday, June 19, 1890, an article about Deschamps appeared in the *Daily Picayune*. According to the piece, two days before, while relaxing in his cell, Deschamps asked to speak to Chief Deputy Sheriff Alcée LeBlanc. He had developed a friendship with LeBlanc while confined at the prison. The officer consented to his request and went to his cell that day.

"I want to clear myself now before dying," Deschamps told LeBlanc in French, "so that the public may see whether I am deserving of dying or not."

LeBlanc hurriedly secured paper, ink, and pen and began to transcribe everything Deschamps said. Deschamps began his story with his life in France, his coming to New Orleans, and then his acquaintance with the Dietsh family. He told LeBlanc of his experimentation with magnetism and his hypnotism sessions with Juliette, the first performed at her father's request. He freely admitted that his relationship with Juliette was friendly at first, then intimate, and then criminal—as though the intimate and criminal were exclusive of one another.

Deschamps indicated that on the day in question, the girls came to his room, not that he had brought them there. Upon returning to his room after securing some kindling, Deschamps discovered that both girls were in his bed and Juliette was dead, having taken some chloroform. He admitted that he had a number of essences or spirits, liquors, and other substances in his room, including a vial of chloroform. When he discovered that Juliette was dead, he left again to acquire more chloroform with the intent of killing himself. He would have likely succeeded in his suicide plan if not for the arrival of the police, Deschamps claimed. In his so-called confession or explanation of events, the Frenchman adamantly professed his innocence of the crime.

"Why should I kill Juliette?" he asked. "I had everything I wanted with her. She was my mistress. Why should I have killed her?"

It is no surprise that Etienne Deschamps never signed his statement, and there is no doubt that George Theard read the article or was made aware of it. If his plan was to convince the court that Deschamps was insane, this was hardly the evidence he needed to prove it. If nothing else, this sham explanation proved that Deschamps was a calculating, manipulating liar who saw nothing evil in what he did to the girls sexually and who appeared to regret only that the affair ended due to Juliette untimely death, not that he was responsible for it.

On June 20, 1890, Theard appeared before Judge Monroe and resigned his appointment, which was accepted. Ironically, the judge then appointed District Attorney Charles A. Luzenberg to assume the duties. In the end, nothing came of the interdiction. In spite of his initial acceptance of the petition, Judge Monroe later ruled that he doubted his civil court had jurisdiction concerning Deschamps's insanity, given the criminal nature of the case. According to Judge Monroe, only the chief executive of the state could take action regarding the matter.

Meanwhile, on June 19, 1890, Léona Queyrouze penned a letter to Gov. Francis Nicholls in which she included a copy of Dr. Havá's June 1889 pamphlet. Her four-page letter chronicled her association with Deschamps—"the demented creature," as she called him—citing evidence of her, her brother's, and Dr. Havá's efforts to aid in his defense, regrettably unsuccessful thus far. Hoping that the governor would read what Dr. Havá had written, Léona concluded, "I come to you alone & unsupported because I believe in you, because I strongly feel that you will hesitate to sign the insane Deschamps's condemnation after learning certain facts." She would be wrong, of course, though the governor wouldn't finalize the first execution date of Etienne Deschamps until late March 1892, an unprecedented delay in those days.

It's not known what Governor Nicholls' reaction was to Léona's letter or if he read Dr. Havá's anatomically graphic rebuttal to Dr. LeMonnier's findings. Léona presumably felt that her letter went nowhere, though she continued to press the governor regarding the Deschamps case until the very day the Frenchman was executed.

In the meantime, having failed in his attempt to declare Deschamps insane, on August 9, 1890, Judge Roman petitioned the governor and Board of Pardons for a commutation of the sentence. Those members included Lt. Gov. James Jeffries and Attorney General Rogers, with the third member always being the judge who presided over the trial—in this case, Judge Marr. The petition filed with the attorney general's office alleged that a misguided public opinion, undoubtedly fueled by a biased press, had led to the guilty verdict, more than any evidence presented at trial. Judge Roman believed that his former client was innocent of the charge and, if sane at the time of the young girl's death, was guilty of manslaughter, not premeditated murder.

Judge Roman further claimed in his petition that Deschamps was a professional magnetizer who was out of his mind the day Juliette Dietsh died. As he had earlier claimed when he sought interdiction, the judge also stated in this petition that if Deschamps was not insane on the day in question, then he lost his mind soon after. Therefore, the law could not rightly execute him under those circumstances, however heinous his charged crime was.

The petition asked that the Board of Pardons take whatever proper steps were necessary to ascertain whether Etienne Deschamps was *non compos mentis* (not of sound mind), either partially or completely at the time of Juliette Dietsh's death. And if he were found to be insane, he should be transferred to an insane asylum until he recovered his mental capacities or the sentence of death should be commuted to life in prison.

□ □ □

Judge Roman was not the only person who sought clemency or a commutation of Deschamps's death sentence. Dr. Havá also wrote the board, including with his petition his pamphlet as evidence of Deschamps's innocence by reason of insanity. On August 25, 1890, Léona Queyrouze also wrote a letter, nineteen legal-size pages long. The epistle contained a litany of reasons why the board should commute his sentence.

She blamed the press for feeding the citizenry of New Orleans a biased, inaccurate, and contradictory account of the happenings on the day young Juliette died, the investigation and charges lodged against Deschamps, and the trials and appeals that followed. To illustrate her point, she told the board what she had heard from so-called "intelligent and cultured individuals" living in the city.

"I don't believe he killed Juliette Dietsh and don't care to know if he did," Léona remembered one person saying. "He ought to be hung for his nastiness, and if I were on the jury, I would have him hung. Besides, he should hang anyhow for his ignorant use of chloroform."

She also questioned the integrity of Laurence's testimony and the coroner's "hypotheses, insinuations, theories, inferences, subtleties, and possibilities, not to speak of impossibilities," which she claimed were far beyond the coroner's expertise.

Léona went to great lengths to prove that Etienne Deschamps was insane, based on his actions on the day in question and his interactions with her and other supporters in the months that followed. She claimed that Deschamps had no motive to kill the young girl—his so-called mistress—and if he did, he surely would not have left a witness to chronicle the murder thereafter. Nothing he did or said afterward made any sense regarding the crime, if the board believed him to be sane.

She closed her letter with a simple plea: "And now, gentlemen, I respectfully and trustfully place this appeal into your hands, with a strong feeling of confidence and hope towards men born in generous America, the refuge of the persecuted."

The Board of Pardons agreed to take the petitions under advisement, but it appeared the body was in no hurry to render a decision. According to an article that appeared in the *Daily Picayune* on October 26, 1890, the board would not decide the matter until at least late November, as two of the three members were out of the city until then. In fact, by year's end, no decision had been reached.

Finally, on February 21, 1891, the Board of Pardons decided to appoint a commission of physicians, a so-called "Commission of Lunacy," to investigate the mental state of Etienne Deschamps. The original intent was to have a commission composed of French-speaking doctors who could interview and observe Deschamps from time to time at the prison, then render their decision on whether he was insane. The board would then act upon their findings, for better or worse. Apparently Dr. Havá was never invited to serve, perhaps because his mind was already made up and the board needed an unbiased panel of experts. Whatever the design, the lunacy commission never got off the ground. The *Daily Picayune* later reported, "An effort was made to appoint a lunacy commission of French speaking doctors, but proper physicians could not be induced to service, and the board had to settle that question for itself." The reason for its failure was less complicated than that—there was no money to pay the commissioners for their work.

On April 11, the board met to consider the application for a commutation of the sentence from death to imprisonment for life filed eight months before by Judge Roman, and separately by Léona Queyrouze and Dr. Havá. (By late September 1890, Léona had distanced herself from Judge Roman and his efforts to commute Deschamps's sentence. She said as much in a September 23 letter to the *Times-Democrat*, which the management refused to print, apparently not wanting to get in the middle of her dispute with Judge Roman. Léona undoubtedly felt that the judge had undermined John MacMahon's efforts at the start of the retrial.) The board likely tabled their decision pending the medical commission's findings that never came. Why the board decided to meet in the first place is a mystery.

By August 1891, it was clear that the Board of Pardons had reached no definitive decision regarding the fate of Etienne Deschamps, in spite of a rumor that a "report of the commission of medical experts as to Deschamps' insanity" was forthcoming and that the commission strongly endorsed a pardon. Nothing was farther from the truth. Whatever its purpose, the Commission of Lunacy vaporized by year's end with the board taking no definitive steps during Deschamps's second full year of incarceration.

Though nothing significant regarding the fate of Etienne Deschamps transpired that year, 1891 was nevertheless newsworthy for other reasons. Two events in particular would touch the lives of New Orleanians and the infamous Frenchman.

The first incident occurred on Saturday, March 7, at 11:00 P.M. Laura Nelson was savagely murdered by Philip Baker, a twenty-five-year-old man employed by Laura's husband, Neil. The Nelsons operated a grocery at 69 Washington Street (then 635 Fern) at the corner of Hampson Street in the New Orleans suburb of Carrollton. A native of Stora Hammar, Sweden, arriving in New Orleans in June 1889, Neil L. Nelson rented the two-story house beginning in September 1889. There he opened his grocery and eventually employed Baker, who had grown up practically across the street from his business. Described as agreeable and pleasant, with blue eyes, medium height, light hair, and a mustache, Baker had prior experience working as a store clerk when he was hired by Nelson. Baker initially worked for $22.50 a month, which was raised to $25, then $30. Besides drawing a salary, he boarded and slept on the premises beginning in November or December 1890. Over time, the employer and clerk became the best of friends, and Baker served as one of Nelson's groomsmen when he married Laura Frank on September 25, 1890. Baker and the Nelsons resided on the second floor above the store; the couple occupied three of the four upstairs rooms.

The day in question was no different from previous days. Nelson and Baker kept the store open until very late each night. On Saturday nights they usually didn't close until 11:00 or midnight. After shutting down that night, Mrs. Nelson retired to her upstairs apartment to await her husband. Meanwhile, Mr. Nelson fed his horse in the stable, located about thirty feet from the building, before reentering the house to count the cash from that day's sales, as was his routine.

Rather than retiring to his upstairs room, Philip Baker remained on the first floor in the kitchen, washing his feet in a bucket of water. Upon entering the house, Nelson passed Baker on his way to the dining room, where Nelson pulled out the table drawer and began courting his money. Meanwhile, Baker passed through the dining room into the grocery, where he picked up a shot bag filled with three pounds of gun pellets. His activity was unbeknownst to Nelson, who remained sitting at the table with his back to Baker. When Baker reentered the dining room, Nelson reached over his shoulder and

Laura Nelson. (Courtesy NOLA.com/ The *Times-Picayune*)

Philip Baker. (Courtesy NOLA.com/The *Times-Picayune*)

Neil Nelson. (Courtesy NOLA.com/The *Times-Picayune*)

Neil Nelson's house and store, at the corner of Washington (Fern) and Hampson streets. (Courtesy NOLA.com/The *Times-Picayune*)

blindly handed him three ten-dollar bills, his monthly wage, which Baker took slowly from his hands. Suddenly Nelson felt a stinging blow to the side of his head, and he fell to the floor while Baker continued to pelt him with the weighted bag. Nelson begged him to stop as he staggered to the store entrance, holding to the counter in a daze. Mrs. Nelson dashed downstairs to see what the commotion was about. As she entered the room, Baker stepped back momentarily but then resumed his attack.

"Don't hurt me, please," Mr. Nelson pleaded as he held up his hands defensively.

"Please don't hurt my husband," Mrs. Nelson added, no doubt horrified at what she saw.

"No, I won't hurt him," Baker said as he jeered at Mrs. Nelson.

Baker soon produced a razor, which Nelson attempted to take away from him without success. He received a cut to his left hand and arm, and his shirt and Canton flannel undershirt were ripped by the blade. Desperate to save her husband's life and thinking nothing of her own safety, Mrs. Nelson grabbed Baker's neck from behind as her husband staggered out the door to find assistance. In such a dazed state, he apparently failed to see the peril that his wife was in.

"Please don't hurt him," Mrs. Nelson said when she initially grabbed hold of Baker.

But Baker then turned his energies toward Mrs. Nelson, slashing at her throat with the bloody razor.

"You have cut me; now don't kill me, Philly!" she cried out as he attempted to lunge at her again.

The *Daily Picayune* reported Mrs. Nelson's final words begging Philly not to kill her two days after her death, though her husband denied that any such dialogue had occurred when he testified at Baker's trial two months later. This was an example of how New Orleans newspapers often created stories rather than reported them. Nevertheless, it made for good reading; Léona Queyrouze undoubtedly believed that this had occurred while the press covered the Dietsh murder.

Cut and badly bleeding, Mrs. Nelson let go of Baker and started toward the side door leading to the yard when he suddenly lunged at her again, cutting her neck from ear to ear. The wound was so deep that it cut her trachea in two, preventing her from crying out. He then shoved her on the stairway, the first few steps leading to a platform where she fell and bled to death, a large trail of blood flowing down the stairs where she lay. The walls were later found splattered with blood from the arterial spray.

Soiled with her blood, Baker took what money remained on the dining-room table and reentered the grocery. His bloody fingerprints on the doors and walls, along with bloody footprints, marked his path. Once in the store he attempted to conceal his crime by setting fire to the house. He lit some kindling and paper that he placed beneath two sixty-gallon zinc tanks partially filled with oil that were located on a stand near the side door leading out to Hampson Street. He then stole what money remained in the cash drawer before exiting the building. Fortunately, the fire burned itself out before the flames could reach the tanks. Racing to the stable, he washed his blood-soaked hands in a bucket of water and changed into fresh clothes he had placed there previously. He then escaped into the darkness.

It was later discovered that Baker had purchased the gun pellets at a neighboring grocery store two days before the murder. The grocer thought it odd that Baker wanted his shots since Nelson's store sold the same item, though that later turned out not to the case. The grocer even asked him if he wanted powder and caps, as he thought Baker was planning a hunting trip, but he only wanted to purchase the pellets. It was clear to the police that this was a premeditated crime, with robbery as the motive. One of the detectives assigned to the murder was Officer Fernand Rancé, and later District Attorney Luzenberg prosecuted the case. The *Daily Picayune* reported that Mr. Nelson had suspected Baker was stealing from him prior to his wife's murder, though he lacked proof to act on his suspicion.

Baker's bloody clothes and hat were later retrieved from the stable, but the razor he used to commit the horrific murder was never found. The shaving case, however, was discovered in a trunk in his upstairs room. The trunk belonged to Neil Nelson, which Nelson had loaned to Baker. The two men were such close friends that Nelson often lent him personal items. The razor was also something both men shared.

Within hours of the murder, the police learned that Baker was courting or engaged to Mamie Alexander of Brookhaven, Mississippi, a small town situated along the Illinois Central Railroad. The tracks ran north from New Orleans between Lake Pontchartrain and Lake Maurepas. Two officers quickly boarded the next available outbound train, which departed New Orleans late in the afternoon of March 8. A few minutes past 6:00 P.M., when the train arrived at Kenner, a town located west of Carrollton, the officers saw Baker board the train. They arrested him soon after while he was sitting at the end of the smoking car. They found a 32-calibre Smith & Wesson revolver and four dollars on him. He had hidden the rest of the stolen money, though he denied stealing any of Nelson's money or committing the murder.

At the next depot, Bayou LaBranche, the threesome exited the car and waited on the platform for the next inbound train. Meanwhile, as the outbound train was leaving the station, Baker lunged forward, striking his head on a log chain bolt hanging alongside the train, which knocked him senseless. There would be no further attempts at suicide or escape. Once back in New Orleans, he was attended to by an ambulance surgeon and then locked up at the First Precinct, the city's central police station at the time, located on Tulane Avenue at the corner of Basin Street (then Saratoga Street, now Loyola Avenue).

Naturally, when the police asked Philip Baker to make a statement, his version of events was quite different. He told the officers that he was innocent of the crime and an unfortunate victim. He stated that he and Nelson got along quite well, but their friendship began to sour after his marriage. The couple often fought with each other, and he was unfortunately caught in the middle of their disputes.

According to Baker, on the night in question, the couple began to argue with each other and Mr. Nelson eventually directed his anger toward him. The accused finally struck Nelson with a shot bag in self-defense. He was shocked to learn of Mrs. Nelson's murder. He told the arresting officers that he had overheard a group of men discussing the murder prior to his boarding the train at Kenner. They had read about it in the newspaper. He also heard his name mentioned as the accused murderer, which he disputed.

"I think that Mr. Nelson did the deed," Baker later said, "as he and his wife were so unfriendly towards each other. He never liked me after his wife told him that she 'liked me very much,' and we were always getting into a quarrel."

At trial, taking the stand on his own defense, Baker testified that he and Mrs. Nelson had been intimate for about two weeks prior to her death, with Mr. Nelson discovering her infidelity two days before her murder.

According to Baker's version of events, after striking Mr. Nelson and fearing his arrest, he went upstairs, got some money, and fled the scene. He walked along the levee to Kenner, where he boarded the train. When he heard about Mrs. Nelson's murder, he was more determined than ever to leave town, knowing he would be blamed. Regarding his head injury, he told police back in New Orleans that when the arresting officers grabbed him, he fell because he was weak from traveling to Kenner. The *Daily Picayune* later reported that the police learned that Baker told one of the railroad employees that Mr. Nelson paid him to murder his wife, although that story was highly suspect.

Not surprisingly, at the coroner's inquest held on Sunday, March 8, Dr. LeMonnier "declared that death was the result of hemorrhage of the blood vessels of the neck . . . the work of a murderer and not self-inflicted . . . [the wound] made by a sharp instrument." He added that Mrs. Nelson was seven to eight months pregnant at the time of her death. The *Daily Picayune* preferred to use the term "delicate condition" to describe her state of pregnancy.

Mrs. Nelson's body was subsequently released to her parents, Jacob and Carrie Frank, and her remains laid out at their home at 333 (then 1130) Dryades Street (the house has since been demolished). She was robed in white, with a wreath of orange blossoms resting on her forehead, and "a constant stream of friends and sympathizers called at the house to see the remains and offer consolation to the afflicted family," the *Daily Picayune* later reported. "The scene was a pitiful one in the extreme, and even the visitors were compelled to shed tears of sympathy with the family." Still suffering the effects of his closed head injury and confined to bed, Neil Nelson was unable to attend his wife's wake or subsequent funeral. The latter took place on Monday morning at 11:00, with Rev. John T. Sawyer of the Felicity Street Methodist Church officiating. Nineteen-year-old Laura Frank Nelson was laid to rest in Lafayette Cemetery No. 2.

On Saturday, May 16, 1891, after a two-day trial and a three-hour deliberation, the jury found Philip Baker guilty of the gruesome murder of Laura Nelson. Sheriff Gabriel Villeré, who was in the courtroom when the verdict was read, immediately telephoned the prison to instruct his men to ready another condemned cell. Baker would share Condemned Box No. 1 with Etienne Deschamps. On June 1, he was formally sentenced to death by Judge Joshua G. Baker (no relation), Section B of the Orleans Parish Criminal District Court. Baker's sentence was appealed to the Louisiana Supreme Court, but unlike Deschamps's first murder conviction, his death sentence was reaffirmed on December 14. There would be no retrial for Philip Baker. His fate would be sealed by the third week of April 1892.

Six days after the murder of Laura Nelson, on Friday, March 13, 1891, the city of New Orleans was rocked by the acquittal verdicts of six men accused of the October 1890 planned murder and/or assassination of David C. Hennessy, the superintendent of police. The jury was unable to reach a unanimous decision on three additional defendants charged with murder, thus mistrials were declared. All of the men were of Italian descent and the verdicts ignited a firestorm in the city, which had been smoldering for years as an anti-immigrant movement was sweeping the city and nation.

The United States had seen such anti-immigrant prejudices before against

Irish and German Roman Catholics before the Civil War and against the Chinese during the 1870s, which culminated in the passage of the Chinese Exclusion Act in 1882. By the late nineteenth century, a large influx of immigrants from Russia, including many Jews, and from Eastern and Southern Europe, including Poles and Italians, brought renewed calls to curb immigration.

Italian Mafia societies, particularly the rival Matranga and Provenzanos families, had an economic foothold in New Orleans. When several members of the Provenzanos family stood trial for the May 6, 1890, ambush of six members of the Matranga family, Hennessy sided with the Provenzanos clan. He was shot down near his house late at night on October 15, 1890, and died early the following morning. The Matranga family was suspected of orchestrating the assassination just days before Hennessy was to allegedly testify against them. Within days of the killing, the police rounded up scores of Italian suspects for questioning. Ten men were eventually charged with the murder of Hennessy and nine others with accessory before the fact. The first nine defendants went on trial beginning on February 16, 1891.

Soon after the verdicts were announced, a mass meeting was called at 10:00 on Saturday morning, March 14, 1891, at the foot of the Henry Clay statue, located in the median on Canal Street at the intersection of St. Charles Street. (This statue was moved to Lafayette Square in 1900.) Meanwhile, the nine Italian defendants were escorted back to Orleans Parish Prison, where city officials thought they would be safe from an angry and disappointed citizenry.

After reading about the mass meeting in the Saturday morning newspaper and expecting possible trouble thereafter, Sheriff Villeré instructed his fourteen officers to take precautions. This included boarding up the vulnerable North Liberty Street entrance to the prison. Ten to twelve New Orleans police officers from the Fourth Precinct reinforced the prison guards.

The massive crowd that assembled on Canal Street on Saturday morning soon called for vigilante justice for Hennessy's murder. At 10:20 A.M., under the leadership of W. S. Parkerson and J. C. Wickliffe, a large group of men arrived at the prison armed with shotguns and rifles. They demanded that Capt. Lemuel Davis relinquish his jail keys, but he refused. Meanwhile, prisoners were ordered locked up in their cells. Before the officers could reach the area that contained the nineteen Italian defendants, the men had fled, seeking shelter wherever they could. Naturally, they assumed they would be shot in their cells if they stayed put.

"Dynamite the jail," the crowd cried out when the keys were refused. "Break it down." As expected, the crowd began to gather at the North

Liberty Street entrance, near where the bedrooms of the captain and clerks were located.

"Shoot the officers if they don't give up the keys," the men shouted.

By then seven planks had been nailed across the doorway, secured by two strong scantlings. Bringing a battering ram with them, the angry mob easily broke through the door and took possession of the prison, forcing Davis to give up his keys or else be cut down by an assortment of weapons. Prison officers thereafter offered no resistance as the mob systematically hunted down the Italian suspects.

Three of the nineteen Italian defendants sought refuge in the unoccupied condemned area on the third floor. Since the conclusion of his second trial, Etienne Deschamps was housed in either Condemned Box No. 3 or No. 4 located below it.

"It was lively for a little while," Deschamps told Dr. LeMonnier, who visited him the day after the prison mayhem. "They shot from down in the yard up to the gallery above. I was on the [second-floor] gallery when the firing started, and I said to myself, 'Deschamps, your place is at the bottom of your cell.' And there I lay until the shooting was over." If Dr. LeMonnier needed any further proof that Deschamps was sane and rational, and not suicidal, he had his evidence then.

Dr. Havá later disputed what Dr. LeMonnier claimed were Deschamps's words regarding the day of the shootings. "On that day my cell was not opened," Deschamps told Dr. Havá in late March 1892. "I was roused from my sleep by several gunshots, and thought they were hunting cats or rats. I did not pay any attention to this. On that day I had been given nothing to eat or drink. The next morning only the door of my cell was opened, and I noticed that my gallery was blood stained, and when I asked what the matter was I was told of the previous day's occurrence." His statement was hard to believe given the chaos that befell the prison that day, even though he had convinced Dr. Havá otherwise.

Among the Italians holding out in the third-floor condemned section, Antonio Marchesi—allegedly the person to fire first at Hennessy—was the first man shot. He was also one of the six defendants found "not guilty" in court the day before. He died that evening, having suffered a massive head wound over his right eye, uncovering and penetrating his brain. The thumb, forefinger, and middle finger of his right hand were blown away as he grasped the gun aimed at his chest. The other two men were murdered outside their cells, one a "not guilty" and the other a mistrial defendant. The mob broke down two doors to reach them and then shot them at pointblank range.

A fourth man, Manuel Politz, another of the mistrial defendants who had locked himself in a cell next to the condemned area, was taken out of the prison and hanged on a lamppost at the corner of St. Ann and North Liberty streets. His corpse was riddled with bullets. A fifth man, Antonio Bagnetto, another "not guilty" defendant, was found on the white female side of the prison, taken out the main entrance, and strung up by his neck on a tree along Orleans Street, opposite the prison.

Six other men were shot to death within the prison walls, including Peter Monasterio, considered by the police to be the mastermind and commander of the assassins and one of the three mistrial defendants. Four of the other men killed had yet to stand trial. Because three of the six "not guilty" defendants were spared their lives and four others who had yet to be tried were killed, many believed that the eleven men killed that day were targeted regardless of the verdicts. Still others, including the district attorney, believed the entire trial was a sham, with the jurors bribed. He was right, and indictments and convictions followed.

After the lynching, the mob returned to the Henry Clay statue. There, a few speeches were made and then the crowd dispersed. No perpetrators of the Italian massacre were ever brought to justice, even though the incident caused an international crisis with the Italian government. That faded away over time.

Sometime after this bloody ordeal, Etienne Deschamps was transferred to the third floor and assigned to a cell in Condemned Box No. 1. There he remained alone until the arrival of Philip Baker.

When leap year 1892 dawned in New Orleans, the Board of Pardons had yet to decide the fate of the Frenchman. They would soon be grappling with the facts surrounding the Baker case as well. With Philip Baker scheduled to be hanged on January 22, the governor received a petition on Wednesday, January 13, seeking a respite for up to thirty days. The petition was immediately forwarded to the board for its consideration. Baker continued to claim his innocence, accusing Nelson of murdering his wife. He also faulted his lawyer for not adequately defending him in court.

The day that Baker's petition was filed with the governor's office, reporters arrived at Attorney General Rogers' office to interview him regarding the two condemned prisoners. He refused to make a statement on the record, though what he said informally was enough to satisfy their curiosities.

According to Rogers, Governor Nicholls had deferred any action regarding Deschamps pending the board's decision. The governor had sent several letters to the board requesting the status; the last one was received several days prior. Reporters were told that the board had informed the governor that the matter was still under advisement and no decision had been reached.

The board had discussed the Deschamps case twice before without reaching a consensus. The insanity claim raised by Deschamps's supporters was a difficult and complicated issue for the board to wrestle with. State officers and the attorney general visited the condemned man at least once to monitor his mental state. Though Rogers didn't say it, the reporters got the notion that the board's majority didn't believe Deschamps was insane at the time of the murder. If the death were accidental, the governor would have grounds to recommend a commutation of his sentence. According to the *Daily Picayune*, "The only question now [was] whether he [would] be executed or sent to the penitentiary for life."

The reporters left the attorney general's office after being told that the board would meet when Lieutenant Governor Jeffries could attend, on January 20. It was then that the case of Etienne Deschamps would be decided. Meanwhile, Baker's thirty-day reprieve would likely be granted.

In spite of what the reporters had been told, the board did not meet until January 25, and no decision was reached in either case because Judge Baker, who was serving with the board in matters related to Philip Baker, was in court all day and couldn't attend the meeting. All was not lost, however, as the lieutenant governor and attorney general visited the criminal court building that afternoon to review the records of Deschamps and Baker. It would take another month for the board to issue its report regarding Philip Baker.

On Monday, February 29, 1892, the day before Mardi Gras, in a unanimous decision involving the lieutenant governor, attorney general, and Judge Baker, the board wrote, "We are unable to advise the governor to commute the sentence rendered or to advise the present case as one warranting executive clemency." Baker was doomed.

Nearly two weeks later, the board finally issued their official report regarding Etienne Deschamps. On Friday, March 11, 1892, close to midnight and following hours of debate, the three-member Board of Pardons delivered their decree to the governor. It read in part, "The board of pardons, by a majority, the attorney general dissenting, declines to recommend the commutation of sentence."

In Baton Rouge, on March 24, 1892, Governor Nicholls signed the death warrants for Philip Baker and Etienne Deschamps. The executions were to take place at Orleans Parish Prison on Friday, April 22, 1892, between the hours of noon and 3:00 P.M. Only a miracle could delay the dual hangings. Fortunately for Deschamps's supporters, the Frenchman had one miracle left.

Chapter Eight

Reprieved and Doomed

*That the commission would have declared the man insane I expected, at least by a
majority; but great was my disappointment.*
Dr. Y. R. LeMonnier, April 14, 1892

When the Board of Pardons issued their official decree regarding Etienne
Deschamps on March 11, 1892, all three members included rationales for
their decisions. Judge Marr refused to modify the verdicts reached by two
sets of jurors, and Lt. Gov. James Jeffries saw no clear evidence of insanity
that would warrant a commutation of sentence. In addition, Jeffries, being
less familiar with the case than the other board members, tended to side with
the juries' decisions and specifically with Judge Marr's opinion. After all, the
judge had presided over both trials. Both men's opinions were short and
concise when they were published in the *Daily Picayune* on March 12. But that
was not the case with Atty. Gen. Walter Rogers' dissenting viewpoint, which
occupied four times the column space.

Having visited Deschamps in prison, Rogers was convinced that the
Frenchman was "a hypnotic enthusiast" who "believed in the power of
mesmerism." Rogers believed that Deschamps, a man clearly not of sound
mind, never intended to murder the child. "Death robbed him of the fruits of
his fancy and labor," Rogers noted. If anything, the attorney general believed
that Deschamps was guilty of manslaughter and deserved imprisonment at
hard labor, not a death sentence.

When the board's decree and opinions appeared in the newspaper, Dr.
Havá and other likeminded physicians seized upon the opportunity opened
by Attorney General Rogers. Havá, apparently running his office in New
Orleans, was able to pen a letter to the governor using Rogers' official
stationery. Convinced that the governor had not been given a complete
psychological picture of the defendant, Havá and seven other physicians
offered their services without compensation to the governor. Their mission
was "to investigate Deschamps' mental condition."

During the late afternoon of March 12, a *Daily Picayune* reporter went to the prison to visit Baker and Deschamps, no doubt to gauge the men's reactions to the published decrees. Deschamps was sitting on his bed eating his dinner when the reporter stepped into his cell, which at the time stood open to the gallery. Upon hearing his footsteps, Deschamps "uttered a lugubrious cry, almost like that of a scared beast," according to the reporter. He then raced to a corner of his cell, crouched down on his knees and elbows, buried his head from view, and appeared to be writing something on a piece of paper. He was obviously trying to impress the reporter with his show of insanity. Baker, who was standing outside his cell watching Deschamps's antics, was amazed by the spectacle. With only Deschamps's shoe soles and the seat of his pants visible to the reporter, the correspondent turned his attention to Philip Baker, who welcomed the visit.

For a half-hour or more, Baker conversed with the reporter on every topic that was brought up. He continued to profess his innocence and thought that in time he would be vindicated, though he knew it would not be in his lifetime. Baker decried the actions of his attorney before and during the trial and criticized one of the jurors who told the judge he wouldn't convict on any grounds but direct testimony. Baker claimed that his conviction was based entirely on circumstantial evidence, since Nelson never saw him murder his wife. The reporter stated that by the end of their conversation, Baker, though putting on a brave face, was "completely despondent." He added, "His whole appearance is a picture of regret and hopelessness."

Even though the reporter painted a sympathetic picture of Baker, he had no such empathy for Etienne Deschamps. He wrote, "He either is, or affects, the insane, but his actions are so marked that he gains no sympathy." Apparently what the reporter saw that day was not an isolated incident. Whenever anyone came to visit Deschamps or Baker, the Frenchman would assume that "strange position in the corner of his cell," not righting himself until his visitors had left the area. In the end, Deschamps only spoke to certain prison officials. "He is ugly and cranky at all times," the reporter wrote, "and the officials feel that his execution will be their gain."

When the above story ran in the March 13, 1892, edition of the *Daily Picayune*, it was accompanied by a chastising editorial piece on Etienne Deschamps's many attempts to evade justice over the past three years. But the editor made one miscalculation by mentioning that the appointed Commission of Lunacy had found no evidence of Deschamps's insanity. Léona Queyrouze, using her alias Constant Beauvais, jumped at the opportunity to correct the editor, writing to him that no such commission was ever formed. Like two small children arguing on a playground, the editor responded in kind by informing his readership that the Board of Pardons had been petitioned to form such a commission "and some action was had," though he skirted the issue of findings by stating: "the details of which are not now at hand."

Dr. LeMonnier finally settled the dispute between Constant Beauvais and the editor of the *Daily Picayune*, surprisingly in favor of the former. When the newspaper interviewed him on March 18, he admitted that no such commission of doctors had ever examined the question of Deschamps's sanity. He alone had done so, and he was convinced beyond a shadow of a doubt that the Frenchman was sane. He also explained that when the Board of Pardons had sought to impanel a group of doctors per Judge Marr's request, there was no money to pay them for their services, as previously mentioned; thus, the commission never got off the ground. Dr. Havá must have known about the money problems when he wrote to the governor stating that his and his colleagues' services would be free of charge.

With the Board of Pardons decree now public knowledge, Dr. Havá wasn't the only Deschamps supporter seeking the governor's ear. Léona once again took the opportunity to write to the chief executive. On March 17, during a visit to his wife's hometown of Thibodaux, Gov. Francis Nicholls wrote back to Léona, acknowledging her letter and informing her that he had also received the physician's application. But he advised Léona that the petition should have been mailed to the board instead of him. For some unknown reason, the governor downplayed his own authority to interfere in matters related to the Board of Pardons. Besides, he told Léona, Deschamps, via his attorneys, had been given two opportunities to plead his insanity defense. At the present moment it was out of his hands, given that the board had already ruled. Therefore, the governor signed the death warrants for Baker and Deschamps on March 25.

Apparently Léona never informed her doctor friend that Governor Nicholls had received his March 12 petition, because Dr. Havá wrote a follow-up letter the same day the governor signed the death warrants. As of March 25, Dr. Havá had yet to hear back from the governor. The doctor was particularly concerned that Nicholls had fixed the Frenchman's date of execution without even considering his proposal. He reiterated that the purpose of this new commission was not to seek a gubernatorial pardon "but an appeal of men prompted by science" to ascertain if Deschamps was insane, by doctors willing to serve without compensation, a factor that seemed to have doomed the last commission.

If for no other reason than to stop Dr. Havá from writing to him again,

Governor Nicholls took action. On March 26, Attorney General Rogers wrote to Dr. Havá and his other colleagues that the governor had forwarded both of their letters to him with the stipulation that the April 22 execution date was set and that he would not entertain any further communications or findings from their proposed commission. However, Rogers added, "[The] board of pardons will receive any report which an investigation conducted by you may suggest, and I am satisfied the board will give it proper consideration." The attorney general concluded his letter by writing, "To that end the public officials in charge of the prison are requested to afford you all necessary facilities in conducting your inquiry, and this letter will be your voucher in the premises."

Dr. Havá wasted little time upon receiving Rogers' letter. Formalizing their assemblage and chaired by Dr. Havá, the self-appointed volunteer Commission de Lunatico Inquirendo ("Commission Inquiring into the Sanity") of Etienne Deschamps sprang into action. Dr. Havá and Dr. Eugène J. Mioton were the first members to arrive at the prison. On Tuesday, March 29, at 9:00 A.M., they presented Capt. Lemuel Davis with a copy of Rogers' communication and were soon escorted to Deschamps's cell, where they conducted a lengthy interview with the condemned prisoner. At 2:30 P.M., Drs. Domingo Bornio and Erasmus Beach arrived at the prison, followed two hours later by Dr. Maximen Fourgette. The remaining members, Drs. Felix Formento, George Lewis, and John Dell'Orto, interviewed Deschamps at a later date. Visiting Deschamps individually or in small groups over the next seven days, each member kept his opinion of Deschamps to himself until they could meet collectively.

On March 30, the editor of the *Daily Picayune* questioned the point of the commission, writing, "There can be perhaps no special objection to permitting a self-appointed deputation of medical men to examine the condemned prisoner . . . , but it is difficult to see what useful purpose is to be [served] by it." In other words, given that over three years had elapsed since the murder, even if the physicians found him insane today, how could that prove he was insane back then? "The Board of Pardons cannot recognize the validity of any such irregular proceedings at this late date," the editor added. He went so far as to state that "the tardiness of justice and the slow moving of the apparently rusty machinery of the law . . . [causes] people in so many instances to distrust judicial proceedings, and drive them to violence." The editor was probably alluding to the Italian massacre that had occurred the year before, violence that his newspaper never condemned.

On Thursday, March 31, Deschamps and Baker were read their respective death warrants, which had arrived at the prison from the governor's office the previous afternoon. Chief Deputy Raoul Arnoult read Deschamps's warrant first; the prisoner showed no emotion. A newspaper reporter from the *Daily City Item* speculated that his lack of understanding the English language played a factor in his flat affect, though "twitching of the thumb of his left hand betrayed his consciousness of the occasion." Arnoult then proceeded to read Baker's warrant. By then he and Baker were sitting on the gallery near Deschamps's cell.

"It's very hard to die when one is not guilty," Baker said, as he stood up after hearing his fate.

Sympathetic to his plight, Arnoult told Baker not to give up all hope. There were still some three weeks before the execution and there was always the chance that something would turn up. Unbeknownst to Arnoult, he was right. Jacob Baker, Jr., Philip's older brother, swore out an affidavit accusing Nelson of murdering his wife. A preliminary examination of the case was set for Saturday, April 23, the day after the scheduled execution. The grand jury met instead on Monday, April 18, and ruled the following Thursday that no cause of action against Nelson was warranted. Philip Baker would walk to the gallows the following day.

Some minutes after Baker was read his death warrant, Deschamps confessed to Arnoult that he acted in such a bizarre manner whenever he was visited by the press because he didn't want them to see him in such a state, "his beard long and ugly and his clothes shabby." There would be no such antics while Deschamps was under the examination of Dr. Havá and the other physicians, though he had not yet given up his verbal peculiarities that helped paint him as insane.

One member of the medical commission who bought into Deschamps's sham was Dr. Bornio. Having visited the Frenchman on four occasions, the doctor concluded that Deschamps suffered from monomania, a psychosis rooted in his obsessions with magnetism and astronomy. Dr. Bornio was convinced that Deschamps could not possibly feign such a mental disorder. His diagnosis was not an isolated conclusion in the medical commission.

On Tuesday, April 5, after completing its investigation into the mental state of Etienne Deschamps, the commission met at the St. Charles Street office of Drs. Bornio and Adrian Havá, one of Dr. John Havá's sons. Their meeting was kept strictly private. There they discussed their respective opinions of the Frenchman and began to formulate their final report, which was forwarded to the Board of Pardons on April 7. The *Daily Picayune* published the commission's physical and psychological assessment of Deschamps six days later.

□ □ □

Their report stressed five points. First, Deschamps suffered from monomania on magnetism and hypnotism, which, in their opinion, constituted a form of "mental alienation"; thus, he was insane. They cited numerous examples in Deschamps's life that pointed to that diagnosis. In particular, they mentioned his obsession with locating buried treasure and his use of magnetism and hypnosis to energize a lucid clairvoyant so that she might lead him to it.

Deschamps easily convinced the physicians that he was also being targeted by persons inside and outside the prison who possessed even stronger magnetic influences than his own, forces that compelled him to act in outlandish ways, creating hatred and ridicule toward him. If the doctors feared for their own safety while in his presence, Deschamps assured them that they were in no immediate danger—as physicians, they were not vulnerable to these same evil influences. According to Deschamps, their science would detect such forces before they could do harm. The Frenchman had thought of every angle while trying to convince the commission of his madness, fabricated as it was.

Second, the commission believed that the etiology of his monomania was a cerebral lesion. On physical examination, they noted that the Frenchman had a slight strabismus and suffered from nystagmus, along with an unequal constriction of the pupils, "the left one more so than the right." In addition, they observed that Deschamps lost his balance when blindfolded. These clinical findings could only point to one thing, a brain tumor. Dr. LeMonnier had observed the unequal constriction of the pupils upon his initial examination of Deschamps on January 30, 1889. Nothing had changed between then and the present.

Third, this cerebral abnormality probably dated back several years, causing the insanity. Fourth, because of that, Deschamps could not be held "responsible for acts suggested by or committed under the influence of his monomania." And finally, fifth (and not surprising), his recovery was very doubtful, in their clinical judgment.

As learned as these physicians were in their day, even the lay editor of the *Daily Picayune* saw holes in their logic. Labeling them a "self-appointed" commission, he stated that according to their own criteria, anyone who believed in hypnotism and clairvoyance and, by extension, magic and astrology was insane. In addition, in spite of the professional zeal shown by these physicians in volunteering their services, the cause and effect of Deschamps's behavior was only their opinion after all, and one that failed to cast any serious doubt on the verdict reached by the last jury.

Of course, as chairman of the commission, Dr. Havá took issue with the newspaper's April 13 editorial, but not for the reasons one might expect. Surprisingly, he had a problem with the phrase "self-appointed" and the word "opinion" used in the commentary. In a letter to the editor that appeared in the *Daily Picayune* the following day, Dr. Havá wrote that "self-appointed" was a misstatement. He stressed that the commission was duly authorized and empowered by the Board of Pardons. Obviously, Dr. Havá was stretching the truth a tad, and the *Daily Picayune* knew it.

Regarding the use of the word "opinion" by the *Daily Picayune*, Dr. Havá responded, "But, pray, what is an opinion expressed formally and conscientiously by a body of honorable men if not the certainty of a fact." He obviously felt snubbed, as if a physician's opinion was not trustworthy.

In a tit for tat, the editor responded the same day that Dr. Havá's letter appeared in his newspaper. He reminded his readership that the attorney general's communiqué with Dr. Havá occurred after the doctor had offered his services—not the other way around. And in responding to the word "opinion," the editor simply quoted the commission's own report when they declared "he is now, in our opinion, an insane man."

The issue of Etienne Deschamps's mental state was far from settled. The Orleans Parish coroner had yet to voice his opinion. On April 15, eight days after the commission's report was forwarded to the Board of Pardons, Dr. LeMonnier's response was printed as a letter to the editor. "That the commission would have declared the man insane I expected," he wrote to the *Daily Picayune*, "at least by a majority; but great was my disappointment at their decision and leaves Deschamps just where he was before those gentlemen saw him, viz: a sane mind in a sane body."

If nothing else, Dr. LeMonnier was highly critical of the commission's opinion that Deschamps suffered from "monomania on magnetism." As the *Daily Picayune* had implied several days before, would this mean that everyone who sought to locate the site of Jean Lafitte's buried treasure would be declared insane? Furthermore, if Deschamps was insane because he was a magnetizer, why wasn't every clairvoyant and medium who fleeces the ignorant of their money or virtue declared insane?

Dr. LeMonnier then tore apart the commission's conclusion that a cerebral lesion was the catalyst for the Frenchman's madness. "What an indefinite conclusion!" he responded. "Have these gentlemen made an ophthalmoscopic examination of the eyes to discover the cause of this supposed brain affection? Of course not." He pointed out to the readership that people afflicted with strabismus and unequal pupils are not insane. Furthermore, such conditions can be treated with surgery to the eye and are not related to the brain. In addressing the commission's third and fifth points that Deschamps's brain affliction "probably dates back several years" and that his recovery was "very doubtful," Dr. LeMonnier responded: "No disease is more difficult to cure than an imaginary one."

But the commission's fourth conclusion—that Deschamps could not be held responsible—troubled Dr. LeMonnier the most. "This is the most extraordinary part of this report," he remarked. "After having so wisely surrounded their conclusions with so much probability and doubtfulness," saying unequivocally that Deschamps could not be held responsible for his actions was a remarkably inept assumption on their part.

And to erase any doubt as to his own ability to judge the difference between the sane and insane, Dr. LeMonnier contrasted his work experience with that of the commission. Their observations involved studying one man for a few hours a day over a week's time. On the other hand, his experiences with the insane spanned years and involved thousands of patients across the city, state, and elsewhere. Regarding Deschamps, Dr. LeMonnier had spent the better part of three years closely observing the man.

"And here I stop," he wrote. "Etienne Deschamps is not insane." Dr. LeMonnier let the readers decide for themselves who was more knowledgeable about Deschamps's mental state.

Not surprisingly, Dr. Havá wanted to have the last word, knowing that the board would act upon their report within days. On April 15 he penned another letter to the *Daily Picayune,* which was printed three days later. "We were particularly struck by the passionate strain of the uncalled for article in which the coroner systematically misconstrues our conclusions," he wrote. "Our report was based upon physical and psychological symptoms, which, taken together as a group, have a deep significance for any unprejudiced mind, but which, taken separately, as it has pleased the coroner to do, signify little or nothing." Dr. Havá reaffirmed his opinion that Etienne Deschamps was insane.

Meanwhile, the attorney general received the medical commission's report

April 7. Copies were made; one was kept by Rogers and the other forwarded to Lieutenant Governor Jeffries in Rapides, Louisiana. Jeffries was instructed to return his opinion to the attorney general's office in New Orleans as soon as possible, since the date of Deschamps's execution was close at hand. In the interim, Rogers handed the original report to Judge Marr for his consideration. Wanting a contrasting viewpoint, Judge Marr asked Dr. LeMonnier to write his opinion regarding the mindset of Deschamps, which he did, providing his report to the judge on April 16. It was no surprise that Dr. LeMonnier continued to insist that the Frenchman was of sound mind.

On April 14, Jeffries wrote to Judge Marr informing him of his receipt of the medical commission's report and his uncertainty regarding their findings of monomania as the causative factor in the murder of Juliette Dietsh. He noted that he would not be able to travel to New Orleans at the present and was content that he and the attorney general would determine the legal validity of the commission's claim. "It is a legal question, and should be largely governed by your opinion if I was there," Jeffries wrote to Judge Marr, a curious thing to write since Jeffries was a lawyer. In other words, with Rogers already supporting a commutation of the sentence, Jeffries was placing the burden of deciding the fate of Etienne Deschamps upon the judge's shoulders. In the end, whatever the judge decided, the lieutenant governor would back.

On Monday evening, April 18, Judge Marr delivered a package to the home of Mr. Rogers. He had tried to deliver it to him at his office early that day but to no avail. In it were three documents: his opinion regarding the matter before the Board of Pardons, that is, the judge's continued insistence that the jury's verdict stand; Dr. LeMonnier's well-known opinion; and in a separate envelope, a short note to the attorney general. The judge wanted to meet with him before making his opinion official, possibly at 8:00 the following morning. "Please say if I can find you at home at that hour, or at your office, as you may prefer," Judge Marr wrote.

"Certainly, my dear judge, I will be at home to meet you," Rogers wrote back. "Sorry I did not know you would be at my office. I would have met you and saved [you the] trouble of coming to me." It's not known if the judge ever received Rogers' reply. Judge Marr never ventured to his home again.

On Tuesday, April 19, Louisiana voters went to the polls to elect a new governor, state legislators, and numerous local officials, including the mayor of New Orleans. Rather than going to see Rogers as planned, Judge Marr left his residence at 359 (now 3321) Coliseum Street at 8:30 A.M. to vote, returning to the general vicinity of his home about thirty minutes later. From there he walked along the Mississippi River levee to Carrollton, where he stopped for a few minutes to watch some boys fishing. He then proceeded to the levee's end before turning around and heading back to town. During the afternoon, a witness saw the judge walking through the old exposition grounds (Audubon Park). And still later that evening he was spotted by Dr. Knapp, a local dentist, again upriver from the grounds. His whereabouts thereafter remain a mystery.

At seventy-two years of age, Judge Marr was described by some as being in feeble health with a history of vertigo, though his son would say otherwise. It was speculated that his long walk that day brought on an attack of vertigo. While strolling along the river, he could have easily fallen in and been swept away by the strong currents. The Mississippi River at New Orleans that day was 14.9 feet above the low-water mark and 1 foot above the danger line.

His son, Judge Robert Marr, Jr., believed that his father's death, whatever the cause, was indirectly related to the Deschamps case and the lieutenant governor's insistence that his father alone decide the fate of the condemned prisoner. According to his son, the judge was in good health and spirits, but the pressure placed upon him at that time was too much for him to bear. He surmised that his father had already made up his mind by the morning of April 19 and therefore saw no need to meet with the attorney general; his final opinion had been delivered the previous day. According to his son, his father may have taken his walk to escape harassment by Deschamps's friends. Though he didn't say so, there's little doubt that he was referring to Dr. Havá and Léona Queyrouze.

When the judge failed to arrive at his house on Tuesday morning, Rogers naturally assumed that it was because of the election or that he had taken ill. Then on Wednesday morning at 4:30, someone banged on Rogers' front door, rousing him from his sleep. It was the judge's son and his acquaintance, Mr. Turner, who were looking for the judge. He had not been seen by family members since 9:00 A.M. the previous day. Rogers explained that Judge Marr did not arrive for his planned appointment and then showed the son what his father had sent him on Monday evening. It was only then that Judge Marr, Jr., became aware of the tremendous pressure placed upon his father by the lieutenant governor's letter.

By Thursday, April 21, it was clear to all rational people that Judge Marr was no more, but that didn't stop the rumor mill from cranking out peculiar theories concerning his disappearance. The *San Francisco Chronicle* reported that the New Orleans police believed the judge had been kidnapped by persons interested in Deschamps. Four days later, Chicago's *Daily Inter Ocean* implied that Judge Marr was alive and in hiding—that he had wandered off intentionally to avoid the "importunities of the reprieve of the murderer Deschamps." The *Daily Picayune* reprinted an April 29 story from the *Republican*, a Springfield, Massachusetts, newspaper, indicating that Judge Marr committed suicide and alleging Deschamps, "a sort of voodoo doctor," had something to do with it. But the most outlandish rumor was published in the *Daily City Item* on July 31. In that story, the Mafia had kidnapped Judge Marr. The police were in possession of a July 29 letter written by P. J. Nunnez, who promised to deliver the judge into their hands for $500 or to liberate him for $100. "This money must reach us before 20 days, unless you will have his right ear for further information," the kidnapper wrote. He didn't get his money and no severed ear was ever delivered as proof of the kidnapping. The judge's body was never found.

On April 21, forty-eight hours after the disappearance of Judge Marr, Attorney General Rogers went to Governor Nicholls' office in New Orleans and placed before him the documents delivered to him by Judge Marr. Rogers advised the governor how he stood on the matter of Deschamps, but in light of Judge Marr's absence, it was unclear if the judge's opinion was to be considered final or not. The burden of deciding the fate of Deschamps now fell upon Lieutenant Governor Jeffries, but he remained out of the city. Until Jeffries could be consulted, Rogers suggested to the governor that he issue a stay of execution for Deschamps. However, Nicholls refused to do so unless Jeffries also asked for one.

Nicholls wired a letter to his lieutenant governor, who was by then in Boyce, a village about five miles northwest of Alexandria, Louisiana. "Your presence here as a member of the board of pardons is absolutely necessary at once," the governor wrote. He informed Jeffries of Judge Marr's disappearance and that action regarding Deschamps's commutation of sentence had to be taken immediately.

Upon receipt of the governor's wire, Jeffries telegraphed the attorney general, notifying him that he had written to Judge Marr about the matter and was not persuaded by the medical commission's report. "If the governor has any doubts, this being new matter, he could respite [Deschamps's execution date] until [the] board could meet," Jeffries wrote.

When Governor Nicholls was informed of Jeffries' message, he sent an order to Sheriff Gabriel Villeré at the prison. "Sir: You will delay the execution of Etienne Deschamps, ordered to be executed to-morrow, April 22, 1892, until further orders from me, a respite being hereby granted Deschamps."

□ □ □

The weather on Friday, April 22 could not have been worse, short of a hurricane. A total of 7.47 inches of rain fell in New Orleans, "flooding the streets and forming miniature lakes in every portion of the city," according to the *Daily City Item*. Though Etienne Deschamps would escape death that day, it was not the case for his fellow prisoner, Philip Baker.

Having been granted permission to remain in the third-floor chapel the night before, Baker received a haircut and shave from the prison barber and then feasted on some oysters and a bottle of wine, his last supper. When Baker woke up at 5:00 A.M., he peered out the chapel window, noticing a steady rainfall. He remarked that it was a horrible day, referring to the weather, but perhaps he was referring to his own fate as well. Immediately afterward he resumed his religious devotions, greeting the nuns who were close at hand. Deputies and newspapermen gathered around him to wish him a good morning, which was an odd thing to say given this was to be his last day on Earth.

After washing his hands and face, Baker put on a fresh white shirt and collar, discarding the old woolen one he had worn, and then knelt down for a short prayer. Afterward he wrote a short note to Deputy Sheriff Myers, asking him if he would accompany his body back to Carrollton for burial.

At 9:30 A.M., Father LeBlanc said Mass; Baker knelt near the altar with his head resting on his hands and his eyes looking downward as he prayed for the deliverance of his soul—or a miracle. When the Sisters of Mercy began to sing during the service, Baker zestfully joined in. The nuns had given him a blessed scapula to wear around his neck, the cloth medallion attached to a string that hung across his chest. From time to time Baker would grab hold of the scapula to confirm its presence. He still had some hope of escaping the hangman's noose.

Prior to Mass, Baker's attorney, Joseph Maille (not his original trial lawyer), visited the prison and informed his client that he was going to apply to Division E, Civil District Court for an injunction to restrain Sheriff Villeré from carrying out the execution. In the petition, Maille set forth specific charges against Mr. Nelson for the murder of his wife. Knowing that the grand jury had failed to find probable cause against Nelson the day before, Baker's attorney tried one last legal maneuver. Maille was at the prison that morning because he needed Baker's signature on the document—along with ten to twelve dollars, the cost to file the injunction. Baker gladly handed over the money after affixing his signature to the petition. After Father LeBlanc heard his confession, he attended Mass, his spirit lifted by this latest legal strategy.

Etienne Deschamps would not receive the news of his respite until 11:00 A.M. Until that morning he had remained in his cell, becoming livid when told the evening before that he would be executed the following day unless the governor intervened. In French, he cursed the sheriffs, the judge, and everyone else who had anything to do with his execution. His rage was silenced only when he collapsed from exhaustion and fell asleep.

When morning came, Deschamps appeared to be more rational in his behavior, though he refused any delicacies that were customary for a prisoner's last meal. Asked if he wanted a haircut and shave, he said no. He then laughed when asked if he wanted to go the chapel and pray. Sometime that morning, Father LeBlanc and the Sisters of Mercy came to his cell and, after a long conversation, enticed him to attend Mass. Unlike Baker, Deschamps took no interest in the service. A reporter with the *Daily City Item* described him as he sat next to Baker: "his long curly locks still uncut and his form habited in the same old well-worn garments that he donned so many weeks ago." When Mass was completed, Deschamps returned to his cell, where he remained "in silence and gloom" awaiting his breakfast, according to the *Daily City Item*. At the meal, he gorged himself on the ordinary prison food.

For his part, Baker began eating his last meal at 10:45 A.M. He had barely started his breakfast when Maille reappeared and requested another five dollars for his trouble. He had apparently miscalculated the court cost. After giving Maille the money, Baker returned to his meal, finishing it at 11:00 A.M.

By that time, Etienne Deschamps was standing on the gallery in front of his cell conversing with Drs. LeMonnier and Havá, which must have been awkward for the two adversaries. Chief Deputy Arnoult and others were also present when Captain Davis appeared with a message from Sheriff Villeré: Deschamps had been given a respite from the governor. Villeré was currently at the Civil Court awaiting Judge Albert Voorhies' decision on the petition Maille filed on behalf of his client.

Captain Davis handed the note over to Dr. LeMonnier, who communicated its content to Deschamps in French. Expecting the worst, Deschamps turned pale, but when the Frenchman was told that he would not hang that day, he simply shrugged his shoulders, and his color returned.

"Well, I'm not sorry for it," Deschamps replied.

He then turned to the people around him and began to chat pleasantly and causally on any topic that was brought up. No doubt, Dr. Havá communicated the good news to Léona Queyrouze immediately upon his departure from the prison. But for the vast majority of spectators in and around the prison, Deschamps's reprieve was viewed "with expressions of extreme dissatisfaction," as reported by the *Daily Picayune*.

"I wish it was Baker instead," some in the crowd murmured. "That Frenchman ought to hang."

Soon all thoughts turned back to Baker's plight. At 11:15 A.M., Baker began to pray the Way of the Cross, accompanied by the nuns. After completing the fourteen-prayer procession, he returned to the sanctuary with Father LeBlanc, where the pair engaged in more prayer.

At 11:58 A.M., Sheriff Villeré arrived at the prison with news of Judge Voorhies' decision. The judge refused to entertain Baker's petition on grounds that he lacked jurisdiction. Unbeknownst to Baker, his lawyer then sped to the Louisiana Supreme Court, but after about a half-hour of deliberation, the court rejected his petition. Philip Baker's fate was sealed.

Shortly after the sheriff's return, Chief Deputy Arnoult swore in the fifteen members of the coroner's jury, Dr. LeMonnier included. Dr. Havá was not among the men and likely left the prison shortly after being informed that Deschamps had been granted a reprieve.

At 12:25 P.M., Villeré, Arnoult, and the jurors filed into the sanctuary, where Baker was seen clutching a crucifix. After Arnoult read the death warrant, Baker rose from his seat and raised the crucifix before him.

"By this, I am as innocent as an unborn babe," he declared.

He then put on a new black alpaca coat and left the chapel in the company of prison officials and the jury, followed by the Sisters of Mercy and Father LeBlanc. The group walked along a corridor, down a flight of stairs to the second floor, and then along another corridor to the gallery and the scaffold. Near the scaffold was a smaller chapel, where Baker knelt in prayer. "There, the jury and others grouped around, all earnest in their responses, the prayers for the welfare of those about to die were said," the *Daily Picayune* reported.

At 12:44 P.M., Baker rose to his feet and walked along the little gallery adjacent to the scaffold, all the while shaking the hands of various people who had become close to him at the prison, four of whom he considered very dear associates. Two of those four gentlemen broke down in tears, unable to conceal their anguish.

Baker's hands were tied together by Hangman Taylor, who was dressed in a black robe. Sheriff Villeré asked if he had any final words.

"I am innocent of this crime, as innocent as a baby," he spoke.

Father LeBlanc was then allowed to say a few words before the sentence was carried out. According to the priest, Baker had been consistent in his worship while confined these many months in prison, and he was completely resigned to the will of the Almighty God. On behalf of the condemned prisoner, Father LeBlanc then wished to thank the nuns, guards, and others who had been so kind to him during his imprisonment. Baker freely forgave anyone who did him injury and prayed that no one would harbor ill will toward him upon his death. Baker then knelt down for his final act of contrition and at 12:50 1/2 stepped upon the trapdoor.

"Goodbye, Phil!" cried out one of the spectators.

"Goodbye, boys," he cheerfully responded. "Boys, I'm innocent of—"

A black cap placed over his head muffled out the remainder of his words, as Hangman Taylor quickly retreated to a neighboring cell to await the signal to cut the rope.

At 12:53 P.M., Philip Baker's descent into eternity began. As he fell seven feet toward the ground, the rope stretched, dampened by the rain, preventing a sudden snap of his muscular neck and the immediate unconsciousness that should have followed. Within seconds, violent convulsions were noted that lasted for almost three minutes, his death a painful suffocation.

At 1:01 P.M., only muscular contractions were noted. By then, he had finally been rendered unconscious. At 1:03 P.M., his body straightened out and went limp and motionless. The body of Philip Baker was cut down at 1:13 P.M. and his death cap was removed, revealing "an ugly knot bruise beneath his left ear, and rough rope marks around the neck and throat," the *Daily Picayune* reported. His eyelids were closed, his mouth slightly opened, "and the whole face was badly cyanosed."

At 1:26 P.M., the body was placed in a silver-mounted, silk-linen black casket, with a plain-looking plate bearing the inscription *Baker* on top. Turned over to his brother, Jacob, the remains were transported to Jacob's home in Carrollton at 68 Washington (now in the 700 block of Fern) Street, diagonally opposite Nelson's grocery and home. Officiated by Fr. René P. Vallée, pastor of Nativity of the Blessed Virgin Mary Catholic Church (or St. Mary's) in Carrollton, Baker's funeral took place at 4:00 P.M. the following day. Prior to Father Vallée's arrival, large numbers of people gathered in front of Jacob's home, hoping to view his brother's body before the casket was sealed. Undoubtedly it was awkward for some who attended the service that the funeral took place across the street from the murder scene, where Neil Nelson still resided. About two hundred people attended the graveyard service that followed; many grieved Philip Baker's passing.

Baker's remains were interred in Carrollton Cemetery, a "quiet little cemetery in the rear of Carrollton," according to the *Daily Picayune*, alongside the remains of his parents, Jacob Baker and Madeline (or Magdelina) Eberhardt Baker, both of German descent. The burial site—"a pretty plot," the newspaper reported—was shaded by a tall, flourishing cedar tree.

It's not known if Neil Nelson witnessed Baker's execution. If Nelson was there, did he derive some satisfaction from seeing that Philip Baker suffered pain prior to his death, as he had inflicted suffering upon his wife thirteen months before? One can only imagine. At a minimum, the fact that Baker had paid the ultimate price for his ghastly offense must have been fulfillment enough for the young widower. Neil Nelson moved on with his life. Philip Baker was no more.

Looking down at the execution from his third-story gallery, Etienne Deschamps knew that his day was coming. The morning after the execution, Dr. LeMonnier visited Deschamps's cell. Over the years, the Frenchman had become accustomed to his visits. The coroner was very much aware that the Board of Pardons would soon be rendering their decision regarding his lot.

"Deschamps, I see that they are trying to say that you are insane. How about that?" Dr. LeMonnier inquired, dumbfounded that such a topic was still being debated at this late stage.

Deschamps quietly responded, "I don't wish to discuss that question at all."

Chapter Nine

The Final Days

Deschamps is dead as you know. To the last moment I expected the contrary.
Léona Queyrouze, May 13, 1892

With Philip Baker dead, all eyes in the city looked toward the fate of Etienne Deschamps. It appeared that Lieutenant Governor Jeffries' communiqué to Attorney General Rogers on April 21 was not the last telegram he would send that day regarding the Frenchman. Addressed to the governor, but sent to the attorney general's office instead, Jeffries told Governor Nicholls that he had changed his mind and joined Rogers' recommendation for commutation to hard labor for life. The problem was that Rogers didn't become aware of Jeffries' decision until Monday, April 25. Beginning sometime on Thursday the twenty-first or Friday the twenty-second, Rogers was confined to his house "by indisposition" and would not return to his office until the beginning of the workweek. Had Rogers been at his office on either of those days to receive the lieutenant governor's message, Deschamps's fate may have changed drastically.

On Monday morning, after Rogers read Jeffries' letter to the governor, Rogers must have been pleased with the news. But just as Rogers finished reading it and was about to forward it to the governor, he received another wire. Jeffries (who was in Alexandria at the time) instructed Rogers not to send his April 21 communiqué to Nicholls but to wait for his letter to arrive instead.

Jeffries sent no fewer than three additional wires directly to the governor, all dated April 21 and sent from Boyce. Governor Nicholls must have been scratching his head in confusion after receiving the dispatches. In his first communiqué, Jeffries wrote, "In case of Deschamps, if you doubt his sanity, might give time for further investigation. Am not much impressed with reports of experts." But his second dispatch, sent at 6:00 P.M., was a complete reversal of the first. "I agree with Rogers to commute. Will send my reasons

163

by mail. If needed, will come down," he wrote. Apparently realizing that his last wire lacked conviction, he sent a third message two hours later. "I will go to New Orleans to-morrow. You will have to respite, as I cannot arrive before night," Jeffries declared.

Returning to the hamlet of Rapides, Jeffries penned his promised letter to the governor, dated the same day as his telegrams. In it he enclosed his recommendations, a copy of which he mailed to Attorney General Rogers. Explaining that he would be unable to reach New Orleans until the following day at 7:00 P.M., and having received no further instructions from Judge Marr regarding his opinion (though he was aware of Marr's disappearance), he told the governor that he would join the attorney general and recommend a commutation of Deschamps's sentence. By then, Jeffries was willing to give Deschamps the benefit of the doubt, having been torn between the opinions of the medical commission and Dr. LeMonnier.

When the governor received his letter on April 23, Nicholls immediately wrote back to him, stating he was wrong regarding Judge Marr. Apparently Jeffries was unaware that the judge had written an opinion against Deschamps's commutation, though the matter was far from settled, since he requested a meeting with Rogers before his opinion went public. Nevertheless, Nicholls stressed to Jeffries that he needed to come to the city and read what Judge Marr had written and then consult with Rogers as to their final recommendation.

Rogers did not receive his copy of Jeffries' letter to the governor until Wednesday, April 27. For some unexplained reason, the lieutenant governor had traveled no farther east than Alexandria. With that said, the urgency of the situation must have finally dawned on Jeffries upon his receipt of the governor's last communiqué. That same day, Jeffries sent a telegram to Rogers stating that he would meet him at his office at 11:00 A.M. on Thursday.

In the interim, Léona Queyrouze took full advantage of the moment, no doubt alerted by the attorney general of the lieutenant governor's change of mind. In a six-page, legal-size letter to the Board of Pardons, she once again laid out her case for commutation of Deschamps's sentence. Léona's letter began by chronicling the mission and opinion of the medical commission and Judge Marr's apparent decision not to interfere with the jury's verdict and the court's imposed sentence. But she reminded the two surviving members of the board that it was possible that Judge Marr was not totally comfortable with his opinion on the day he disappeared. If he was, why did he ask to see Rogers before finalizing it? The judge failed to keep his appointment and was apparently dead. To that end, Léona wrote, "What is the result? A terrible doubt. Who is to get the benefit of that doubt, if not the condemned?"

Knowing that the board also had a copy of Dr. LeMonnier's opinion, Léona again took the opportunity to publicly chastise the coroner, referring to him as "Mr. LeMonnier" throughout her letter. "Does the opinion of Mr. LeMonnier, known for three years, published repeatedly in the papers and many times reaffirmed, overthrow the opinion of eight physicians prominent in their profession?" she asked. She accused Dr. LeMonnier of being prejudiced against Deschamps from the very start. In addition, she argued, his opinion of the Frenchman's mental state, as biased as it was, should not be allowed to outweigh the educated medico-legal opinion of Dr. Havá.

She then lectured the board, stating that their very existence was "instituted for *clemency,* and when, as in this particular case, they cannot come to an understanding, the doubt which forcibly arises, is equivalent, in the eyes of Justice, to a recommendation for mercy." In all likelihood she delivered her essay personally to Attorney General Rogers prior to his meeting with Jeffries.

Léona was not the only one who ventured into the vacuum created by Judge Marr's disappearance. On the other side of the debate, the judge's son, Robert Marr, Jr., was astonished that doubt still existed regarding how his father felt about the commutation of sentence.

"I don't think that Lieut. Gov. Jeffries was aware of the fact that my father had written an opinion refusing Deschamps a pardon," he told a *Times-Democrat* reporter, the interview later printed in the *Daily City Item* on April 25. "If he was aware of that, then he is very inconsistent, having written my father that he would be governed by his opinion and then to telegraph the Executive requesting a respite for Deschamps."

The respite made no sense to the younger Marr. He admitted to the reporter that his father was very troubled over the untold pressured both men placed upon him. "Finding that my father was very much worried over this case," he said, "I told him that if those people wanted to let that old fellow off to let them do it."

According to Marr, Jr., shortly before his death, his father had met socially with Attorney General Rogers and told him he didn't think it was right that all the burden of choosing Deschamps's lot rested upon him. But Rogers clarified his own position by informing the judge that he alone had wanted to commute Deschamps's sentence. Rather, it was Jeffries who was vacillating between the hangman's rope and life with hard time served, with the lieutenant governor waiting for Judge Marr's opinion before he decided. Nevertheless, Rogers conceded that the judge was under tremendous pressure.

"This thing will cause my death," Judge Marr told Rogers at one of their meetings.

"Don't let it worry you," Rogers responded. "You are simply doing your duty. Don't mind anything else." Judge Marr, however, repeated his concerns.

When Jeffries arrived in New Orleans on Wednesday evening, April 27, Rogers greeted him at the station; both men decided to meet that night rather than waiting until the next morning. Jeffries had every opinion in hand, including that of the late Judge Marr and, no doubt, the epistle written by Léona Queyrouze. When the gentlemen parted ways that night, Jeffries informed Rogers he would notify him of his decision the following day.

As part of his official duties at the prison, Dr. LeMonnier went to visit Deschamps on Thursday morning.

"Doctor, have they done anything in my case yet?" the Frenchman asked, a query made supposedly by an insane man. LeMonnier would be unable to answer that question until later that evening, when the board's decision was publicized.

"The case of Deschamps has been passed upon on the merits," Jeffries wrote to the governor on April 28, after informing the attorney general of his opinion, "and the only question now before us is want of responsibility on account of his mental condition." In spite of the report written by Dr. Havá's commission (all "reputable physicians," according to Jeffries), no evidence was presented that Deschamps suffered from "mental alienation" on the day of the crime. "It is not shown to my satisfaction that a monomaniac on the subjects mentioned should not be held responsible for his acts," the lieutenant governor concluded.

Though Rogers maintained that Deschamps's sentence should be commuted, without the signature of another board member, the original sentence stood. "There is, therefore, no recommendation from the board to the executive for interference with the sentence of the court," Rogers wrote to the governor. Etienne Deschamps would hang for the murder of young Juliette Dietsh.

Making one last attempt to persuade the governor to her way of thinking, Miss Queyrouze wrote to him on April 29, knowing what the board had just declared.

"Dear Governor, again Deschamps seems lost, and on what grounds?" she asked.

She again implored the governor to weigh the opinion of the eight physicians against that of Dr. LeMonnier. By the tone of her letter, she had nothing but contempt for the coroner, whom she accused of defaming her name both in the press and verbally when he had spoken to the International

Medico-Legal Congress in June 1889. It was her final rant directed toward Dr. LeMonnier, but she mailed it to the governor instead. "In the name of Divine and human Justice, can an insane man hang?" she queried. Whether or not the governor saw her letter is not known. It's clear he never replied, because she wrote him on May 3 and then again on May 11. Regardless, Governor Nicholls made it clear he would not counter the board's recommendation— or lack of one.

Deschamps was finally informed of the board's findings on the morning of April 29 and, according to the *Daily City Item*, "took the news with his usual undemonstrativeness."

"All right," Deschamps declared, "let him hang me."

Retiring to his favorite corner of his cell, he refused to see anyone thereafter. He reportedly cried softly during the greater part of Friday night.

By Saturday morning, April 30, Etienne Deschamps had regained his composure and conversed freely with reporters and prison officials, proclaiming his innocence though he refused to talk directly about his case. He told Sheriff Villeré that he wasn't afraid to die but was bothered that his death would bring shame to his family's name back in France. Up to that point, his surname was deemed honorable in the Old Country. He then echoed what he had said many times before: that he was browbeaten from the very start.

"My trial was in English," he noted in French. "I did not understand it at all. I was railroaded into this stall, and they keep railroading me."

But he had even harsher comments about Dr. LeMonnier when he came to visit the Frenchman that day. According to Deschamps, the coroner was more powerful—in an evil way, one can only assume—than the commission of physicians who declared him insane. It was a remarkable statement from a man who supposedly had lost his mind. But Dr. LeMonnier reminded Deschamps that he was not insane and that the coroner had acted to fulfill his oath of office.

Sometime that same day, a member of the "knights of the shear" came into Deschamps's cell and shaved off his ragged beard and neatly trimmed his mustache and long, grayish hair. By the time the barber finished, Deschamps looked as he did when he was first convicted of his crime, though thinner after more than three years confined behind bars.

Affirming his innocence and declaring he was not deserving of hanging, Deschamps wanted nothing to do with the preparation of his immortal soul. While Father LeBlanc and the Sisters of Mercy were kept at bay, Deschamps

Etienne   Deschamps,   1892.   (Courtesy
NOLA.com/The *Times-Picayune*)

meditated or yakked freely with his guards or other visitors. Thirteen days
before his death, he wanted nothing to do with Catholicism or the Rites of
the Church. However, his attitude toward religion would change on the day
of his execution.

On Thursday evening, April 28, Governor Nicholls received the Board of
Pardons' report, but it wasn't until Friday, May 6, that he signed Deschamps's
death warrant. The date and time of his execution were set for Friday, May
13, between the hours of noon and 3:00 P.M. At noon the following day,
Chief Deputy Sheriff Arnoult received the warrant at the prison; six hours
later, he went to Condemned Box No. 1.

Deschamps was feeling "cast down" by then, having already been told he
would die after the Board of Pardons had failed to recommend a commutation
of his sentence. By May 7, Deschamps had shunned all reporters, feeling they
had contributed to his plight. The *Daily Picayune* stated, "He drew within
himself, retired to his cell's inner gloom, and spent the long hours in quiet
meditation, his arms folded, his chin dropped forward upon his breast."

When Arnoult arrived at his cell to read the death warrant, Deschamps
had already walked out onto the gallery to meet him. Standing like a statue
at the very spot where he had witnessed Philip Baker's hanging two weeks
before, the Frenchman braced himself for the news. Arnoult translated the

English wording into French for the benefit of the condemned man, but Deschamps already knew what he was about to say. He had heard the same pronouncement a little over a month before, when he learned he would die on April 22. Now, only the date had changed. At first Deschamps showed no emotion, but afterward, "in his excitable French fashion," according to the *Daily Picayune*, he stated that he had done nothing deserving of a hanging "and that it was unjust to kill him like a rat." Still refusing the company of Father LeBlanc and the nuns, he retired to his cell.

With less than a week to live, Etienne Deschamps abandoned all pretenses of insanity. The *Daily City Item* reported, "All of his old spirit of bravado has disappeared, and he makes no more attempts to convey the impression that his brain is disordered." Instead, he woke early each day and spent time reading or conversing with prison officials. If he was visited by an outsider and chose not to speak to them, he was at least polite about it. When pressed for details surrounding the murder, he would only admit that he never intended to kill young Juliette, though he continued to modify his story and the circumstances of her death until the very day he hanged.

By May 10, Deschamps had begun a limited dialogue with Father LeBlanc, the Jesuit priest who had visited him on a daily basis. Deschamps still refused to take the sacraments or attend Mass when offered. He suffered frequent spells of nervousness and despondency.

Only the direct intervention of Governor Nicholls, whose successor would be inaugurated on Monday, May 16, could save him from the gallows. That seemed highly improbable by that late date, but it didn't stop Dr. Havá from trying. In a letter mailed the day before Deschamps hanged, the governor's office informed Dr. Havá of the receipt of his letter and advised him that the chief executive had not the authority to take any further actions regarding Deschamps, though that was clearly not the case. Obviously, Governor Nicholls believed that the Frenchman was guilty.

Dr. Havá was not alone in his efforts to save Deschamps. On April 30, Léona's brother, J. Maximé Queyrouze, wrote a legal brief to the governor, though what became of it is not known. In addition, hoping to persuade the lieutenant governor to secure a commutation of Deschamps's sentence, the French acting consul, Charles H. G. Meyrier, traveled to Baton Rouge from New Orleans and met with Jeffries on May 11. Meyrier danced around the legal issues, indicating instead that he needed to intervene on behalf of Deschamps simply because of his French citizenship. But Jeffries politely informed the consul that he had carefully examined the facts surrounding the case and saw nothing to be gained by renewing a discussion about it. With great diligence he had probed the matter "and added that the mysterious character of the crime, coupled with the fact that Deschamps was a French subject, had induced the Board of Pardons to give the case more time and attention than if Deschamps had been an American citizen," as reported in the *Daily Picayune*. The matter between them was closed.

On Thursday, May 12, on the last full day of his life, Etienne Deschamps continued to maintain his innocence and to blame everyone else for his situation. He cursed his fate and as well as the authorities for suspecting him of a crime that he could not possibly have committed. According to Deschamps, the evidence clearly showed that Juliette Dietsh had died from the inhalation of chloroform administered by a person who had minimal knowledge of its application. Of course, this implied that he had substantial knowledge of the drug's properties and he should have therefore been ruled out as a suspect early in the investigation. It appeared that his story surrounding the events of January 30, 1889, was changing almost every day.

He also insisted that he wasn't afraid to die and so continued to refuse when Father LeBlanc tried to persuade him to attend Mass. He even refused to enter into prayer with the Sisters of Mercy who accompanied the clergyman. All he agreed to do was to talk to them in a casual manner on any subject but the crime or God. Not believing in religion himself, Deschamps told Father LeBlanc and the nuns that they didn't know any more about the future—implying the afterlife—than he did.

Sometime on May 12, the French consul returned to the city and visited Deschamps, undoubtedly to inform him of his failed attempt to persuade the lieutenant governor. It was at that meeting that Deschamps expressed a need to write a last will and testament. Before Théodule Buisson, a notary public, and in the presence of Sheriff Villeré, Jacques Villeré (a relative of the sheriff), Joseph Judice, and Charles Meyrier, Etienne Deschamps let it be known that he was sixty-two years old, which was contrary to what was recorded in the 1870 U.S. census and his enlistment age during the Crimean War. He also stated that he was a native of Rennes, France, never married or had children, and both of his parents were dead. He had four brothers, Louis, Pierre, Jean Maria, and Frédéric, all living in Paris, and three sisters, Marie, a nun, Rose, married to Mr. Giquel, and Joséphine, married to Mr. Derniau, all residents of Brittany.

Deschamps designated his siblings as universal legatees of his earthly possessions, except those items left in his cell, which he gave to Edgar White, one of his jail keepers. To Dr. Havá he left his illustrated anatomical posters and various books on chemistry, pharmacology, and other medical subjects. In addition, his body was to be donated to Dr. Havá so that he might perform an autopsy, though Havá was not notified of Deschamps's final wish until midafternoon on May 13. Obviously, Deschamps hoped that Dr. Havá would find something abnormal with his brain to confirm his insanity. He would never know that Dr. Havá did not perform the autopsy; it was performed instead by Dr. LeMonnier's associate, thirty minutes after his death.

The trunks and saddlebag in Deschamps's possession the day of the crime, along with a gold watch valued at $300 and pawned from Lewis Fishel loan office at 8 (then 109) Camp Street for $35, were entrusted to the French consul, who was named as testamentary executive and detainer of his aforementioned possessions. Somehow these belongings would be shipped back to his siblings in France.

In spite of his animosity toward them, Deschamps entertained questions from the press on his last full day on Earth. (They had literally camped out on the gallery in front of his cell, hoping to engage in a conversation one last time with the child murderer.) Continuously elusive about the crime, Deschamps never admitted his guilt. Shortly before dark, he asked to speak to Sheriff Villeré. When the sheriff arrived at his cell, the condemned prisoner requested that the gallery be cleared of everyone but the death watchman, Edgar White. Deschamps didn't want the reporters gawking at him while he slept. Orders were issued and Etienne Deschamps spent his last night in relative peace and quiet.

All preparations for the hanging were complete, the witnesses notified, and the gallows made ready. One of the last things done that night occurred just before midnight, when Hangman Taylor rechecked the rope that he had stretched and tallowed with animal fat, then shortened. There would be no repeat of the Baker hanging; Deschamps's execution was flawless.

Everyone assumed that Deschamps had left a considerable sum of money behind, but upon examination of his cell, all that White received was some old clothes, a plate picture, and two pairs of old, worn shoes. A thorough search of his cell, including his mattress, revealed nothing else, though Dr. LeMonnier remembered seeing a letter belonging to Deschamps that stated he had 2,000 francs in a bank in France. It was likely the same document that Deschamps had shared with Judge Roman at their first meeting three years before.

Even after Deschamps's death, Léona Queyrouze wasn't finished with the governor. Writing to him on May 13, she stated, "Deschamps is dead as you know. To the last moment I expected the contrary." And then for some odd reason, perhaps to satisfy herself that she had done all in her power to save the Frenchman, she asked Governor Nicholls if he had received her brother's brief and her letters of April 29, May 3, and May 11. She feared that they had been lost in the mail. More than likely they were discarded by the governor's secretary as unnecessary distractions during the closing days of the Nicholls administration.

Sometime around 3:00 P.M. on Friday, May 13, Dr. Havá received notification from Buisson that Deschamps had willed his body to him. The doctor had chosen not to be among the spectators within the prison walls to view the execution. He had arrived at the prison thinking he could perform the autopsy; instead, he was informed that the operation had already occurred. Furious, he refused to accept the mutilated corpse. What was the point?

At 3:30 P.M., Dr. Havá witnessed a group of people gathered at the front gates of the prison. Apparently unbeknownst to him, they were taking the body to Potter's Field for burial. At that point Dr. Havá was under the false impression that the interment would not occur until the following morning. Who claimed the body was a mystery to him, and he said so in a short note written to Léona Queyrouze at 4:30 P.M.

On Saturday morning, May 14, the *Daily Picayune* chronicled the gruesome details of Etienne Deschamps's execution, his abbreviated life story, his crime, and the legal maneuvers that followed. But Dr. Havá considered the article in the May 13 evening edition of the *Daily City Item* to be "the most correct and moderate of any published by our dailies." He did take the opportunity to write their editor to correct some misinformation about the autopsy published in his and other newspapers.

Printed in the *Daily City Item* on Sunday, Dr. Havá's letter let it be known that the autopsy performed by those "self-appointed authorities" at the prison violated Deschamps's will. He then informed the readership that he was notified of the will's directive after the fact and that he refused to accept the body post-autopsy for obvious reasons. "And, moreover, could I accept conscientiously, the legacy of a man whom I have always considered as insane and irresponsible, which opinion I still retain?" he wrote, trying to distance himself from Deschamps. To illustrate that point further, Dr. Havá also informed the readership that, contrary to what some newspapers printed, he was not at the prison at the time of the execution.

The news of the execution of Etienne Deschamps received not only city and state exposure but national coverage as well. From the *Los Angeles Herald* to the tinier markets within the spheres of the *Worthington Advance* in southwestern Minnesota and *The Fisherman and Farmer* in Edenton, North Carolina, the news of the Frenchman's crime and final punishment was printed. And then there was nothing; not even the location in Potter's Field where he was buried is known. He had committed a horrible crime and paid with his life for his actions. The memory of his life was all but forgotten as the years progressed, except for the occasional mention of his name and crime when another condemned man met a similar fate in the city. Etienne Deschamps was dead!

Epilogue

In Memoriam

I am at peace now.
Léona Queyrouze Barel, August 18, 1933

At 10:00 on Sunday morning, July 17, 1892, Fred Meyer, who owned a plantation below New Orleans, telephoned the *Daily Picayune* asking for a description of Judge Marr. About two hours before, he had found a body along a batture in front of the Mississippi River levee that ran along his property. For the past five to six weeks, the batture had been covered with muddy water from the swollen river, but with the river now receded, the ground beneath was visible. The decomposed body, five feet five inches tall with little left but the skeleton, was dressed in a dark suit, with size-eight shoes clinging to the feet. The face was unrecognizable and the corpse had no hair on its head. Meyer was able to retrieve a pair of silver spectacles and a little leather purse from inside the coat pocket. It was later determined not to be the body of the judge but of Christian Keller, a forty-nine-year-old man who went missing on June 27. A dental examination revealed that Keller was missing a considerable number of teeth (the judge was not), he wasn't the same height, and the clothing was all wrong. Judge Marr was wearing a black, double-breasted Prince Albert frock coat the day he disappeared.

Long before Meyer's discovery, on May 25, 1892, a resolution was offered in the Louisiana Senate to formulate a bill declaring the judge's seat vacant. The Senate Judiciary Committee was to consult with Gov. Murphy J. Foster and the attorney general on such a bill. The resolution passed the following day, but Governor Foster's eventual appointee, John H. Ferguson, did not assume the unexpired term of Judge Marr until June 30.

The mysterious and sudden disappearance of Judge Marr shook the entire city of New Orleans but especially his family and close friends, none more so than Rev. Dr. Benjamin M. Palmer, pastor of the First Presbyterian Church, which was located on Lafayette Square, a block from the courthouse. Judge

175

Marr was one of his parishioners. Dr. Palmer wrote an eloquent tribute to his memory, which the *Daily Picayune* reprinted on September 25.

Robert H. Marr was born on October 29, 1819, in Clarksville, Tennessee, of Scottish and English descent. His parents were Presbyterian, hence the judge's eventual connection with Dr. Palmer. Dr. Palmer greatly admired Judge Marr's "blending hereditary and somewhat opposing traits in a composite character" and claimed that the judge derived his caution, shrewdness, purpose, and strength of conviction from his paternal Scottish side. From his mother he acquired a "gentleness of manner, the tenderness of feeling, and that sweetness of courtesy which united in him the delicacy of the woman with the intellectual vigor of the man."

Graduating from the old University of Nashville in 1838, the same school his father attended, Marr was admitted to the bar in 1840 and opened his law office in Paducah, Kentucky, remaining there until autumn 1844. He relocated to Baton Rouge, Louisiana—Dr. Palmer did not say why—and then to New Orleans in early 1845. He would remain there for the next forty-seven years, except between 1863 and 1865 "when he was spilt out with so many others," a victim of the war.

On February 7, 1850, Judge Marr married Mary Elizabeth Jane Marr

Judge Robert H. Marr. (Portrait by Andres Molinary, courtesy the Louisiana Supreme Court)

of Tuscaloosa, Alabama, the same lineage as he, "though some degrees removed," according to Dr. Palmer. Their union lasted almost thirty-five years, until Mary's death on February 2, 1885. All told, the couple had seven children, three of whom died in infancy. The remaining four children included three girls and a son, Robert H. Marr, Jr., born in March 1860, who would be elected judge of the Fourth City Court in New Orleans in 1888. The Marr family joined Dr. Palmer's fellowship on August 6, 1872, and Judge Marr was a consistent member of the church over the next twenty years.

The only controversy to arise during his adult life, unrelated to the war, came in September 1874. Two years before, during the November 1872 gubernatorial election, William Pitt Kellogg, a Republican and former brigadier general in the Union Army, ran against John McEnery, a Democrat, former lieutenant colonel in the Louisiana Fourth Battalion, and brother of the future governor Samuel D. McEnery. The State Returning Board, which oversaw the election, declared McEnery the winner, but an opposing board declared that Kellogg had won. The dispute wasn't settled until September 1873, when President Grant issued an executive order declaring Kellogg the legal governor.

For many whites in the state, especially those who had sided with the former Confederacy and were members of the Democratic Party, the election was yet another example of the Republican-controlled federal government usurping the state's power. Corruption plagued the Kellogg administration and violence ensued on several occasions during his first two years in office.

By mid-September 1874, the festering wounds of that disputed election and the events that followed erupted into violence in the streets of New Orleans, the capital of Louisiana at that time. At 11:00 on the morning of September 14, Robert Marr, an attorney and president of the Committee of Seventy, read an address to a large gathering of New Orleanians standing outside Crescent Billiard Saloon, located on St. Charles Street at the corner of Canal Street. Affiliated with the Crescent City White League, men who sought to restore Democratic Party control over the state and remove Republican rule, Marr demanded Governor Kellogg's immediate resignation and the restoration of Governor McEnery's administration. Though not advocating violence to achieve his goal, Marr would not shy away from it if Kellogg chose not to resign.

Within hours of his speech, and Kellogg naturally refusing to step down, violence erupted in the streets between 5,000 White Leaguers and 3,500 police and state militia. The bedlam resulted in over a hundred casualties, including scores of men who were killed in the crossfire. Though the White League won the day, President Grant sent federal troops to the city three days later, erasing any gains made by the league. Kellogg remained governor until the election of Democratic candidate Francis Nicholls in 1876. Reconstruction ended the following year, with Louisiana, the last former Confederate state to be governed with Northern support.

Having been nominated by Governor Nicholls and confirmed by the Senate on January 9, 1877, Robert H. Marr assumed his place as associate justice on the Louisiana Supreme Court for the first time. Joining him was Alfred Roman, who had been appointed a clerk to the High Court. When a new state constitution was adopted in 1879, it vacated all public offices. Therefore, Judge Marr's tenure with the High Court ended in April 1880. When Nicholls was elected to his second, non-sequential term in 1888, he again appointed Judge Marr, this time to Orleans Parish Criminal District Court, Section A, where he served until his death.

In Dr. Palmer's words, "Judge Marr may truly be said to have been the soul of honor. He was, withal, simple in his tastes and habits . . . averse to all display, he withdrew from public gaze, never sunning himself in the applause of the outer world." He was a gentleman in every sense of the word. Judge Robert Harding Marr was seventy-two years old.

Within months of Judge Marr's death, Alfred Roman passed away from complications of a stroke, having suffered from hemiplegia in his last months. His death occurred at his home at 92 (now in the 800 block of) Esplanade Avenue (between Bourbon and Dauphine streets) on September 20, 1892. The funeral took place at his residence at 4:30 the following afternoon and was widely attended by a representative group of citizens, including his old military commander, Gen. P. G. T. Beauregard. Rev. Jean R. Ritter of St. Louis Cathedral performed his last rites, whereupon his "handsome casket," as described by the *Daily Picayune*, was taken by a carriage to St. Louis Cemetery No. 1 for interment. The Honorable Alfred Roman was sixty-eight years old.

Dr. John G. Havá was the next prominent figure in the Deschamps saga to pass away. He died at his home on January 15, 1894. His passing was not unexpected by his family and close friends. It was only after his considerable absence from city life that the general public learned that Dr. Havá was dying.

For some months prior to his death, Dr. Havá battled epithelioma of the mouth. "All that medical science and surgery could do to relieve the suffering man was done," according to the *Daily Picayune*, "but to no avail." The death certificate suggested that the tumor eroded a neighboring blood vessel. The term "hemorrhagic" was included in his cause of death.

Though it's not known if Dr. LeMonnier visited him during his final days, the doctor informed the *Daily Picayune* in November 1903 that Dr. Havá had written him a letter admitting that he had been right all along regarding the Frenchman's sanity. In spite of what some newspapers reported—that Dr. Havá died still believing Etienne Deschamps was insane—Dr. LeMonnier told the *Daily Picayune* that after much reflection, Dr. Havá had come to realize that that was not the case. Dr. LeMonnier promised to deliver the Havá letter, written in French, to the newspaper when he located it. Apparently the letter was never found, so one can only trust the man's word that Dr. Havá wrote what he said.

Dr. Havá's funeral took place at the family residence at 252 (now in the 1000 block of) Burgundy Street (between St. Philip and Ursuline [now Ursulines] streets) at 3:00 P.M. on the day following his death. Survived by his wife and three sons, Dr. Juan (John) G. Havá was sixty years old.

James Dowling, Deschamps's first defense attorney, died from influenza at his home at 4126 Magazine Street at noon on February 11, 1896. During the previous spring, he had been stricken by an undisclosed illness that prevented him from performing his duties as a lawyer. Whatever the root cause, Dowling was able to resume his practice later that year, though he remained in poor health for several months prior to his death, according to a newspaper report. By February he was in the midst of representing another accused murderer at trial when he was stricken with pneumonia.

Dowling was born in the city in 1867, the eldest child of Thomas Dowling and Mary F. McAuley, both natives of Ireland. In 1888, at the age of twenty-one, he was admitted to the bar and was able to establish an excellent legal practice over the next eight years, undoubtedly helped by his exposure to the Deschamps case. For a time he also served as an assistant recorder for the Third Recorder's Court.

With the Deschamps saga behind him—a career footnote for him—the learned counsel married twenty-eight-year-old Cecile Martin on December 20, 1893. Their marriage lasted a scant twenty-six months before his untimely death. Dowling's funeral took place at St. Stephen's Catholic Church at 4:00 P.M. on February 12. Survived by his parents and wife—Cecile never remarried and died in December 1961—James J. Dowling was twenty-eight years old.

Charles Luzenberg, the district attorney who prosecuted Deschamps twice, died at his home at 4691 North Peters Street at the corner of Jourdan Avenue on July 20, 1897, from complications of a stroke he suffered on May

5. (That portion of North Peters Street no longer exists, due to a change in topography.) The ischemic attack initially left him with only partial paralysis of his left side, with his mental abilities and speech unimpaired, though his disability rendered him bedridden. But as the days and weeks passed, his conditioned worsened until he lapsed into unconsciousness five days before his death. His official cause of death was listed as "cerebral apoplexy [an archaic term for stroke] causing softening of the brain."

Luzenberg was born in the city on June 20, 1837, the only child of Charles A. Luzenberg, a prominent physician, and Mary Clement. After being schooled in New Orleans, Luzenberg attended Princeton University, where he earned a bachelor of arts degree. He then transferred to Yale University, where he earned his master's degree in 1857. Just prior to the Civil War, Luzenberg was awarded a law degree at the University of Louisiana in New Orleans.

With the war raging, Luzenberg enlisted in the Thirteenth Louisiana Infantry on September 11, 1861. Like so many other participants in this story, he fought at the Battle of Shiloh for the Confederacy. As a second lieutenant and acting adjutant, Luzenberg bore the regimental colors in battle, "never for a moment [letting] go his hold of the staff of the colors and through all the long hours of Sunday and Monday, from daylight until

Charles H. Luzenberg. (Courtesy NOLA. com/The *Times-Picayune*)

dark through successful charges and disastrous repulses, kept it aloft at the rallying point of the regiment," as noted in a *Daily Picayune* tribute to the man. By October 1862, the remnants of the old regiment were joined with what remained of the Twentieth Louisiana Regiment to form the Thirteenth and Twentieth Consolidated Regiment, with Luzenberg fighting at the Battle of Murfreesboro in December 1862-January 1863. Promoted to captain, Luzenberg was seriously wounded at the Battle of Chickamauga in September 1863, which ended his battlefield experiences. He spent the rest of the war detailed to the Mobile (Alabama) Ordnance Department.

Returning to New Orleans after the war, Luzenberg opened his law practice and soon entered politics. He was elected for two terms as district attorney of Orleans Parish during the late 1860s and early 1870s. In 1880, Gov. Louis Wiltz appointed him judge of Section B, Orleans Parish Criminal District Court, a seat he occupied until he resigned in 1883 to resume his law practice. He was elected district attorney again in 1888 for Orleans Parish, serving honorably until May 1892.

In February 1864, Luzenberg married Alabama native Anna Rebecca Chandler and they would have four sons, though the youngest, John Henry, died of congestive fever (malaria) at six months of age. Anna passed away from postpartum complications on November 25, 1869, six months before John's death and twelve days after his delivery. Luzenberg would be remarried by the time of his death.

For many years, Luzenberg served as a member of the Louisiana Division of the Benevolent Association of the Army of Tennessee, a Confederate veteran's organization that was founded in New Orleans in May 1877. He was serving as its president at the time of his death. He was also on the board of directors of the Soldiers' Home of Louisiana, later referred to as Camp Nicholls, an infirmary located on Bayou St. John at the head of Esplanade Avenue. Established in 1866 by an act of the state legislature, the facility took care of the state's war-maimed and disabled Confederate veterans. At the time of his death, Luzenberg was a prominent member of Louisiana Lodge No. 102 Free and Accepted Masons.

Luzenberg's funeral took place at his home at 3:00 P.M. on July 21, 1897. His interment was in Lafayette Cemetery No. 1. Judge Charles Henry Luzenberg was sixty years old.

Elizabeth "Lizzie" Hilroy, Etienne Deschamps's widowed landlady, died on October 27, 1899, from chronic hepatitis, still residing at the St. Peter Street property. Elizabeth Bastian (or Basten) was born circa 1834 in what would later become Germany. Her history is unclear, but she may have arrived in New Orleans aboard the *Moses Taylor* from Le Havre, France, in November 1854. At some point, she married a gentleman by the name of Bachthallor; what became of him is unknown. Lizzie was remarried in the city on April 12, 1875, to Joseph Hilroy, a painter who died about eleven years later. His last listing in the city directory appeared in 1886. By 1888, his widow's name, Lizzie Hilroy, began appearing in the city directory, residing at 64 St. Peter Street. Elizabeth Hilroy was sixty-five years old at her passing.

Lemuel "Lem" Davis, who served as captain and warden of Orleans Parish Prison during Deschamps's incarceration, died at his home at 641 Congress Street of relapsing pneumonia on February 21, 1901. By then, he had all but disappeared from the public's eye.

Davis was born in the city on January 15, 1858, one of two children of James Davis, a native of Sweden, though Lem believed his father was born in Scotland; his mother, Bedelia J., was from New York. His father died when Lem was two years old and his mother passed away from an unspecified pulmonary disease, likely tuberculosis, on October 9, 1869, at age thirty-five. Lem's schooling was put aside at that latter point and he was compelled to enter the workforce at an early age. Taking an assortment of jobs to make ends meet, he first worked as a messenger boy, then a laborer, and finally a

Capt. Lemuel "Lem" Davis. (The Illustrated American, April 1891)

news dealer and paper carrier, a job he held during the early 1880s. At twenty-five years old, he joined the New Orleans police, serving as a court officer for the Second Recorder's Court. By 1885, he was promoted to sergeant, working his way up to captain by 1888. In June of that year, Sheriff Gabriel Villeré appointed him as the warden of Orleans Parish Prison, a position he held until June 1892, when Villeré's term expired. Villeré's successor did not reappoint Davis. In 1878, Davis married Jane McLaughlin, a New Orleanian whose parents were natives of Ireland. That union produced six children, one of whom died at an early age.

Davis left the police force in the summer of 1892 and operated various saloons in the city until his passing. He apparently failed at this endeavor, although that was likely related to his declining health. At the time of his death, he had "dwindled away from a splendid specimen of manhood to a mere living skeleton," the *Daily City Item* reported. He undoubtedly had other diseases underlying his chronic pneumonia. Like his mother, Lem may have developed a pulmonary anomaly. He left behind a wife and five children, the youngest an eleven-year-old boy. Lemuel J. Davis was forty-three years old.

Walter Rogers followed Lem Davis in death, passing away quietly at his home at 1724 Canal Street on Monday, April 16, 1906. (His home was later demolished. The property is now commercial real estate.) For the last three weeks of his life, he had battled pneumonia, with acute pleurisy exacerbating his condition. Antibiotics that could have saved his life, such as penicillin, were yet to be discovered.

Walter H. Rogers was born in New Orleans on October 12, 1843. His parents were natives of Ireland who settled in the city during the early 1800s. His father, Wynne Grey Rogers, became a prominent merchant, and his mother, Jane Eastman Carter, a loving caregiver.

Rogers was schooled in New Orleans, graduating from Boys' High School in 1860. In the spring of 1861, he planned to attend the University of Virginia, but Louisiana was organizing an army by then. Therefore, on April 11—less than twenty-four hours before the first shots were fired at Fort Sumter, South Carolina—Rogers enlisted for twelve months as a private in the Orleans Cadets, the first volunteer company mustered into the war from the state. Initially commanded by Capt. Charles D. Dreux, who was later promoted to lieutenant colonel, the Orleans Cadets were shipped off to Pensacola, Florida, and later incorporated into Dreux's First Louisiana Battalion as Company F.

From Florida, Rogers was sent to a camp in Richmond, Virginia,

Walter H. Rogers. (Courtesy NOLA.com/
The *Times-Picayune*)

transferring thereafter to the garrison defending Yorktown. When Dreux was killed on July 5 in a skirmish near Newport News, Maj. N. H. Rightor was promoted and assumed command of the battalion. Rogers remained in Virginia and fought during the early days of the 1862 Peninsula Campaign, serving beyond the expiration of his enlistment. Rightor's battalion finally disbanded on May 1, after Gen. Joseph Johnston's retreat to Richmond.

Many of the former battalion members, including Rogers, joined Charles Fenner's battery when it mustered into Confederate service in mid-May 1862. (Fenner was the former commander of Company A, "Louisiana Guards," in Rightor's old battalion.) The battery saw action in Mississippi, Georgia, and Tennessee. At some point during Rogers' service, he was attached to the Military Court and, by war's end, surrendered himself at Meridian, Mississippi, in mid-May 1865. He left the battlefield "with the highest honors to which the soldier who had done his full duty is entitled," according to a feature story about Rogers' life and passing that appeared in the *Daily Picayune*.

After the war, Rogers returned to New Orleans to study law, graduating from the University of Louisiana in 1866. One year later, he married twenty-four-year-old Elizabeth Goelet of Buncombe Hall, North Carolina, and from that union had three daughters. Over the years he became a highly respected attorney. Early in his career, Rogers was drawn into state politics, serving as a representative from Orleans Parish.

Like Judge Marr, Rogers was an outspoken critic of Reconstruction and was in the forefront when the Crescent City White League was organized. On September 14, 1874, he served as a lieutenant in one of the companies that battled with the Metropolitan Police and state militia.

In November 1876, Rogers was elected judge of the Fifth District Court of Orleans Parish, serving until 1880, when he was elected to the Louisiana State Court of Appeal. He resigned in May 1884 to resume his law practice and for a time served as city attorney beginning that summer. Four years later, he worked tirelessly as the chairman of the Campaign Executive Committee for the election of Governor Nicholls. His efforts were recognized when Nicholls appointed him attorney general in 1888, his term lasting until mid-May 1892.

Judge Rogers' body lay in state in the parlor of his home from Monday night until Wednesday morning, with hundreds of people paying their final respects over that thirty-six-hour period. His funeral took place at Grace Episcopal Church on South Rampart Street, with his body interred in the Tomb of the Army of Tennessee in Metairie Cemetery. Among the pallbearers was his former commanding officer and retired Louisiana Supreme Court Justice Charles E. Fenner. The late jurist and attorney general was survived by his wife and three daughters. The Honorable Walter Henry Rogers was sixty-two years old.

Sheriff Gabriel Villeré died of acute dysentery at his home at 2309 Columbus Street on September 17, 1907. He came from a long line of French and Louisiana dignitaries. His great-grandfather Jacques Phillippe Villeré served as the general of the Louisiana militia during the War of 1812 and later became the second governor of Louisiana under United States authority. His plantation, located approximately ten miles below New Orleans at Chalmette, was the site of the climactic Battle of New Orleans. It was General Villeré's son and Sheriff Villeré's grandfather and namesake, Major Gabriel Villeré, who warned Gen. Andrew Jackson of the British Army's location below Chalmette in late December 1814.

Though he lived most of his adult life in New Orleans, Gabriel Villeré was born in neighboring St. Bernard Parish on November 27, 1851. Prior to assuming his position as the Orleans Parish criminal sheriff in 1888, a position he held until May 1892, Villeré was actively engaged in commercial affairs in the city. In 1877 he married twenty-two-year-old Uranie P. Lewis and that union produced eight children. After leaving office, Villeré worked as an agent for Charles B. Slack & Company, a coal and coke distributing enterprise located on Carondelet Street. For the last six years of his life, he

Orleans Parish Criminal Sheriff Gabriel Villeré. (The Illustrated American, April 1891)

worked for Menard Brothers, a wine and liquors wholesale business located on Conti Street.

The *Daily Picayune* wrote, "He was generous to a fault, and was never known to have refused a request for aid at any time in his life and was one of sterling worth and strong character." Villeré was buried in St. Louis Cemetery No. 1. Survived by his wife—she died in 1954—and three children, Gabriel Phillip Villeré was fifty-five years old.

Neil L. Nelson died of tuberculosis on May 20, 1909, in Covington, Louisiana. Though he was not a participant in the Deschamps saga, he was somewhat connected through his wife's murder and the execution of Philip Baker, Deschamps's nearby cellmate.

Initially, practically everyone who knew Nelson was concerned that the blow Baker administered to his head would render him permanently disabled or worse. However, he made a full recovery and later testified against Baker at his trial. On June 6, 1894, he married Laura's younger sister, Catherine "Katie" Frank, and the couple would have four children.

In spite of the tragedy that befell him on March 7, 1891, Nelson continued to operate his grocery on Washington (now Fern) Street in Carrollton until as late as 1907, when his health began to fail. Business partners Frederick

T. Bosworth and Percy Backes assumed ownership of the grocery. Forced into an early retirement due to his pulmonary disease, Nelson moved his family north across the lake to Covington, where he presumably believed the climate was more hospitable toward his condition.

Nelson's body was returned to New Orleans on May 21. His funeral took place at 3:00 the following afternoon at 3710 Constance Street, the home of his widowed mother-in-law, Carrie Frank. He was later laid to rest in Greenwood Cemetery. Survived by his wife and children, Neil L. Nelson was forty-three years old.

The two-story corner house and grocery at Fern and Hampson streets was demolished years ago. It was replaced by a brick home that was demolished in 2012 and superseded by a New Orleans-style, two-story house. Its front entrance now faces Hampson Street.

Oddly, Jacob Baker, Philip's only sibling and older brother, continued to reside diagonally across the street from Neil Nelson. Staunchly believing his brother was innocent, Jacob remained in the neighborhood with his family (he married on November 4, 1890) until relocating elsewhere in Carrollton sometime between 1896 and 1898. Baker died of carcinoma of the larynx and trachea on February 28, 1919, at his home at 1736 Cambronne Street. (That address and presumably the house no longer exist.) Survived by his wife, Annie Harmeyer Baker, and four of his seven children, Jacob Baker, Jr., was fifty-six years old.

Lt. Gov. James Jeffries died of heart failure on January 18, 1910, at his home at 851 Jordon Street in Shreveport. (His house was long ago demolished. The property is now commercial real estate.) Jeffries had a thirty-year history of mitral regurgitation, his official cause of death, which was exacerbated by a ten-day bout of pneumonia prior to his passing.

Jeffries was born in Kentucky on October 3, 1836, to James Jeffries, Sr., and Rebecca Eubank, both natives of Virginia. He was raised in Texas, probably moving there as an infant. His parents were undoubtedly interested in the newly established Republic of Texas. On July 27, 1859, he married Annie J. Munson, a native of Mississippi, in Washington County, Texas, and from that union had one child, Annie, who was born on May 22, 1861. Tragically, Annie, who was only twenty-one years old at the time, died four days later, probably due to postpartum complications. She was buried in Cameron Pioneer Cemetery in Cameron, the small East Texas town where she undoubtedly gave birth to her daughter.

Jeffries became a lawyer and eventually partnered with Thomas Neville

Lt. Gov. James J. Jeffries. (Courtesy NOLA. com/The *Times-Picayune*)

Waul, his senior by seventeen years. During the Civil War, Waul commanded the famed Waul's Texas Legion, initially attached to the Department of Mississippi and East Louisiana fighting in the Vicksburg Campaign. After Vicksburg fell in July 1863, Waul was eventually exchanged, promoted to brigadier general, and returned to Texas. In the meantime, Jeffries served as a private in Company F, Eighth Texas Infantry (also known as the Twelfth Texas Infantry). The regiment was organized in May 1862 and defended various Texas coastal cities before it transferred to East Texas in December 1863. By the spring of 1864, Jeffries' regiment was part of Waul's brigade, John G. Walker's Division, which participated in the Red River Campaign, seeing action at Mansfield and Pleasant Hill in April 1864. Jeffries served as a staff officer under Waul and was later promoted to command Walker's Division. Later in his life, Louisiana newspapers would often refer to him as Captain or Colonel Jeffries.

After the war, Jeffries and his daughter, Annie, moved to central Louisiana, where they settled in Rapides Parish in and around the Alexandria area. There Jeffries met thirty-year-old Mary Elizabeth "Lillie" Mead, and they married on July 27, 1865. The couple had one child, who died prior to 1880. Living in Rigolette near Pineville by June 1880, the Jeffries family eventually moved across the Red River just west of Alexandria to Rapides, his designated hometown while he served as lieutenant governor. In Alexandria, Jeffries established a law practice with J. R. Thornton; they remained partners for many years and their friendship lasted until Jeffries' passing. Thornton, a judge by the time of Jeffries' death, held his old friend in his arms when he took his last breath. By then, James and Lillie Jeffries were living in Shreveport, where Annie and her husband, E. H. Randolph, resided.

The law was not Jeffries' only vocation. Farming became very much a part of his life; it was listed as his sole occupation by the time of the 1880 U.S. census. In April 1875, he was elected as one of thirteen directors of the Rapides [Parish] Agricultural Fair Association.

Jeffries entered state politics during the latter turbulent years of Reconstruction; he represented Rapides Parish in the state legislature for two terms during the mid-1870s. In January 1876 he was elected chairman of the House Committee of Ways and Means. In April 1888 he was elected lieutenant governor and served one term during the Nicholls administration. As part of his state constitutional duties, he served as president of the Senate.

Though he was out of office by the summer of 1892, Jeffries continued to dabble in state and national politics. In August 1892, he was appointed to the National Democratic Executive Committee, which basically picked the sites of the Democratic Party conventions that were held every four years. During the 1890s, he served as the chairman of the Democratic Executive Committee of Rapides Parish.

Two days after Jeffries' death, his funeral was conducted at his home with members of the General Leroy Stafford Camp #3, United Confederate Veterans, attending. The lieutenant governor was a member. Described as simple, the services were conducted by Rev. Claude L. Jones, pastor of the First Christian Church, and Rev. J. K. Smith, pastor of the First Presbyterian Church. Out of respect for the former lieutenant governor, who for many years had practiced law across the state, municipal and state courts adjourned that day. Survived by his wife, who lived until 1924 (his daughter died in October 1907), Jeffries was laid to rest in Greenwood Cemetery in Shreveport. On his tombstone is written: *A Believer in Christ / A Confederate Soldier.* James J. Jeffries was seventy-nine years old.

Governor Nicholls followed Jeffries in death two years later. At his home, Ridgefield Plantation, located on the western outskirts of Thibodaux, the former general, governor, and jurist quietly passed away on Thursday, January 4, 1912. His death had been expected, as he had been confined to bed since the previous Saturday. He had contracted a bad cold that quickly turned into pneumonia, resulting in heart failure. "Seldom had it come to pass that any single man has ever been so tried as was Francis [Redding] Tillou Nicholls," Judge Taylor Beattie of Thibodaux wrote.

Nicholls was born on August 20, 1834, in Donaldsonville, Louisiana, the son of Thomas C. Nicholls and Louisa Hanna Drake. His initial education came at Jefferson Academy in New Orleans. Wanting to be a soldier, Nicholls received an appointment to West Point in 1851, graduating in 1855, whereupon he was assigned duty at Fort Myers, Florida, and later at Fort Yuma, California, located along the Arizona Territory border. Failing health, hardships experienced while living in such rugged terrain, and homesickness caused him to resign his commission the following year. He eventually entered the University of Louisiana and began to study law in 1857. After one year, Nicholls easily passed the bar examination and began practicing law in his hometown. He eventually entered into a partnership with his older brother, Lawrence, and a friend. Lawrence handled clients in Donaldsonville, while Francis and the third partner directed their energies toward acquiring business contacts south of town along Bayou Lafourche. Nicholls set up his law office in Napoleonville. On April 26, 1860, he married Caroline Zilpha Guion of Thibodaux; her father owned Ridgefield Plantation. The couple had seven children.

Gov. Francis R. T. Nicholls. (Courtesy NOLA.com/The *Times-Picayune*)

When the war broke out, Nicholls became the captain of the Phoenix Guard, a company organized in his hometown. It was eventually incorporated into the Eighth Louisiana Infantry, and he served as its lieutenant colonel. The regiment served as a reserve unit guarding supplies during the Battle of First Manassas or Bull Run in July 1861. It later saw action as part of "Stonewall" Jackson's army during the Shenandoah Valley Campaign, where Nicholls lost his left arm during the Battle of Winchester on May 25, 1862. Captured at the battle by the Federals, Nicholls was later exchanged and elected colonel of the newly organized Fifteenth Louisiana Infantry. Before assuming command, however, on October 14, 1862, he was promoted to brigadier general. On January 16, 1863, he was assigned command of the Second Louisiana Brigade, Colston's Division, Jackson's Second Corps. As Nicholls fought in May at the Battle of Chancellorsville, a solid shot blew off his left foot and killed his horse. An ambulance crew saw him unconscious on the ground but, noticing that he was also missing his left arm, assumed he was dead and passed him by. His men later found him and brought him to a field hospital.

After losing a part of his left leg and arm, Nicholls was disqualified from further battlefield service. In 1864, he was assigned to desk duties as the commander in Lynchburg, Virginia, a post he held until he transferred to the Trans-Mississippi Department in December. From then until the war's close, he served as the superintendent of the Bureau of Conscription headquartered in Shreveport.

Nicholls resumed his law practice in Napoleonville after the war and by the mid-1870s was drawn into state politics. He was elected governor in 1876 in a bitter contest, which saw dual governorships in January 1877 until federal authorities recognized Nicholls as the legitimate governor of the state. His four-year term of office was cut short by a year when the 1879 State Constitution was ratified. He declined to run again in 1880. He was reelected governor in April 1888, pledging to end the corrupt Louisiana Lottery, and he served until May 1892. Governor Foster then appointed Nicholls as the chief justice of the Louisiana Supreme Court, with the Senate confirming his twelve-year term on May 24, 1892. When the State Constitution was amended in 1890, which required Supreme Court justices to be elected, Nicholls ran in 1904 and was elected as an associate justice of the High Court. He held that position until 1911, when he was forced to retire due to a service clause in the Constitution.

Dividing his time between New Orleans and Thibodaux for the bulk of his court years, Nicholls settled in Thibodaux after his retirement, residing at Ridgefield Plantation until his death. His funeral service took place at 11:00 A.M. on January 6 at St. John's Episcopal Church in town, and hundreds of people came to pay their final respects. He was later entombed in the church cemetery.

At 4:00 the following afternoon in Donaldsonville, townspeople; other citizens from Ascension Parish; a delegation from Major Victor Maurin Camp #38, United Confederate Veterans; and nearly every member of the bar from the Twenty-Seventh Louisiana Judicial District crowded into Judge Paul Leche's courtroom. Their purpose was to honor the memory of their favorite son. In spite of a driving rain that commenced shortly before the ceremony, the courtroom was filled to capacity. Judge Taylor Beattie of Thibodaux was to deliver the eulogy but at the last moment was unable to attend. His prepared text was read by Walter Lemann, a local attorney. Beattie's closing words spoke volumes about the man: "His sacrifices in the field, as his unmaimed character, enforced his policy in the cabinet; who rendered to public inestimable service by showing that a man can fill political office and leave it without a stain." Survived by his wife and six of his children, former general, governor, and jurist Francis Redding Tillou Nicholls was seventy-seven years old.

Fr. Louis LeBlanc, who attended to the spiritual needs of Philip Baker and Etienne Deschamps, died of chronic myocarditis on March 17, 1913, on the campus of Loyola University in New Orleans. He suffered from a long history of rheumatism, which led to heart failure that confined him to his bed for the last two weeks of his life.

Louis LeBlanc was born on October 11, 1846, near Montreal, Canada, and entered the priesthood on August 15, 1883. His uncle was credited with building Mary, Queen of the World Cathedral in Montreal, a smaller version of St. Peter's Basilica in Rome, though he died before the project was finished.

As a Jesuit priest, Father LeBlanc immigrated to the United States in 1885. His first assignment took him to Tampa, Florida, then farther south along the Gulf Coast to the Ten Thousand Islands region of the state, near the western edge of the Everglades. His stay in that semitropical region was short-lived due to ill health, probably the beginning of his rheumatism. He was then transferred to New Orleans and later to Shreveport but would return to Florida on numerous occasions over the next twenty-eight years, especially during the last eight years of his life. In his later years, wishing to better serve Cuban immigrants in the Tampa area, Father LeBlanc learned to speak

Fr. Louis LeBlanc, S.J. (Courtesy NOLA.
com/The *Times-Picayune*)

Spanish. For a time while living in New Orleans between 1906 and 1908, he taught at Jesuits' College. During his last two years he taught French at Loyola University.

Father LeBlanc was also the chaplain for the school and Holy Rosary Convent on St. Charles Avenue. At the time of his death, he was the assistant pastor of Church of the Holy Name of Jesus on the Loyola campus.

On March 18, his body lay in state at Holy Name of Jesus; a requiem Mass was held at 9:30 A.M. His body was transported the following day to Spring Hill College in Mobile for burial. The Reverend Louis LeBlanc, S.J., was sixty-six years old.

John Journeè, the captain of the Third Precinct police station who responded to the Dietsh murder, died from complications of a stroke, hypertension, and chronic nephritis at his home at 926 North Carrollton Avenue during the early-morning hours on November 15, 1927. The night before, he had attended a meeting of the Fireman's Charitable and Benevolent Association, for which he served as secretary treasurer. He suffered the fatal cerebral hemorrhage several hours later.

John Journeè was born in January 1854 in New Orleans. Too young to fight in the war, he took a position as an apprentice in a carpenter and joiner's shop while attending a private school at night. By the war's end, he had become a master carpenter and joiner who specialized in furniture making. Like Judge Rogers, Journeè led a squad of men against the Metropolitan Police and state militia in September 1874, and his name would become well known in the city. In 1877, when carpentry could no longer support him, Journeè asked Mayor Edward Pilsbury for a job as a police officer. Pilsbury knew of Journeè's courage under fire and gave him a commission on the force. Six years later, Captain Journeè married eighteen-year-old Amelia Avalard and from that union had two children.

Over the years, Journeè's popularity with the police force and his ability to get things done earned him praise from everyone in city government. He served as Police Superintendent David Hennessy's alternate during his official absences and planned vacations. When Hennessy was assassinated in 1890, Mayor Joseph A. Shakespeare appointed Journeè as temporary head of the police; by that time, he was the senior captain on the force.

Jumping into the political ring in 1892, Journeè placed his name in nomination for superintendent of police, but he didn't make it through the caucus vote. He was eventually elected in 1901 and served as the top law-enforcement officer in New Orleans until 1905. Besides being affiliated with the Fireman's Association, Journeè was a member of the Elks Club and Knights of Pythias beneficial societies.

Chief Journeè's vigil began at 6:00 P.M. on the day of his death, his body lying in state at the Elks Club on South Saratoga Street until the funeral the following day at 3:30 P.M. His body was then taken by a police escort to Greenwood Cemetery. Survived by a son (his wife died in September 1922), former captain and superintendent of police John D. Journeè was seventy-three years old.

At his office on June 1, 1892, Dr. Yves R. LeMonnier wholeheartedly greeted the newly elected coroner of Orleans Parish, Dr. Charles L. Seemann, and presented his commission from Governor Foster. After orienting him to his duties, Dr. LeMonnier resumed his life as a surgeon and farmer. He divided his time between New Orleans and his farm, appropriately named "Shiloh" for his Tennessee war experience and as a place of peace and respite. It was located a few miles south of Amite City, Louisiana, in Tangipahoa Parish, along the old Illinois Central Railroad. In August 1892, Dr. LeMonnier became a founding member of the Fruit and Vegetable Association in Amite City.

When not at his farm he ran a private practice out of his home at 273 (now 1129) North Rampart Street; served as house surgeon of the Soldiers' Home of Louisiana; volunteered as a member of the Games Commission at Jesuits' College, a sporting organization at the school; and served as member and later an officer of the Benevolent Association of the Army of Tennessee.

In April 1896, Dr. LeMonnier was reelected coroner of Orleans Parish, in which capacity he would serve until June 1900. After leaving the coroner's office a final time, Dr. LeMonnier retired to his farm with his wife, Marie. He returned to the city when she died in April 1906.

Dr. LeMonnier passed away at his residence at 1224 North Galvez Street on January 14, 1928, after a long history of heart disease, specifically arteriosclerosis and angina pectoris. Funeral services were held the following day at 3 P.M. at St. Ann's Episcopal Church, with interment at St. Louis Cemetery No. 3 on Esplanade Avenue near Bayou St. John. No immediate family members survived him. Dr. Yves René LeMonnier was eighty-four years old.

Léona Queyrouze died at her home at 1448 North Villere Street on January 3, 1938, from heart failure brought on by a long history of cardiac valvular disease, cardiac dilatation, and arteriosclerosis. (Léona's side of the street is now part of McDonogh 35 Senior High School.) By the time of her death, she had also lost most of her vision.

On December 26, 1901, she married widower Pierre Marie Etienne Barel at St. Mary's Catholic Church in the city. The marriage was later described by others as one of convenience for both parties. Barel, a carpenter and contractor by trade, was born on February 27, 1850, in Saffré in the Loire-Inférieure (now Loire-Atlantique) Department in western France and came to the United States in 1876. Settling in New Orleans, Barel married Marie Julia Juilliat, also a native of France, on May 29, 1876. They had at least one child, Eugénie, who was born in the city in September 1879. She died at an early age, followed by Barel's wife, who passed away on November 26, 1898, from a stroke at age forty-three. At that time, the couple resided at 421 Exchange Alley or Place. (That portion of the street no longer exists. It was incorporated into the property borders of the present-day Louisiana Supreme Court complex.)

Sometime after Barel's arrival in the city, before or after his wife's death, he befriended the Queyrouze family, who resided near his home at 17 (now 525) St. Louis Street. By 1901 he was lonely and Léona was available, though she was eleven years his junior, and they married. Barel passed away on November 23, 1913, from glomerulonephritis and massive generalized edema and was interred in St. Louis Cemetery No. 3. He was sixty-three years old.

Prior to her marriage, the only gentleman in Miss Queyrouze's life of any substantial emotional worth was Lafcadio Hearn, who, during the late 1880s, worked briefly for the *Daily City Item* and *Times-Democrat*. During his lifetime (he passed away in 1904 at age fifty-four), he was a noted journalist, author, educator, and translator. Hearn was drawn to Léona and she to him, as they shared an interest in literature and poetry. She likely would have married him had he asked. He did not, and he left the city for Japan before the Deschamps saga began.

In August 1933, Léona published *The Idyl: My Personal Reminiscences of Lafcadio Hearn*, the manuscript she patiently worked on for ten years. "I am at peace now," she told a reporter with the *Times-Picayune*. "I wanted to do this for him. I have been almost blind and ill so much of the time, but I can be content now." She died four and a half years later.

Léona's funeral took place at her residence, with a requiem Mass held at St. Augustine Catholic Church on St. Claude Avenue (that portion of the avenue is now Henriette Delille Street) at the corner of Governor Nicholls Street. Her body was interred at St. Louis Cemetery No. 3. Marie Léona Queyrouze Barel was seventy-six years old.

Léona's brother, J. Maximé Queyrouze, was the last of the major Deschamps participants to die. On August 11, 1952, he suddenly passed away at his home at 3104 De Soto Street, twenty minutes after suffering a coronary artery thrombosis. He had a history of arteriosclerotic heart disease and generalized arteriosclerosis. At the time of his death, he lived with his only surviving child, Harold J. Queyrouze, a Marine Corps veteran, and Harold's wife, Rebecca Marie Weinberg. Harold was employed as a traveling automotive-parts salesman, but he passed away a few months after his father's death while on a business trip in Lafayette. Like his father, Harold suffered a coronary thrombosis and died on November 18, ten minutes after his first symptoms. Undoubtedly, coronary artery disease ran in the family. Harold was forty-three years old.

The elder Queyrouze was born in New Orleans on November 27, 1866. Married three times and three times a widower, he had two children with his first wife, Marie Adele Sorio, whom he wed on April 23, 1902. His son, Harold, once remarked that one of his father's favorite sayings was: "I don't know which is the mightiest, the pen or the sword. Both have served me well." Like his sister, Léona, J. Maximé was an avid fencer who won the Southern Fencing Championship as a young man. As a well-respected attorney in the city, he wielded a pen with much success.

Queyrouze's funeral took place at his residence at 9:45 A.M. on August 12, with a requiem Mass held thereafter at Our Lady of Most Holy Rosary Church. His was interred in St. Louis Cemetery No. 3. Jacques "J." Maximé Queyrouze was eighty-five years old.

A month after Queyrouze's death, his son began the laborious task of going through a lifetime's worth of his father's personal effects, which had been stored at their home. A tattered and seemingly worthless cloak discovered among his father's belongings was quickly tossed into the trashcan. Harold learned later after reading an old newspaper clipping that it had been a gift from Napoleon to Simon Queyrouze, Harold's great-grandfather, as a token of affection to a fellow officer in exile.

Among the various other items discovered were the correspondences of Léona Queyrouze, including those referenced in this book, and her unpublished manuscript about the life of Paul Morphy, a New Orleanian and friend of the family who was considered one of the greatest chess masters of his era. The chessboard and pieces that Morphy used to learn the game were among Queyrouze's personal effects.

What became of Jules Dietsh and his younger daughter, Laurence, is a mystery. There is no record of a death certificate filed for either one in the Louisiana State Archives in Baton Rouge. Jules' name and occupation—either carpenter or cabinetmaker, depending upon the year—continued to appear in the *Soards' New Orleans City Directory* through 1898. Then there was nothing. He and his daughter, who would have turned nineteen on November 23, 1898, seemed to have vanished from the city and the state. In addition, if Laurence married, it likely didn't occur in Louisiana, as there is no marriage certificate with her maiden name on file in the state archives, nor does Orleans Parish have any such record, assuming she stayed in the parish.

The fate of Charles Serra, Deschamps's next-door neighbor, is likewise unknown, though it appears at the very least he lost his ability to earn a living as a night watchman. It seems a woman's scorn cost him dearly.

Serra had been a much-respected watchman for at least a couple of years prior to the Dietsh murder. He and his business partner, William Sears, had contracts with a number of business establishments in the French Quarter, which they patrolled each night. On April 21, 1887, Captain Price, a riverboat captain by all appearances and "a resident of Bayou Lafourche," seemed to have gone on a spending spree while in the city and had somehow made the acquaintance of Serra and Sears, who escorted him back to his room at the close of his festivities. The following morning, Price discovered that he was missing four $100 bills. He complained to police that he had been robbed. Obviously, some suspicion was cast upon the watchmen, but without proof, nothing could be done. A year later, the lottery office on Royal Street, between Conti and St. Louis streets, was robbed of money, jewelry, and other valuable papers valued at over $400. The place was one of the businesses patrolled by Serra and Sears. Again, nothing came of it.

During this time, Sears was seeing an unidentified young lady who happened to be living at 64 St. Peter Street under the watchful eye of Elizabeth Hilroy. For whatever reason, he ended the relationship and married someone else in early December 1889. On December 13, the scorned female took revenge by informing Chief Hennessy that Sears and Serra had indeed robbed Captain Price of his money and that Hilroy had made change for the four stolen $100 bills.

When questioned by the chief of police, Serra admitted that he found the money, implying it wasn't stolen, and was going to return it to Captain Price the next day but felt ashamed for not acting sooner. He ended up not returning it and gave Sears $100 to keep quiet. Both parties denied any knowledge of the lottery robbery.

Chief Hennessy later learned that, upon his return to Bayou Lafourche, Captain Price had committed suicide over the loss of his money. With that known, any possibility of criminal prosecution of Serra and Sears was put to rest, though both men lost their contracts as private watchmen.

◻ ◻ ◻

The demise of young Juliette Dietsh was not the first death at 64 St. Peter Street or the last, though it may have been the only murder to occur at the residence (the address changing to 714 St. Peter Street by 1894). The fact that any deaths occurred within the confines of that building was not unusual. Virtually every home in the city built during the 1700s and 1800s served as the death house and funeral parlor of someone's loved one. The public's view of death was drastically different in those days. Going to the hospital to die was not a choice or a desire for most families, and there were few established funeral parlors in those days. The cost of using such an establishment may have been prohibitive for the poorer families. In addition, most bodies had to be quickly entombed or buried within twenty-four hours of death. Modern American embalming, which began during the Civil War, was the exception rather than the rule during the late nineteenth and early twentieth centuries.

In cases such as young Juliette's, where the body could not be buried quickly, preventing decomposition during public viewings was more commonly accomplished by placing manufactured ice inside the open coffin, rather than using chemicals such as formaldehyde.

Besides the Dietsh murder, which was the second known death on the property, and not counting the death of Elizabeth Hilroy—who was number three—there were apparently two additional deaths at 64 (714) St. Peter Street. The first known death involved a yellow fever victim, a twenty-three-year-old woman named Louise Sabathier who succumbed to the mosquito-spread viral disease on September 16, 1878. The 1878 yellow fever epidemic was an especially brutal plague in New Orleans, claiming 4,046 lives out of 23,707 reported cases in the city, an unofficial total. A fifth of the population eventually fled the city when the first cases of yellow fever appeared in late July.

In addition to her death, three other people who lived on the same side of the block died that month. One was a thirty-two-year-old Frenchman who lived next door, closer to Royal Street at 62 (now 710), and the others were a thirty-two-year-old father and his four-year-old son, who lived near the corner of Bourbon Street at 76 St. Peter Street.

The fourth death at the property occurred ten years after Mrs. Hilroy's passing on November 26, 1909, when "marasmus" or malnutrition, likely caused by a birth anomaly or from unsuitable foods, claimed the life of two-month-old Bernadette M. Miller.

There may have been a fifth death at the property. On December 26, 1915, sixty-year-old Andrew Sobsas, a native of Austria, died from chronic endocarditis and chronic nephritis. However, the address listed on his death certificate was 716 St. Peter Street. It's possible the undertaker who reported the death to city officials meant to say 714. It's also possible that there was a 716 St. Peter Street address, since the property once constituted 64 and 66 St. Peter Street. No such address currently exists.

The upstairs front portion of 714 St. Peter Street no longer resembles the space once occupied by Etienne Deschamps or, for that matter, by Charles Serra and his wife. The inner wall and door separating the two rooms was removed, creating a larger reception room for private parties. The original fireplace that Deschamps used to burn incriminating evidence is no more, replaced instead by a wall-length wallpaper mural depicting a nineteenth-century Mississippi River scene. Serra's fireplace along the Bourbon Street side of his room was replaced with a wall-length bar to serve the needs of guests when the room is rented out.

The solid "rear" door for both rooms off the inner gallery is gone too, replaced with glass-pane French doors, with the second set of doors slightly off center to where Serra's original door was located. In addition, a five-foot-wide by six-foot-high nine-pane window occupies a portion of the wall space along the inner gallery within Deschamps's portion of the upstairs. To accommodate patrons of the downstairs restaurant, two restrooms were constructed years ago that replaced the original water closet. The second-floor side rooms are now one large room used for food storage. In addition, the exterior walkway is home to several air-conditioning and heating units. Tucked at the end of the side-room portion of the walkway is a vertical metal duct connected to the exhaust ventilation system from the kitchen below. For safety reasons, this walkway is only accessible to employees, though the three exterior French doors leading to the old rooms (two of which are sealed off) are still visible from the patio below.

Whatever claim the second floor had to infamy, the lower floor has had an equally checkered past, not for murder but related instead to its culinary history and, for a very brief period, its association with retail sales. Beginning in 1885, John P. Lewis, who lived on the first floor at 66 St. Peter Street, sold "Chinese goods" and the following year operated a grocery, though both businesses only lasted a year. The initial eatery or coffee shop was allegedly established in 1894, but the first mention of a restaurant at that location appeared in the city directory four years earlier when Lewis opened a restaurant.

Lewis appeared to be a fickle entrepreneur. Before opening his restaurant on St. Peter Street, he operated a similar business at 102 (now in the 800 block of) St. Louis Street. He moved his eatery a final time to 116 (now 910) Toulouse Street in 1891. The St. Peter Street building's association with the January 1889 murder might have driven business away, or perhaps he just got a better deal by relocating one street over. Nevertheless, Lewis lived continuously at 64/66 St. Peter Street between 1885 and 1894, in spite of his various business moves.

From 1897 through 1910, an assortment of "lunch houses" operated next door and continuing up the street to 726 St. Peter Street, though none at the same time. A Chinese restaurant opened at 728 St. Peter Street in 1911 but lasted only a year.

Taking aside Antoine Alciatore's 1860s affiliation with the house and the restaurant businesses he operated up and down the street from there, starting in 1926 and continuing through the 1930s, the adjacent property at 710 (currently a gift shop) was referred to as the Green Shutter Coffee-House. Its name was derived from the colored shutters that adorned the four French-door entry points to the one-story building. By the 1940s, the Green Shutter was referred to as the Coffee Pot and, by the mid-1950s, the Coffee Pot Restaurant. Other than the 1890 Lewis restaurant, no such eatery at 64/66 or 714 St. Peter Street was ever listed in the city directories prior to the 1950s, though it appears that meals were prepared on the premises for the tenants or at least for the owner who lived there. In November 1903, the property advertised for a female cook, promising an easy work environment and good treatment if hired.

Furthermore, the building was oddly never listed in the city directories as a "boardinghouse" or "lodging home," though it clearly had boarders from time to time. In June 1902 the entire property, nine rooms in all, was listed for rent at $22.50 a month. More than likely, it remained a private home whose various owners rented out the property or the upstairs rooms as the need arose.

For a brief period during the mid-1920s, the building also served as the first domicile for Le Petit Salon, an exclusive and prestigious women's organization that was formed in New Orleans in October 1924. By late 1925, the ladies moved to their permanent headquarters down the street at 620 St. Peter Street, one door up from the Le Petit Theatre.

The house at 714 St. Peter Street continued to operate as a nonregistered boarding home for many years, under the supervision of an assortment of owners. But the modern era of the eatery appears to have gotten its start during the early 1950s, certainly by 1951. On April 12, 1951, the *Times-Picayune* printed an advertisement seeking a female to help in the "Four Seasons Pastry Shop" located at 714 St. Peter Street, though this location was listed in city directories under its French spelling—Pâtisseries Aux Quatre Saisons. (The owner had a second shop located at 505 Royal Street.) Two months later, a feature article announced that the "dining and the pastry shop [at 714 St. Peter Street] . . . had been cooled" with air conditioning. The business was described as "one of the French Quarter's more picturesque spots where elegant entertaining [was] done." For a time, Four Seasons, listed in the 1958 city directory as "The Coffee Pot," and the Coffee Pot Restaurant located next door were open simultaneously.

The Four Seasons or the Coffee Pot closed its doors sometime during 1958-59, in spite of the restaurant being described in the newspaper as a "'Luxurious Must' of discriminating gourmets." It reopened in September

1959 under its prior business name. Unfortunately, the new restaurant failed or was consolidated with the 505 Royal Street property, now a jewelry store. In November 1962, the St. Peter Street property was listed in the commercial real-estate section of the *Daily Picayune* for rent at $250 a month.

The current establishment, the Old Coffee Pot Restaurant, acquired by its present owner in May 2010, remains a very popular eatery in the French Quarter. Whether their clientele know what occurred on the second floor, only time will tell.

On Friday, May 13, 1892, Etienne Deschamps swung by his neck until dead. Whether he was truly guilty of premeditated murder, or whether his criminality rose no higher than manslaughter instead, the fact that the crime involved the death of a nude, twelve-year-old girl was something the citizenry of New Orleans could not get beyond. During the waning years of the Victorian era, Deschamps was seen by virtually everyone in the city as a sexual predator, regardless of whether he was ever charged with rape. For *that*, his sin was unforgivable. And for *that*, he paid with his life.

The Old Coffee Pot Restaurant, 714 St. Peter Street, in 2014.
(Courtesy Gerard Peña)

Bibliography

Archdiocese of New Orleans, Office of Archives and Records

Mater Dolorosa Church, Funerals, Vol. 1, 1870-1912. Fr. R. Vallée officiating. Pastor of St. Mary's Catholic Church in Carrollton (founded in 1848), he assisted with clerical duties when called upon by Mater Dolorosa Church, a neighboring German Catholic parish (founded in 1871). The two churches merged in 1899. For unknown reasons, Philip Baker was cited in the volume as *J. Baker.* The Baker family were undoubtedly members of Mater Dolorosa Church, as they were of German ancestry.

St. Louis Cemetery No. 2, Burials, 1888-97. Juliette Dietsh, Square No. 1, Oven No. 12, Second Row, St. Louis Aisle near (North) Robertson (Street). The wall vaults on the street side of St. Louis Aisle or Alley resembled three tiers of baker's ovens, a common architectural style of aboveground tombs in New Orleans at the time. Juliette's tomb was the twelfth and middle wall vault on the left, beneath the tomb of François and Adelaide Theard.

Books and Periodicals

Arthur, Stanley Clisby. *Old New Orleans: Walking Tours of the French Quarter.* 1936. Reprint, Gretna, LA: Pelican, 2014.

Bergeron, Arthur W., Jr. *Guide to Louisiana Confederate Military Units 1861-1865.* Baton Rouge: Louisiana University Press, 1989.

Biographical and Historical Memoirs of Louisiana in Two Volumes. Chicago: Goodspeed, 1892.

Booth, Andrew B. *Records of Louisiana Confederate Soldiers and Louisiana Confederate Commands, in Three Volumes.* New Orleans.

Brooksher, William Riley. *War Along the Bayous: The 1864 Red River Campaign in Louisiana.* Washington, DC: Brassey's, 1998.

Buck, Albert Henry. *The Dawn of Modern Medicine: From the Early Part of the Eighteenth Century to About 1860.* New Haven: Yale University Press, 1920.

"Bulletin of the International Medico-Legal Congress, Held June 4, 5, 6, and 7, 1889 at New York." *The Medico-Legal Journal* (1891): vi-ix, 8-9, 25.

Castellanos, Henry C. *New Orleans As It Was.* 1895. Reprint, Gretna, LA: Pelican, 1990.

Coleman, William H. *Historical Sketch Book and Guide to New Orleans.* New York: Astor House, 1885.

Dimitry, John. *Confederate Military History.* Vol. 10, *Louisiana.* Atlanta: Confederate, 1899.

Duffy John, ed. *The Rudolph Matas History of Medicine in Louisiana, Volume 1.* Baton Rouge: Louisiana State University Press, 1958.

"First Volunteers from Louisiana." *Confederate Veteran* 3, no. 5 (1895): 146.

Larson, Susan. *The Booklover's Guide to New Orleans.* 2nd ed. Baton Rouge: Louisiana State University Press, 2013.

Marr, Robert H., ed. *The Criminal Statutes of Louisiana.* New Orleans: F. F. Hansell & Bro., 1929.

Odem, Mary E. *Delinquent Daughters: Protecting and Policing Adolescent Females' Sexuality in the United States, 1885-1920.* Chapel Hill: University of North Carolina Press, 1995.

Peña, Christopher G. *Scarred by War: Civil War in Southeast Louisiana.* Bloomington, IN: Authorhouse, 2004.

Remini, Robert V. *The Battle of New Orleans.* New York: Penguin, 1999).

Renaud, J. K. "The Orleans Cadets." *Confederate Veteran* 29, no. 6 (June 1921): 207-8.

Revised Civil Code of Louisiana. New Orleans: F. F. Hansell & Bro., 1888.

The Revised Civil Code of the State of Louisiana. New Orleans: 1879.

Sears, Stephen W. *Chancellorsville.* Boston: Houghton Mifflin, 1996.

Sifakis, Stewart. *Compendium of the Confederate Armies: Texas.* New York: Facts on File, 1995.

Tallant, Robert. *Ready to Hang: Seven Famous New Orleans Murders.* 1952. Reprint, Gretna, LA: Pelican, 2012.

Warner, Ezra J. *Generals in Gray: Lives of the Confederate Commanders.* 2nd ed. Baton Rouge: Louisiana State University Press, 1987.

Dissertation

Meletio, Donna. "Léona Queyrouze (1861-1938), Louisiana French Creole

Poet, Essayist, and Composer." PhD diss., Louisiana State University, 2005.

Louisiana State Archives, Baton Rouge

Certificates of Birth

Orleans Parish, Secretary of State, Vital Records, January 15, 1858-November 27, 1866.

Certificates of Death

Lafayette Parish, Secretary of State, Vital Records, Secretary of State, Vital Records, November 18, 1952.

Orleans Parish, Secretary of State, Vital Records, October 9, 1869-December 25, 1961.

Shreveport, Caddo Parish, Secretary of State, Vital Records, January 18, 1910-December 10, 1924.

Certificates of Marriage

Orleans Parish, Secretary of State, Vital Records, May 29, 1876-June 22, 1943.

Louisiana State Museum, New Orleans

Detail, 700 block of St. Peter Street, sketch for Historic American Survey; E. E. Loving, delineator; June 23, 1941.

Manuscript Collections

Leona Queyrouze Barel Papers, Mss. 1204, 1222, 1278, 1314, 1323, 1335. Letters and documents from April 1, 1889, to May 13, 1892. Louisiana and Lower Mississippi Valley Collections. Louisiana State University Libraries, Baton Rouge.

National and State Documents

National Archives and Records Administration, Washington, D.C. *Index to the Compiled Military Service Records for the Volunteer Soldiers Who Served During the War of 1812.*
————. *Passenger Lists of Vessels Arriving at New Orleans, Louisiana, 1820-1902.*
Reports of Cases Argued and Determined in the Supreme Court of Louisiana, Vol. 41—For the Year 1889, Henry Denis, reporter (New Orleans: E. Marchand, State Printer, 1890).
Reports of Cases Argued and Determined in the Supreme Court of Louisiana, Vol. 42, 44—For the Year 1890, 1892, Henry Denis, reporter (New Orleans: F. F. Hansell & Bro., 1891, 1893).
War of the Rebellion: A Compilation of the Official Records of the Union and Confederate Armies. 128 vols. 1894-1927. Reprint, Harrisburg, PA: 1995.

New Orleans Public Library, Louisiana Division/City Archives

Inquest held on January 31, 1889, into the death of Juliette Dietsh at 64 St. Peter Street on January 30, 1889.
Inquest held on March 8, 1891, into the death of Louisa (*sic*) Frank, wife of Neil Nelson, at southwest corner of Washington and Hampson streets on March 7, 1891.
Orleans Parish Coroner's Office. *Records of Inquests and Views, 1844-1904.* Vol. 35. January 10, 1887-July 28, 1897. TH420, microfilm roll #903980.
State v. Etienne Deschamps, Orleans Parish District Court, Docket #11915.

Newspapers

Alexandria Gazette & Virginia Advertiser. November 24, 1853.
Alexandria Louisiana Democrat. April 7, 1875-January 19, 1876.
Baltimore American & Commercial Advertiser. December 19, 1853.
Baton Rouge Advocate. May 28, 1890-April 15, 1892.
Bridgeton (NJ) Evening News. January 31, 1889.
Canton (OH) Repository. February 27, 1890.
Chicago Daily Inter Ocean. April 25, 1892.
Colfax (LA) Chronicle. January 29, 1910.

Courrier des États-Unis (New York). May 3-15, 1889.
Donaldsonville Chief. January 6-8, 1912.
Edenton (NC) Fisherman and Farmer. May 27, 1892.
Evansville (IN) Courier. May 14, 1892.
Galveston Daily News. March 7, 1882.
Los Angeles Herald. May 14, 1892.
New Orleans Daily City Item. September 17, 1879-November 24, 1903.
New Orleans Daily Picayune. June 30, 1844-November 25, 1913.
New Orleans Item. December 27, 1915.
New Orleans Times-Picayune. March 2, 1919-October 25, 1987.
New Orleans Tribune. October 17, 1866.
New York Times. June 5, 1889.
St. Francisville True Democrat. January 13, 1892.
San Francisco Chronicle. April 21, 1892.
Shreveport Caucasian. January 7, 1912.
Winnfield (LA) Comrade. January 21, 1910.
Worthington (MN) Advance.

Web Sites

http://connecticuthistory.org
http://drvitelli.typepad.com
http://files.usgwarchives.net
http://louisianalodgeofresearch.org
http://nutrias.org
http://trees.ancestry.com
http://www.ancestry.com
http://www.biography.com
http://www.findagrave.com
http://www.gsa.gov
http://www.hancockcountyhistoricalsociety.com
http://www.historyofhypnosis.org
http://www.lasc.org
http://www.newadvent.org
http://www.orleanscivilclerk.com
http://www.psanes.org
http://www.storyvilledistrictnola.com

http://www.sunypress.edu
https://archive.org
https://familysearch.org

Index

209

CPSIA information can be obtained
at www.ICGtesting.com
Printed in the USA
LVOW11*1927240217
525403LV00001B/3/P